BUSINESS VOCABULARY IN USE

Self-study and classroom use

Third Edition

Intermediate

Bill Mascull

Shaftesbury Road, Cambridge CB2 8EA, United Kingdom

One Liberty Plaza, 20th Floor, New York, NY 10006, USA

477 Williamstown Road, Port Melbourne, VIC 3207, Australia

314–321, 3rd Floor, Plot 3, Splendor Forum, Jasola District Centre, New Delhi – 110025, India

103 Penang Road, #05–06/07, Visioncrest Commercial, Singapore 238467

Cambridge University Press & Assessment is a department of the University of Cambridge.

We share the University's mission to contribute to society through the pursuit of education, learning and research at the highest international levels of excellence.

www.cambridge.org
Information on this title: www.cambridge.org/9781316629987

© Cambridge University Press & Assessment 2002, 2010, 2017

This publication is in copyright. Subject to statutory exception and to the provisions of relevant collective licensing agreements, no reproduction of any part may take place without the written permission of Cambridge University Press & Assessment.

First published 2002
Second Edition 2010
Third Edition 2017

20 19 18 17 16 15

Printed in Malaysia by Vivar Printing

A catalogue record for this publication is available from the British Library

ISBN 978-1-316-62998-7 Book with Answers
ISBN 978-1-316-62997-0 Book with Answers and Ebook

Cambridge University Press & Assessment has no responsibility for the persistence or accuracy of URLs for external or third-party internet websites referred to in this publication, and does not guarantee that any content on such websites is, or will remain, accurate or appropriate. Information regarding prices, travel timetables, and other factual information given in this work is correct at the time of first printing but Cambridge University Press & Assessment does not guarantee the accuracy of such information thereafter.

Contents

| INTRODUCTION | 8 |

JOBS, PEOPLE AND ORGANIZATIONS

1 Work and jobs   10
- A What do you do?
- B Word combinations with 'work'
- C Types of job and types of work

2 Ways of working   12
- A Working hours
- B Nice work if you can get it
- C Nature of work

3 Recruitment and selection   14
- A Recruitment
- B Applying for a job
- C Selection procedures

4 Skills and qualifications   16
- A Education and training
- B Skilled and unskilled
- C The right person

5 Pay and benefits   18
- A Wages, salary and benefits
- B Compensation 1
- C Compensation 2

6 People and workplaces   20
- A Employees and management
- B Management and administration
- C Labour
- D Personnel and HRM

7 Companies and careers   22
- A Career paths
- B Company structure
- C In-house staff or freelancers?
- D Leaving a company

8 Problems at work   24
- A Discrimination
- B Bullying and harassment
- C Health and safety

9 Managers, executives and directors   26
- A Managers and executives: UK
- B Managers and executives: US

10 Businesspeople and business leaders   28
- A Businesspeople and entrepreneurs
- B Leaders and leadership
- C Magnates, moguls and tycoons

11 Organizations 1   30
- A Business and businesses
- B Commerce
- C Enterprise

12 Organizations 2   32
- A Self-employed people and partnerships
- B Limited liability
- C Mutuals
- D Non-profit organizations

PRODUCTION

13 Manufacturing and services   34
- A Manufacturing and services
- B Countries and their industries

14 The development process   36
- A Market research
- B Development and launch

15 Innovation and invention   38
- A Innovation and invention
- B Research and technology
- C Patents and intellectual property

16 Products and services   40
- A Products
- B Mass production
- C Capacity and output

Business Vocabulary in Use Intermediate

17 Materials and suppliers 42
A Inputs
B Suppliers and outsourcing
C Just-in-time

18 Business philosophies 44
A Mass customization
B Wikinomics
C The long tail
D Benchmarking

MARKETING

19 Buyers, sellers and the market 46
A Customers and clients
B Buyers, sellers and vendors
C The market

20 Markets and competitors 48
A Companies and markets
B More word combinations with 'market'
C Competitors and competition

21 Marketing and market orientation 50
A Marketing
B The four Ps
C The market orientation

22 Products and brands 52
A Word combinations with 'product'
B Goods
C Brands and branding

23 Price 54
A Pricing
B Word combinations with 'price'
C Upmarket and downmarket
D Mass markets and niches

24 Place 56
A Distribution: wholesalers, retailers and customers
B Shops
C Direct marketing

25 Promotion 58
A Advertising
B The sales force
C Promotional activities

26 E-commerce 60
A B2C, B2B and B2G
B Web 2.0
C E-commerce companies
D Word combinations with 'online'

MONEY

27 Sales and costs 62
A Sales
B Costs
C Margins and mark-ups

28 Profitability and unprofitability 64
A Profitable and unprofitable products
B Budgets and expenditure
C Economies of scale and the learning curve

29 Getting paid 66
A Shipping and billing
B Trade credit
C Accounts

30 Assets, liabilities and the balance sheet 68
A Assets
B Depreciation
C Liabilities
D Balance sheet

31 The bottom line 70
A Accounts
B Results
C Financial reporting

32 Share capital and debt 72
A Capital
B Share capital
C Loan capital
D Security
E Leverage

33 Success and failure — 74
A Cash mountains
B Debt and debt problems
C Turnarounds and bailouts
D Bankruptcy

34 Mergers, takeovers and sell-offs — 76
A Stakes and joint ventures
B Mergers and takeovers
C Conglomerates

FINANCE AND THE ECONOMY

35 Personal finance — 78
A Traditional banking
B Internet banking
C Personal investing

36 Financial centres — 80
A Financial Centres
B Stock markets
C Other financial markets
D Derivatives

37 Trading — 82
A Market indexes
B Market activity: good times …
C … and bad

38 Indicators 1 — 84
A Finance and economics
B Inflation and unemployment
C Trade
D Growth and GDP

39 Indicators 2 — 86
A Going up
B Going down
C Peaks and troughs
D Boom and bust

DOING THE RIGHT THING

40 Wrongdoing and corruption — 88
A Wrongdoing
B Bribery and corruption
C Fraud and embezzlement

41 Business ethics — 90
A Professional behaviour
B Social issues
C Environmental issues

PERSONAL SKILLS

42 Time and time management — 92
A Timeframes and schedules
B Projects and project management
C Time tips

43 Stress and stress management — 94
A When work is stimulating
B When stimulation turns to stress
C Downshifting

44 Leadership and management styles — 96
A Leadership
B Modern management styles
C Empowerment

CULTURE

45 Business across cultures 1 — 98
A Cultures and culture
B Power and distance

46 Business across cultures 2 — 100
A Individualism
B Time
C Cross-cultural communication

TELEPHONING AND WRITING

47 Telephoning 1: phones and numbers 102
- A Telephones and beyond
- B 'Phone', 'call' and 'ring'
- C Numbers
- D Doing things over the phone

48 Telephoning 2: trying to get through 104
- A Asking to speak to someone
- B Voicemail 1
- C Voicemail 2

49 Telephoning 3: getting through 106
- A Getting through
- B Giving and taking messages
- C Spelling names
- D Taking messages: checking information

50 Telephoning 4: arrangements and ending calls 108
- A Phoning again
- B Making arrangements
- C Closing the conversation
- D Changing arrangements

51 Business communication 1: staying in touch 110
- A Business cards 1
- B Business cards 2
- C Staying in touch

52 Business communication 2: email 112
- A Email
- B Email expressions
- C Beginnings and endings

53 CVs, cover letters and emails 114
- A CV tips
- B Parts of a CV
- C Cover letters and emails

54 Interns, trainees and apprentices 116
- A Interns
- B Experience or exploitation?
- C Trainees and apprentices

BUSINESS SKILLS

55 Meetings 1: types of meeting 118
- A Word combinations with 'meeting'
- B Types of meeting
- C How was the meeting?

56 Meetings 2: the chair 120
- A The role of the chair: before the meeting
- B The role of the chair: running the meeting
- C Follow-up

57 Meetings 3: points of view 122
- A Opening the meeting
- B Asking for and expressing opinions

58 Meetings 4: agreement and disagreement 124
- A Agreeing
- B Disagreeing

59 Meetings 5: discussion techniques 126
- A Interrupting, referring back, checking understanding, avoiding confrontation
- B Agreement, consensus or compromise?
- C Concluding

60 Presentations 1: key ideas 128
- A Types of presentation
- B What makes a good presentation?
- C Presentation tools and visual aids

61 Presentations 2: key steps 130
- A Key steps: introduction
- B Key steps: main part
- C Key steps: closing

62 Presentations 3: audience interaction   **132**
   A Closing and dealing with questions
   B Intercultural aspects

63 Negotiations 1: situations and negotiators   **134**
   A Types of negotiation
   B Word combinations with 'negotiations'
   C Bargaining

64 Negotiations 2: preparing   **136**
   A Preparing to negotiate
   B Opening the negotiation
   C Negotiating styles

65 Negotiations 3: win-win   **138**
   A Probing
   B Positive positions
   C Negative positions
   D Concessions and trade-offs

66 Negotiations 4: reaching agreement   **140**
   A Deadlock and mediators
   B Agreements and contracts
   C Checking the deal

Answer key   **142**

Index   **161**

Also available   **176**

Introduction

Who is this book for?

Business Vocabulary in Use Intermediate is designed to help intermediate and upper-intermediate learners of business English to improve their business vocabulary. It is for people studying English before they start work and for those already working who need English in their job.

In addition to improving your business vocabulary, the book helps you to develop the language needed for important business communication skills.

You can use the book on your own for self-study, with a teacher in the classroom, one-to-one or in groups.

How is the book organized?

The book has 66 two-page units. The first 46 of these are **thematic** and look at the vocabulary of business areas such as people, organizations, production, marketing and finance.

The other 20 units focus on the language of **skills** you need in business, such as those for presentations, meetings, telephoning and negotiations.

The left-hand page of each unit explains new words and expressions, and the right-hand page allows you to check and develop your understanding of the words and expressions, and how they are used through a series of exercises.

There is **cross-referencing** between units to show connections between the same word or similar words used in different contexts.

There is an **Answer key** at the back of the book. Most of the exercises have questions with only one correct answer. But some of the exercises, including the **Over to you** activities at the end of each unit (see below), are designed for writing and/or discussion about yourself and your own organization or one that you know.

There is also an **Index**. This lists all the new words and phrases which are introduced in the book and gives the unit numbers where the words and phrases appear. The Index also tells you how the words and expressions are pronounced.

The left-hand page

This page introduces new vocabulary and expressions for each thematic or skills area. The presentation is divided into a number of sections indicated by letters: A, B, C, etc., with simple, clear titles.

In *Business Vocabulary in Use Intermediate*, explicit reference is made to the business material in the **Cambridge International Corpus (CIC)** – business pages of newspapers, business textbooks, and business meetings and discussions. The texts are stored in a database, which is searchable in various ways to reveal the patterns of business usage. The database has been exploited to identify typical word combinations found in the data, and there are notes about their relative frequency.

As well as explanations of vocabulary, there is information about typical word combinations and grammar associated with particular vocabulary, for example operative verbs – the verbs that are typically used with particular nouns. Again, the CIC has been a prime source of information about these.

There are notes about differences between British and American English.

- BrE: **CV**; AmE: **résumé** or **resume**

The right-hand page

The exercises on the right-hand page give practice in using the new vocabulary and expressions presented on the left-hand page. Some units contain diagrams to complete, or crosswords.

'Over to you' sections

An important feature of *Business Vocabulary in Use Intermediate* is the **Over to you** section at the end of each unit. There are sometimes alternative **Over to you** sections for learners who are in work and for those who are studying pre-work. The **Over to you** sections give you the chance to put into practice the words and expressions in the unit in relation to your own professional situation, studies or opinions.

Self-study learners can do the section as a written activity. In many **Over to you** sections, learners can use the internet to find more information.

In the classroom, the **Over to you** sections can be used as the basis for discussion with the whole class, or in small groups with a spokesperson for each summarizing the discussion and its outcome for the class. The teacher can then get students to look again at exercises relating to points that have caused difficulty. Students can follow up by using the **Over to you** section as a written activity, for example as homework.

The Answer key contains sample answers for the **Over to you** questions.

How to use the book for self-study

Find the topic you are looking for by using the Contents page or the Index. Read through the explanations on the left-hand page of the unit. Do the exercises on the right-hand page. Check your answers in the Answer key. If you have made some mistakes, go back and look at the explanations and the exercise again. Note down important words and expressions in your notebook.

How to use the book in the classroom

Teachers can choose units that relate to their students' particular needs and interests, for example areas they have covered in coursebooks, or that have come up in other activities. Alternatively, lessons can contain a regular vocabulary slot, where students look systematically at the vocabulary of particular thematic or skills areas.

Students can work on the units in pairs, with the teacher going round the class assisting and advising. Teachers should get students to think about the logical process of the exercises, pointing out why one answer is possible and the others are not (where this is the case).

We hope you enjoy using *Business Vocabulary in Use Intermediate*.

1 Work and jobs

A What do you do?

To find out what someone's job is, you ask **'What do you do?'**

Kerstin talks about her job:

'I **work for** a large European car maker. I **work on** car design. In fact, I **run** the design department and I **manage** a team of designers: 20 people **work under** me. It's very interesting. One of my main **responsibilities** is to make sure that new model designs are finished on time. I'm also **in charge of** design budgets.

'I **deal with** a lot of different people in the company. I'm **responsible for** coordination between design and production: I **work with** managers at our manufacturing plants.'

> **Note**
>
> **in charge of** + noun
> **responsible for** + verb + -ing
> **responsibility** + infinitive / -ing
> One of my responsibilities is to make sure that …
> One of my responsibilities is making sure that …
> You don't say: 'I'm a responsible.'

B Word combinations with 'work'

If you **work** or **have work**, you have a job. But you don't say that someone has 'a work'. **Work** is also the place where you do your job. You don't say for example, 'at the work' or 'to the work'.

Here are some phrases with 'work'.

The economy is growing fast and more people are **in work** – have a job – than ever before. The percentage of people **out of work** – without a job – has fallen to its lowest level for 30 years.

Frank talks about his job:

'I work in a bank in New York City. I leave **for work** at 7.30 every morning. I **go to work** by train and subway. I **get to / arrive at** work at about 9. I'm usually **at work** till 6. Luckily, I don't get ill very much so I don't often take **time off work** – away from work due to illness.'

C Types of job and types of work

A **full-time job** is one for the whole of the normal working week; a **part-time job** is for less time than that. You say that someone **works full-time** or **part-time**.

A **permanent job** does not finish after a fixed period; a **temporary job** finishes after a fixed period.

You talk about **temporary work** and **permanent work**.

Business Vocabulary in Use Intermediate

Exercises

1.1 Look at A opposite. Margaux is talking about her work. Correct the expressions in italics.

'I work for a large French supermarket company. It is an international company and **(1)** I work *about* the development of new supermarkets abroad. **(2)** In fact, I *running* the development department and **(3)** I *am manage for* a team looking at the possibilities in different countries. It's very interesting. **(4)** One of my *main* is to make sure that new supermarkets open on time. **(5)** I'm also *charged with* financial reporting. **(6)** I deal *at* a lot of different organizations in my work. **(7)** I'm *responsible of* planning projects from start to finish. **(8)** I work closely *near* our foreign partners, and so I travel a lot.'

1.2 Complete each gap in the text with one of the prepositions from B opposite.

Rebecca lives in London and works in public relations. She leaves home for work at 7.30 am. She drives **(1)** _____ work. The traffic is often bad and she worries about getting **(2)** _____ work late, but she usually arrives **(3)** _____ work at around 9. She finishes work quite late, at about 8. 'Luckily, I'm never ill,' she says. 'I could never take time **(4)** _____ work.'

She loves what she does and is glad to be **(5)** _____ work. Some of her friends are not so lucky: they are **(6)** _____ of work.

1.3 What is being advertised in each of these job advertisements (1–6)? Use an expression from C opposite, including the words in brackets. The first one has been done for you.

1 Librarian required for public library, afternoons 2 till 6. (job) — *a part-time job*

2 Personal assistant needed for busy office, 9 am to 5.30 pm. (work)

3 Experienced barman wanted, 8 pm until midnight. (work)

4 Teacher needed for summer course, 1 to 31 August. (job)

5 Salesman required for showroom – good prospects for right person. (work)

6 Lawyer wanted for law firm – long hours, 4 weeks holiday per year. (job)

Over to you

If you work, answer these questions.

- What do you do? What are you in charge of? What are your responsibilities?
- What time do you leave for work? How long does it take you to get to work? What time do you arrive at work? Do you take a lot of time off work?
- Why do some people prefer to work part-time or to have temporary jobs?

If you don't work, answer these questions.

- What sort of job would you like to do?
- What sort of routine would you like to have?

2 Ways of working

A Working hours

'I'm an **office worker** in an insurance company. It's a **nine-to-five** job with regular **working hours**. I need my **swipe card** to get into the office. The work isn't very interesting, but I like to be able to go home at a reasonable time.'

 You can also say **clock in** and **clock out**.

 BrE: **flexitime**
AmE: **flextime**

Swiping a card

'I'm in computer programming. There's a system of **flexitime** in my company, which means we can work when we want, within certain limits. We can start at any time till 11, and finish as early as 3 – as long as we do enough hours each month. It's ideal for me as I have two young children.'

'I work in a car plant. I work in **shifts** and I have to **clock on** and **clock off** at the beginning and end of every shift. I may be on the **day shift** one week and the **night shift** the next week. It's difficult changing from one shift to another. When I change shifts, I have problems changing to a new routine for sleeping and eating. When the company is selling lots of cars, they ask us to work **overtime** – more hours than usual for more money.'

'I'm a commercial artist in an advertising agency. Unlike most other people in my department who **commute** to work every day, I **work from home** and avoid the long journeys that some **commuters** experience every day. That's the benefit of **teleworking** or **telecommuting** – working from home and using the computer and phone to communicate with other people.'

B Nice work if you can get it

All these words are used in front of **job** and **work**.

- **satisfying**, **stimulating**, **fascinating**, **exciting** – the work is interesting and gives you positive feelings
- **dull**, **boring**, **uninteresting**, **unstimulating** – the work is not interesting
- **repetitive**, **routine** – the work involves doing the same things again and again
- **tiring**, **tough**, **hard**, **demanding** – the work is difficult and makes you tired

C Nature of work

My work **involves** I **like / dislike / prefer / enjoy**	**+ noun** human contact long hours teamwork
	+ -ing working with figures dealing with customers solving problems

12   Business Vocabulary in Use Intermediate

Exercises

2.1 Look at the six expressions (a–f) from A opposite. Which person (1–6) is most likely to do each of the things described?

a work in shifts
b work under a flexitime system
c telecommute
d commute to work
e clock in and out at the same time every day
f work overtime

1 A designer in a website design company. Has to be in the office, but can decide when she wants to start and finish work each day.
2 A manager in a department store in a large city. Lives in the country.
3 A construction worker on a building site where work goes on 24 hours a day.
4 A worker in a chocolate factory in the three months before Christmas.
5 A technical writer for a computer company. Lives in the country and visits the company offices once a month.
6 An office worker in a large, traditional manufacturing company.

2.2 Look at the words and expressions in B and C opposite. Five people describe their jobs. Match the jobs (1–5) with the descriptions (a–e) and put the words in brackets into the correct grammatical forms.

| 1 accountant   2 postwoman   3 flight attendant   4 software developer   5 teacher |

a 'Obviously, my work involves _____ (travel) a lot. It can be quite physically _____ (demand), but I enjoy _____ (deal) with customers, except when they become tired and anxious about arriving. This doesn't happen often, but it can be very frustrating for us and the other passengers.' ☐

b 'I love my job. It's very _____ (stimulate) and not at all _____ (repeat): no two days are the same. The children are fine: you see them learn and develop. The parents can be more of a problem.' ☐

c 'I was good at maths at school and I like _____ (work) with figures. But my job is much less _____ (bore) and routine than people think. The work _____ (involve) a lot of human contact and teamwork, working with other managers.' ☐

d 'You've got to think in a very logical way. There's a lot of teamwork between the developers. The work can be mentally _____ (tire), but it's very satisfying to write a program that works.' ☐

e 'Of course, it involves getting up quite early in the morning. But I like _____ (be) out in the open air. And you get a lot of exercise. I walk two or three miles every day.' ☐

Over to you

If you work, answer these questions.

- Do you have a nine-to-five job? Do you have to clock on and off? Is there a flexitime system in your organization? Are there people who do shiftwork in your company?
- Could you do your job working from home? If so, would you like to?
- What do you like most about your job? What do you like least?

If you don't work, answer these questions.

- What sort of working hours would you like to have when you start working?
- Would you like to work from home?
- What kind of job would you like? Complete this sentence in five ways to talk about yourself.

  I'd like a job that involves …

3 Recruitment and selection

A Recruitment

The process of finding people for particular jobs is **recruitment** or, especially in American English, **hiring**. Someone who has been **recruited** is a **recruit**, or in AmE, a **hire**. The company **employs** or **hires** them and they **join** the company.

A company may recruit employees directly or use outside **recruiters**, **recruitment agencies** or **employment agencies**. Outside specialists called **headhunters** may be used to find people for very important jobs and to persuade them to leave the organizations they already work for. Key people recruited like this are **headhunted** in a process of **headhunting**.

B Applying for a job

Fred is an accountant, but he was fed up with his old job. He looked in the **situations vacant** pages of his local newspaper, where a local supermarket was advertising for a new accountant's position. He **applied for** the job by completing an **application form** and sending it in.

Harry is a building engineer. He'd been working for the same company for ten years, but he wanted a change. He looked at jobs with different engineering companies on a **jobs website**. He **made an application**, sending in his **CV** (**curriculum vitae** – a document describing your education, qualifications and previous jobs, that you send to a prospective employer) and a **covering letter** explaining why he wanted the job and why he was the right person for it.

An application form

> **Note**
>
> **Situation**, **post** and **position** are formal words often used in job advertisements and applications.
> BrE: **CV**; AmE: **résumé** or **resume**
> BrE: **covering letter**; AmE: **cover letter**

C Selection procedures

Dagmar Schmidt is the head of recruitment at a German telecommunications company. She talks about the **selection process**, the methods that the company uses to recruit people.

'We advertise in national newspapers and on the internet. We look at the **backgrounds** of **applicants** – their **experience** of different jobs and their educational **qualifications**.

> **Note**
>
> **Internet** is sometimes written with a capital letter when it is a noun.
> **internet** (noun): mostly BrE
> **Internet** (noun): mostly AmE

A job interview

'We invite the most interesting **candidates** to a **group discussion**. Then we have individual **interviews** with each candidate. The head of the department is also present. We also give the candidates written **psychometric tests** to assess their intelligence and personality.

'After this, we **shortlist** three or four candidates. We check their **references** by writing to their **referees** – previous employers, teachers, and so on that candidates have named in their applications. If the references are OK, we ask the candidates to come back for more interviews. Finally we **offer** the job to someone, and if they **turn it down** we have to think again. (Some applicants may get other **job offers** at the same time as ours.) If they **accept** it, we hire them. We **appoint** someone only if we find the right person.'

Business Vocabulary in Use Intermediate

Exercises

3.1 Complete the crossword with the correct form of words from A, B and C opposite.

Across
5 I phoned to check on my application, but they said they'd already .... someone. (9)
6 This job is so important; I think we need to .... someone. (8)
8 The selection procedure has lasted three months, but we're going to .... someone next week. (7)

Down
1 and 2 I hope she .... the job, because if she .... it .... , we'll have to start looking again. (7, 5, 4)
3 The last applicant was very strong, but I understand he'd had two other job .... already. (6)
4 They've finally .... a new receptionist. She starts work next week. (5)
7 Computer programmers wanted. Only those with UNIX experience should .... (5)

3.2 Now divide the words in 3.1 into two groups.
1 what a company personnel department does
2 what a person looking for work does

3.3 Replace the underlined phrases with correct forms of words and expressions from A, B and C opposite.

Fred had already **(1)** <u>refused</u> two job offers when he went for **(2)** <u>a discussion to see if he was suitable for the job</u>. They looked at his accountancy degree and contacted **(3)** <u>previous employers Fred had mentioned in his application</u>. A few days later, the supermarket **(4)** <u>asked him if he would like</u> the job and Fred **(5)** <u>said yes</u>.

Harry didn't hear anything for six weeks, so he phoned the company. They told him that they had received a lot of **(6)** <u>requests for the job</u>. After looking at the **(7)** <u>document describing his education, qualifications and previous jobs</u> of the **(8)** <u>people asking for the job</u> and looking at **(9)** <u>what exams they had passed during their education</u>, the company had **(10)** <u>chosen six people to interview</u> and then given them **(11)** <u>tests on their personality and intelligence</u>. They had then given someone the job.

Over to you

If you work, answer these questions.
- Where did you see the jobs advertised?
- What did you send to apply for the job?
- What was the selection procedure?

If you're a student, answer these questions.
- When you applied for your course did you use an online application form or send an application in?
- Did you need to provide referees?
- Did you have an interview?

4 Skills and qualifications

A Education and training

Two company managers, Kasia Gutowska and Nils Olsen, are talking.

KG: The trouble with **graduates** – people who've just left university – is that their **paper qualifications** are good. They might have **qualifications in** interesting subjects, but they have no **work experience**. They just don't know how business works.

NO: I disagree. Education should teach people how to think, not **train** them **for** a particular job. One of last year's recruits **graduated from** Oxford University **with** a **degree in** philosophy and she's doing very well!

KG: Philosophy's an interesting subject, but for our company, it's more useful to do **training in** a practical subject: it's better for us if you **train as** a scientist, and **qualify as** a biologist or a doctor, for example.

NO: Yes, but we don't just need scientists. We also need good managers, which we can achieve through **in-house training** – courses within the company. You know we put a lot of money into **management development**, where managers regularly **go on** specialized **courses** in leadership (see Unit 10), finance (see Unit 38), etc. You need to **acquire experience** – get knowledge through doing things – for that. It's not the sort of thing you can learn when you're 20!

> **Note**
> In AmE, you can also say that someone **graduates from** high school – the school that people usually leave when they are 18.

> **Note**
> A **master's degree** is a qualification you can get after one or two years of **graduate study**. A **Master's of Business Administration (MBA)** is a master's degree in advanced business studies.

B Skilled and unskilled

A **skill** is a particular ability to do something well, especially because you have learned and practised it.

Jobs, and the people who do them, can be described as:

- **highly skilled**, e.g. car designer
- **skilled**, e.g. car production manager
- **semi-skilled**, e.g. taxi driver
- **unskilled**, e.g. car cleaner

You can say that someone is:

skilled at or skilled in	+ *noun* customer care electronics	+ -ing communicating using Excel

You can also say that someone is:

good with	computers figures people

C The right person

These words are often used in job advertisements. Companies look for people who are:

a **methodical**, **systematic** and **organized** – working in a planned, orderly way
b **computer-literate** – good with computers
c **numerate** – good with numbers
d **motivated** – very keen to do well in their job because they find it interesting
e **talented** – very good at what they do
f **self-starters**; they must be **proactive**, **self-motivated**, or **self-driven** – good at working on their own
g **team players** – people who work well with other people

> **Note**
> **Self-starter** and **team player** are nouns. The other words in bold are adjectives.

Business Vocabulary in Use Intermediate

Exercises

4.1 Look at A opposite. Complete each sentence with the correct word.

1. Ravi graduated .... Mumbai University .... a degree .... philosophy and politics.
2. He taught for a while, but didn't like it. He wanted to get a qualification .... accountancy and decided to train .... an accountant at evening classes.
3. He qualified .... an accountant and joined a big accountancy firm in its Mumbai office.
4. After he had acquired some experience, he went .... a number of management courses to get training .... team-building and other skills.

4.2 Look at B opposite. Are these jobs generally considered to be highly skilled, skilled, semi-skilled or unskilled? Use each expression twice.

1. teacher
2. software engineer
3. car worker on a production line
4. cleaner
5. office cleaner
6. airline pilot
7. bus driver
8. office manager

4.3 Complete these extracts from job advertisements using words from C opposite.

1. You'll be researching developments on the internet, so you have to be _ _ _ _ _ _ _ _-_ _ _ _ _ _ _ _. You must be _ _ _ _ _ _ _ _ _, able to work on your own initiative, and a _ _ _ _-_ _ _ _ _ _ _ _. But as part of a team of researchers, you'll need to be a good _ _ _ _-_ _ _ _ _ _ _ too.

2. You'll need to be _ _ _ _ _ _ _ _, as you'll be working on financial budgets.

3. As part of our sales team, you'll be working independently, so you have to be self-_ _ _ _ _ _ _ _ _ and self-_ _ _ _ _ _ .

4. We're looking for someone who can work on ten projects at once, without being told what to do. You must be a _ _ _ _-_ _ _ _ _ _ _ _ – _ _ _ _ _ _ _ _ _ _, _ _ _ _ _ _ _ _ _ _ and _ _ _ _ _ _ _ _ _.

5. We need _ _ _ _ _ _ _ _ journalists who are very good at their job and extremely _ _ _ _ _ _ _ _ _ – very keen to find out as much as they can about news stories.

Over to you

Write an extract from a job advertisement for your job or one you would like to have, using words from C opposite.

Business Vocabulary in Use Intermediate 17

5 Pay and benefits

A Wages, salary and benefits

'My name's Luigi and I'm a hotel manager in Venice. I get paid a **salary** every month. In summer, we're very busy, so we do **overtime** – work a lot of extra hours. The pay for this is quite good. Working in a hotel, we also get some nice **perks** – for example, free meals!'

'I'm Ivan and I work as a waiter in Prague. I like my job even if I don't **earn** very much: I get paid **wages** every week by the restaurant. We get the **minimum wage** – the lowest amount allowed by law. But we also get **tips** – money that customers leave in addition to the bill. Some tourists are very generous!'

'Hi, I'm Catherine, and I'm a saleswoman in luxury goods, based in Paris. I get a **basic salary**, plus **commission** – a percentage on everything I sell. If I sell more than a particular amount in a year, I also get a **bonus**, which is nice. There are some good **fringe benefits** with this job: I get a **company car**, a BMW; there's a **health plan** to pay the costs of medical treatment if I get ill; and the company makes payments for my **pension** – money that I'll get regularly after I stop working. So, with the bonuses, the car, the health plan and the pension, I've got a very nice **benefits package**. And the **working conditions** are good too: I have a nice office and I don't have to travel too much.'

B Compensation 1

Catherine mentioned her **pay and conditions**. **Remuneration** and **compensation** are formal words used to talk about pay and conditions, especially those of senior managers. **Remuneration package** and **compensation package** are used especially in the US to talk about all the pay and benefits that employees receive. For a senior executive, this may include **share options** (BrE) or **stock options** (AmE), the right to buy the company's shares (see Unit 36) at low prices. There may be **performance (-related) bonuses** if the manager reaches particular objectives for the company.

C Compensation 2

Compensation is also used to talk about money and other benefits that someone receives if they are forced to leave the organization, perhaps after a disagreement with other managers in what newspapers call a **boardroom row**. This money is in the form of a **compensation payment** or **severance payment**. If someone also receives benefits with this, the payment and the benefits form a **compensation package** or **severance package**.

In Britain, executives with very high pay and benefits may be referred to as **fat cats**, implying that they do not deserve this level of remuneration.

Exercises

5.1 Xavier and Yvonne are talking about Xavier's new job as a photocopier salesman. Sometimes, they don't use the exact names for things that they are talking about. Complete these expressions, using items from A opposite.

1. X: I get paid every month, rather than every week.
   Y: I see. You get a ...., not wages.
2. X: I usually have to work late: I don't get paid for it, but I do get a percentage for every photocopier I sell.
   Y: So you don't get ...., but you do get .... That's good.
3. X: And the people in production get a .... if they reach their targets.
   Y: Oh right. They get an extra payment if they produce more than a certain amount.
4. X: And the extras are great: the company pays for medical treatment if we get ill and the company restaurant is fantastic.
   Y: Wow! The company .... sound very nice.
5. X: And they've given me a .... to go and visit clients.
   Y: So you don't have to buy a car then.
6. X: What's more, there's a very good scheme where the company pays in money for us to get when we don't work any more.
   Y: Yes, it's important to get a good ....
7. X: The total .... is brilliant.
   Y: Yes, all those extras are really worth having.

5.2 Which expressions from B and C opposite could be used to complete each of these newspaper extracts?

1. **KEVIN DAVIS QUITS AS MF GLOBAL CHIEF**
   Shareholder anger boiled over at the company's annual meeting in July, with Greg Newton, one activist, saying Mr Davis 'should be taken out and shot'. MF Global said Mr Davis's .... (2 possibilities) would be worth $7.5 million.

2. **PUBLIC ANGER AT BANKING EXECUTIVES' PAY**
   Anger at the ....s (2 possibilities) of bank executives is high. Henry Waxman, the California Democrat, this week sent letters to nine of the biggest investment banks asking why they have set aside $108 billion for salaries and bonuses in a year when they have received $125 billion in government aid.

3. **Underachieved? Have a ....-........................ !**
   When things get tough, senior executives should get a pay rise, right? Top executives at Kingfisher, which owns B&Q, and at Vodafone seem to think that directors should be entitled to large amounts of extra pay even when their companies are doing badly.

4. **NEW THINKING**
   Following the UK government's rescue of the banks, voters will say, 'If you could find the money to clear up the mess left by a few greedy ...., then you can find the money to fund this bus service / save this village school / renationalize the railways.'

Over to you

In what order of attractiveness would you put these benefits in relation to your job or one that you would like to have? Give your reasons.

| salary | share options | company car | performance-related bonus |
| commission | pension | health plan | |

Business Vocabulary in Use Intermediate

6 People and workplaces

A Employees and management

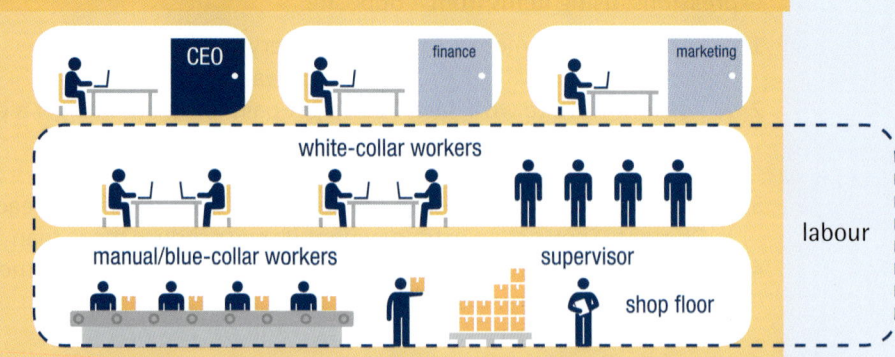

The people who work for a company are on its **payroll**. They are its **employees**, **personnel**, **staff**, **workers** or **workforce**. These words can also refer just to the people carrying out the work of a company, rather than the **management** – those leading and organizing the company.

Note: Workforce, work-force and work force are all possible.

B Management and administration

A company's activities may be spread over different **sites** in different places. A company's most important managers usually work in its **head office** or **headquarters (HQ)**. Some managers have their own individual **offices**, but often employees work in **open-plan offices** – large areas where many people work. **Administration** or, informally, **admin** – the ordinary work supporting a company's activities – is often done in offices like these by **administrative staff** or **support staff**. For example, those giving technical help to buyers of the company's products are in **technical support**.

C Labour

You use **labour** to talk about everyone except the management who works for a company, especially a company that makes things.

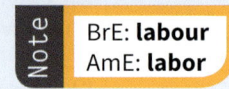

Note: BrE: **labour** AmE: **labor**

labour	costs	what companies have to pay for labour, rather than materials, etc.
	dispute	a disagreement between management and labour
	leader	someone in charge of an organization that represents workers
	relations	the relationship between management and employees in general
	shortage	a period when there are not enough people available to work
	unrest	a period of disagreement between management and employees

Labor unions (AmE) and **trade unions** (BrE) defend the interests of workers.

When workers are not happy with pay or conditions, they may take **industrial action**:
- a **strike**, **stoppage** or **walk-out** – workers stop working for a time
- a **go-slow** – workers continue to work, but more slowly than usual
- an **overtime ban** – workers refuse to work more than the normal number of hours

D Personnel and HRM

In larger organizations there is a **human resources department (HRD)** that deals with pay, recruitment, etc. This area is called **human resources (HR)** or **human resource management (HRM)**. Another, older, name for this department is the **personnel department**.

Business Vocabulary in Use Intermediate

Exercises

6.1 Complete the crossword with the correct form of words from A, B, C and D opposite.

Across

2 and 15 Office workers may be described this way. (5, 6)
5 all of the people working for a company (5)
6 workers who use their hands are of this type (6)
7 when people stop working to protest (6)
9 one of the people working for an organization (8)
10 occasions when workers stop working in order to protest: walk-_____ (4)
12 another name for the human resources department (9)
13 workers seen as a group (6)

Down

1 Everyone working for a company is on this. (7)
2 everyone, or everyone except top managers (9)
3 These are *trade* in the UK and *labor* in the US. (6)
4 and 15 across Manual workers are this, even if they don't wear this. (4, 6)
5 A place in a factory where the production lines are. (9)
8 when people stop work to complain about something (8)
14 and 11 Workers do this when they intentionally produce less. (2, 4)

6.2 Manuel Ortiz is the founder of a Spanish computer sales company. Use the words in B and D opposite to complete what he says about it.

'I founded Computadoras Creativas 20 years ago. We started with a small **(1)** _____ in Madrid. Our **(2)** ____ _____, our **(3)** _____ is still here, but now we have sites all over Spain, with about 500 employees. Many of the offices are **(4)** ____-____ – everyone works together. This includes managers to **(5)** _____ _____ – secretaries and people who support the company's activities, and people in technical **(6)** _____ giving help to customers over the phone.

Recruitment is taken care of in Madrid, by the **(7)** _____ _____ _____ or **(8)** ___.'

> **Over to you**
>
> Answer these questions about the company you work for or would like to work for. Look at the company website to help you.
> - Where is its head office? How many sites does the company have? How many employees?
> - Do people have their own offices or are there open-plan offices? Which do you or would you prefer to work in?

7 Companies and careers

A Career paths

Many people used to work for the same organization until they reached **retirement**, the age at which people **retire** – end their working life. **Career paths** were clear: you could **work your way up the career ladder**, getting **promotion** to jobs that were more **senior** – more important with greater responsibility. You would probably not be **demoted** – moved to a less senior job.

B Company structure

Like many other companies, Tel Italia has reorganized and **restructured** in order to become **flatter** – with fewer layers of management – and **leaner** – with fewer, more productive employees. The number of management levels in the **company hierarchy** has been reduced, and many managers have lost their jobs.

In other words, to reduce costs and cut the payroll (see Unit 6), Tel Italia has **downsized** and **delayered**. The company said that **downsizing** and **restructuring** were necessary to reduce costs, increasing **efficiency** and **profits**.

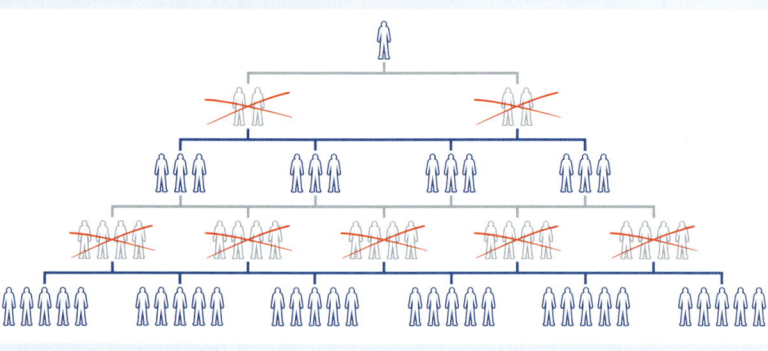

Delayering

C In-house staff or freelancers?

Companies that downsize often **outsource** many jobs previously done by **in-house** personnel: outside companies clean the offices, transport goods, and collect money from customers. This allows the companies to concentrate on their main business activities. **Downsized** companies use more **freelancers** – independent people who work for several different companies – or they may ask **contractors** to work for short periods on **temporary contracts**. They often expect **flexibility**, with people moving to different jobs when necessary: but for many employees, this means **job insecurity** – the feeling that they may not be in their job for long.

The way that an employee is doing their job is discussed at **performance reviews** – regular meetings with their manager.

Note: You can say **freelancers** or **freelances**.

D Leaving a company

To leave a company, you can **resign** or **hand in your notice**.

If you do something wrong and are forced to leave a company, you are: **dismissed**, **terminated**, **fired** or **sacked / given the sack**.

If you've done nothing wrong, you are: **laid off**, **made redundant** or **offered early retirement**.

> **Note**
>
> You can also say that someone's **contract has been terminated**.
> **Fired**, **sacked** and **given the sack** are informal expressions. **Sacked** and **given the sack** = BrE only.

Employees who are made redundant may get **outplacement** – advice about how to find another job, retraining, etc.

Business Vocabulary in Use Intermediate

Exercises

7.1 Complete the tables with words from A, B and C opposite. The first one has been done as an example.

Noun	Verb
retirement	retire
demotion	
lay-off	
dismissal	
termination	

Noun	Adjective
seniority	
	freelance
redundancy	
	insecure
	flexible

7.2 Match the sentence beginnings (1–5) with the correct endings (a–e). The sentences all contain words from A and B opposite.

1 Career paths aren't what they used to be. Companies won't
2 He worked his way up from
3 The new management have restructured and delayered the company,
4 We used to do printing in-house,
5 Employees are afraid their organizations will be downsized

a and that they will be replaced by temporary workers, or made redundant by technology.
b take care of us for life any more. We have to take care of ourselves.
c but now we outsource it.
d factory worker to factory manager.
e reducing the number of management levels in the company hierarchy from five to three.

7.3 Carla used to work for an Italian magazine publishing company. She talks about how she lost her job. Choose the correct form of the word in each case.

Edizione Fenice is a big magazine publishing company. I was director of a monthly magazine called *Casa e Giardino*.

Then Fenice was bought by an international publishing group. We had to have regular performance (1) .... (review / reviews / reviewer) with one of the new managers. After a few months they started laying staff (2) .... (off / on / out). Our own journalists were put on temporary (3) .... (contracts / contractual / contracting) or replaced by (4) .... (freelancer / freelancers / freelanced).

Then they started (5) .... (laid / lying / laying) off more senior people like me. The new owners said they wanted to make the company

(6) .... (flat / flatter / flatten) and (7) .... (lean / leant / leaner). So I was made (8) .... (redundant / redundancies / redundancy). They offered to help me to find another job with (9) .... (outplacement / outplaced / outplacing) services, but I refused.

Over to you

If you work, answer these questions.
- Do you think you will work for the same company until you retire? Why? / Why not?
- What kind of structure does your company have?
- What kind of work does your company outsource?

If you study, answer these questions.
- Do you think you will look for a job in a company where you can work your way up the career ladder until you retire, or do you think you will work for a lot of different companies?
- Do you know any companies which have restructured or downsized?

8 Problems at work

A Discrimination

If people are treated differently from each other in an unfair way, they are **discriminated against**.

If a woman is unfairly treated just because she is a woman, she is a victim of **sex discrimination**. In many organizations, women complain about the **glass ceiling** that prevents them from getting further than a particular level.

If someone is treated unfairly because of their race, they are a victim of **racial discrimination** or **racism**. Offensive remarks about someone's race are **racist** and the person making them is **a racist**.

Equal opportunities, **positive discrimination** or **affirmative action** is when help is given in education and employment to groups who were previously discriminated against.

Some companies have a **dignity at work policy** covering all the issues described in A and B.

> **Note**
>
> BrE: **equal opportunities**
> BrE/AmE: **positive discrimination**
> AmE: **affirmative action**

B Bullying and harassment

If someone such as a manager **bullies** an employee, they use their position of power to hurt or threaten the employee. Someone who does this is **a bully**. The **bullying** can often be verbal.

Sexual harassment is when an employee behaves sexually towards another in a way that they find unwelcome and unacceptable. The related verb is **harass**.

C Health and safety

Health and safety issues for people at work contribute to a **bad working environment**. The government sends officials called **health and safety inspectors** to make sure that factories and offices are safe places to work. They check what companies are doing in areas like:

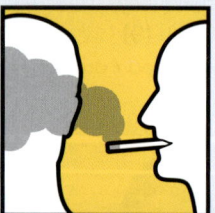
a **passive smoking**

b **repetitive strain injury** or **RSI**

c **dangerous machinery**

d **hazardous substances**

e **fire hazards**

f **heating and air-conditioning**

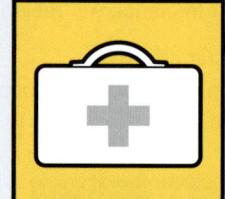
g **first aid**

Of course, dangerous machinery and hazardous substances can cause **industrial accidents**.

> **Note**
>
> **Compensation** (see Unit 5) can also be used to mean money or other benefits that someone receives after an injury caused by a work accident.

Exercises

8.1 Complete these headlines and articles with expressions from A and B opposite. Use one expression twice.

1.
   OFFICE MANAGER ACCUSED OF ....
   A court heard today how an office worker was almost driven to suicide by a bullying office manager. James Blenkinsop, 27, told how boss Nigel Kemp victimized him by shouting at him, criticizing his work in front of others, tearing up his work and telling him to do it again.

2.
   NATIONAL RESTAURANT CHAIN FACES .... **CLAIMS**
   Four waitresses claim they were repeatedly .... by male bosses in a branch of a well-known national restaurant chain. All four waitresses said they were subjected to sexist remarks at the restaurant.

3.
   JAPANESE WOMEN BREAK THROUGH ....
   Naomi Tanaka, 23, last year started working on the Tokyo Stock Exchange as a trader. She complained about traditional .... and said she did not want to be a 'counter lady' answering phones and serving tea at a Japanese bank. Instead she got a job as a trader at Paribas, a French firm.

4.
   SHOP MANAGERESS IN .... **CASE**
   A clothing shop's half-Burmese manageress, 24-year-old Marion Brown, claims her boss continually made .... remarks, and sacked her from her £110-a-week job when she objected. She claims that the company that owns the shop has racially .... against her.

5.
   .... **ABOLISHED AT TEXAS LAW SCHOOL**
   Last year federal law court made affirmative action at the University of Texas law school illegal, and supporters of .... have said that it was a 'disaster'. The University of Texas law school last year admitted a class that was 5.9 per cent black and 6.3 per cent Hispanic. This year the black percentage stands at just over 0.7 and the Hispanic at 2.3.

8.2 Match the employees' complaints (1–7) with health and safety issues (a–g) in C opposite.

1. I do a lot of data entry, and recently I've started getting really bad pains in my wrists. ☐
2. My doctor says there's something wrong with my lungs, but I've never smoked. ☐
3. It's either too cold and we freeze, or too hot and we all fall asleep. ☐
4. There's all this waste paper, but there no fire extinguishers in the building. ☐
5. The containers are leaking – one day someone is going to get acid burns. ☐
6. There are no safety guards on the machines – you could easily get your hand caught. ☐
7. There are all these problems, but no-one is trained to give medical assistance. ☐

Over to you

Think about the industry you work in or would like to work in. Look at a health and safety website, for example the UK government site at www.hse.gov.uk, and identify key hazards in the industry.

9 Managers, executives and directors

A Managers and executives: UK

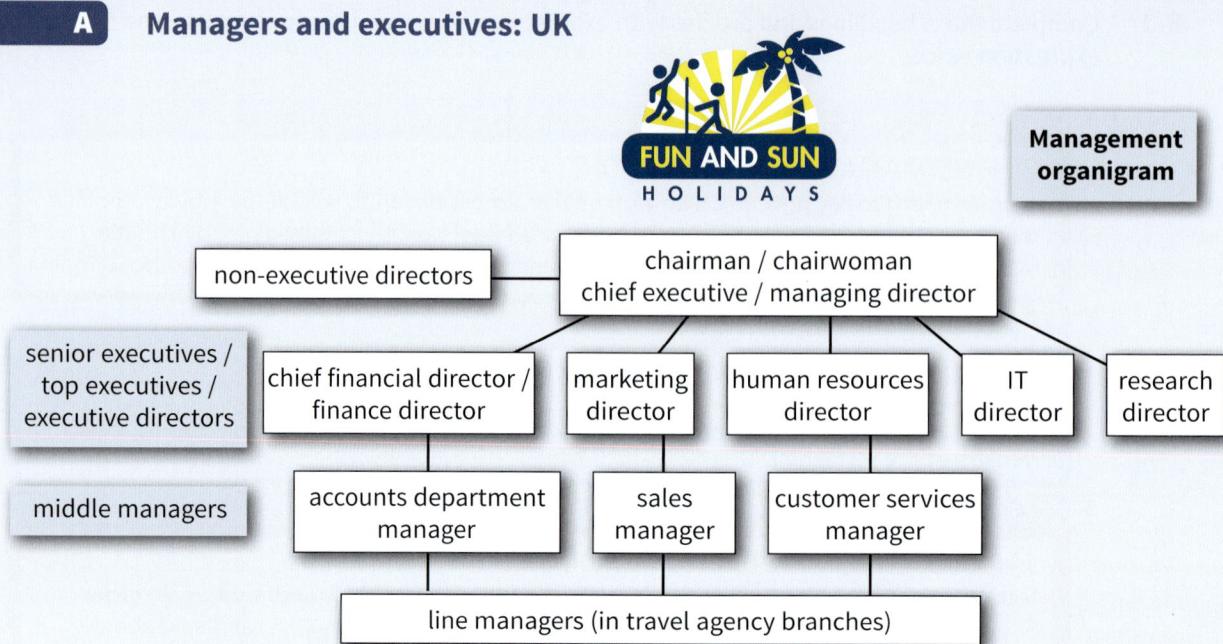

Management organigram

All the directors together are the **board**. They meet in the **boardroom**.

Non-executive directors are not managers of the company; they are outsiders, often directors of other companies with specialist knowledge of the industry or of particular areas.

The marketing director is the **head of marketing**, the IT director is **head of IT**, etc. These people **head** or **head up** their departments. Informally, the head of an activity, a department or an organization is its **boss**.

An **executive**, or informally, an **exec**, is usually a high-level manager, as in **senior executive**.

> **Note**
>
> Executive can be used in other contexts to suggest luxury – as in **executive car** and **executive home**. It can even be used for things that are not actually used by executives.

B Managers and executives: US

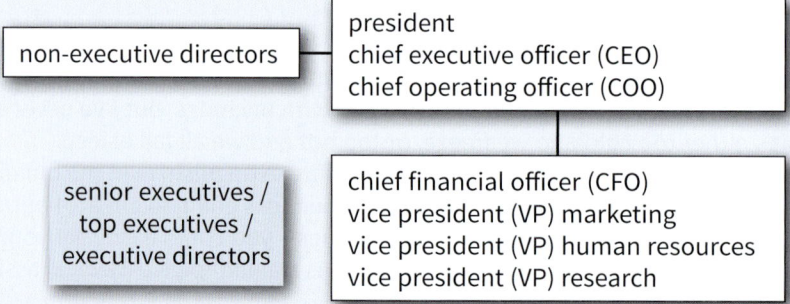

In the US, the top position may be that of **chairman**, **chairwoman** or **president**. This job is often combined with the position of **chief executive officer (CEO)**. Some companies have a **chief operating officer** to take care of the day-to-day running of the company. The finance director may be called the **chief financial officer (CFO)**.

In a US company, the senior managers in charge of particular areas are often called **vice presidents (VPs)**.

Business Vocabulary in Use Intermediate

Exercises

9.1 Look at the executives and managers listed in A opposite. Match each task (1–6) with the particular person most likely to be responsible for doing it.

1. Meet with advertising agency to discuss new advertisements for the company's holidays.
2. Study possible new holiday destinations in detail.
3. Analyse last year's profits in relation to the previous year's.
4. Contact newspaper to advertise new jobs.
5. Deal with complaints from customers.
6. Discuss sales figures with sales team.

9.2 Who's who on this company board? Look at B opposite and complete the diagram.

> My name's Maria Montebello, and I'm president and CEO. We have some excellent people on our board, including two who are not involved in day-to-day running of the company: George Gomi and Julia Jones.

> My name's Stan Smith and it's my job to look after the accounts. I work closely with Clarissa Chang and Richard Roberts, as they tell me what their departments need for marketing and research, and I allocate them an annual budget.

> My name's Deirdre Dawes and I head up personnel, on the same level in the company as Clarissa Chang and Richard Roberts.

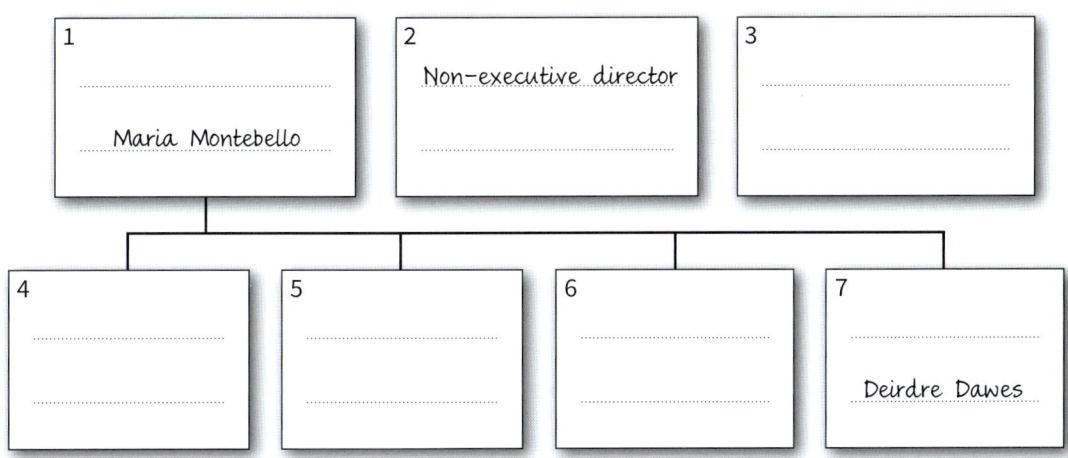

Over to you

If you work, draw an organigram of your organization and practise describing it to a new colleague.

If you don't work, think of a job you would like in an organization and write about why you would be good at the job.

10 Businesspeople and business leaders

A Businesspeople and entrepreneurs

A **businessman**, **businesswoman** or **businessperson** is someone who works in their own business or as a manager in an organization.

An **entrepreneur** is someone who starts or **founds** or **establishes** their own company. Someone who starts a company is its **founder**. An entrepreneur may found a series of companies or **start-ups**. **Entrepreneurial** is used in a positive way to describe the risk-taking people who do this, and their activities. Some entrepreneurs leave the companies they found, perhaps going on to found more companies. Others may stay to develop and **grow** their businesses.

> **Note**
>
> The plural of **businessperson** is **businesspeople**. **Businessperson** and **businesspeople** can be spelled as two words: **business person**, **business people**.
>
> **Found** is a regular verb: past tense and past participle are **founded**.
>
> **Establishment** is used to talk about the act of founding something as well as a particular organization, or part of one.
>
> Some English speakers believe it is not correct to use **grow** as a transitive verb in this context.

> **Note**
>
> **Entrepreneur** is used in combinations such as **internet entrepreneur**.

B Leaders and leadership

A large group of companies mainly owned by one person or family is a **business empire**. Successful businesspeople, especially heads of large organizations, are **business leaders**, or in slightly old-fashioned journalistic terms, **captains of industry**.

There is a lot of discussion about whether people like this are born with **leadership skills**, or whether these can be taught.

C Magnates, moguls and tycoons

People in charge of big business empires may be referred to, especially by journalists, as **magnates**, **moguls** or **tycoons**. These words often occur in combinations such as these:

- media magnate
- property mogul
- software tycoon

Business Vocabulary in Use Intermediate

Exercises

10.1 Use words from A and B opposite to complete the missing words.

The big place for people starting their own companies – for (1) _ _ _ _ _ _ _ _ _ _ _ _ – is, of course, the internet. Take Sergey Brin and Larry Page. They met while doing their doctorates at Stanford, where they were encouraged to develop their mathematical research on the world wide web. Brin and Page are both very (2) _ _ _ _ _ _ _ _ _ _ _ _ _ _ _. They (3) _ _ _ _ _ _ _ Google together in 1998: some of the investment in the (4) _ _ _ _ _-_ _ came from Andy Bechtolsheim, one of the founders of Sun Microsystems.

Now Brin and Page are both very rich, with their own Boeing 767. In 2006, Brin and Page appointed Eric Schmidt to develop and (5) _ _ _ _ the business. Like many entrepreneurs, they felt that they did not have the (6) _ _ _ _ _ _ _ _ _ _ skills to head up and inspire a large business (7) _ _ _ _ _ _.

10.2 Who are these famous businesspeople? Use the expressions below to describe them.

| electric car entrepreneur | e-commerce mogul | social media website founder |
| property tycoon | retail entrepreneur | banking entrepreneur |

Güler Sabancı (b. 1955)

Cath Kidston (b. 1958)

Jack Ma (b. 1964)

Elon Musk (b. 1971)

Zhang Xin (b. 1965)

Mark Zuckerberg (b. 1984)

```
Over to you
```
- Who is your country's most famous entrepreneur? What is this person famous for?
- In your opinion, are entrepreneurs born or made?

Business Vocabulary in Use Intermediate

11 Organizations 1

A Business and businesses

Business is the activity of producing, buying and selling goods and services. A **business**, **company** or **firm,** or more formally a **concern**, is an organization that sells goods or services. Large companies considered together are referred to as **big business**.

You can talk about a company or a particular activity as an **enterprise**, especially to emphasize its risk-taking nature.

Businesses vary in size, from the **self-employed** person working on their own, through the **small or medium enterprise (SME)** to the large **multinational** with activities in several countries.

A large company, especially in the US, is a **corporation**. The adjective is **corporate**, used to talk about a big company – or big companies in general. **Corporate** is often used in these combinations:

corporate	culture	the way a company's employees think and act
	ladder	the different levels of management in a company
	headquarters	a company's main office
	logo	a symbol used by a company on its products, advertising, etc.
	image	all the ideas, opinions, etc. that people have about a company
	profits	the money made by companies

B Commerce

Commerce is used:

- to refer to business in relation to other fields: 'literature, politics and commerce'.
- for government departments that deal with business: US **Department of Commerce**.
- in the names of organizations that exist to help business: **chambers of commerce**.
- to refer to business on the internet: **electronic commerce** or **e-commerce**.

The adjective **commercial** describes money-making business activities: for example, **commercial airline**, **commercial artist**, **commercial disaster**.

C Enterprise

In 1970s Britain, there were **state-owned** or **government-owned companies** in many different industries, such as car manufacturing. Some industries, such as coal and electricity, had been **nationalized** – they were entirely state-owned. In the 1980s, the Thatcher government believed that **nationalized companies** were inefficient, so many of them were **privatized** by selling them to investors. Supporters of **privatization** believed that **bureaucracy** – the system for running government departments, with its rigid rules and slow decisions – was not good for business: state-run companies were too **bureaucratic**.

Enterprise is used in a positive way to talk about business, emphasizing the use of money to invest in new activities with a certain amount of risk involved. **Enterprise** is often used in these combinations:

| free / private | enterprise | business activity owned by individuals rather than the state |

enterprise	culture	when people are encouraged to make money through their own activities and not rely on the government
	economy	an economy where there is an enterprise culture
	zone	part of a country where business is encouraged because there are less strict laws, lower taxes, etc.

Business Vocabulary in Use Intermediate

Exercises

11.1 Match the two parts of these sentences containing expressions from A opposite.

1. Managers who themselves often worked long hours in order to climb the corporate
2. Analysts forecast a slowing of economic growth because of lower corporate
3. 3M continues to improve its corporate
4. Retailer Best Buy is allowing employees at its corporate
5. The only corporate
6. Listening to customers is part of the corporate

a. image by showing environmental leadership.
b. logo in view was the Haagen Dazs name on three table umbrellas.
c. profits, capital gains taxes and slow job growth.
d. ladder may demand the same thing from their employees.
e. culture at Lowe's, and managers use a variety of methods to ensure that it's happening.
f. headquarters to set their own hours and work outside the office.

11.2 Someone is talking about words and expressions in B and C opposite. Which are they referring to each time?

1. They're not companies in which people can buy shares. (3 expressions)
2. It carries passengers and goods in order to make a profit.
3. It's so slow and inefficient: no way to run a business!
4. It's going to be used for offices and factories, not houses.
5. It's owned and run by private companies, and the programmes are interrupted by advertising.
6. We need to encourage this in order for the economy to grow and modernize.
7. He does advertisements: you can't find his work in art galleries.
8. It was an artistic success, but unfortunately it lost a lot of money.

11.3 Use expressions with 'enterprise' from C opposite to complete this text.

Margaret Thatcher often talked about the benefits of **(1)** _____ or **(2)** _____. She said that her achievement was to establish an **(3)** _____ in Britain, an economy based on free enterprise. She wanted a society where people were encouraged to start their own companies and where it was acceptable to get rich through business: an **(4)** _____.

In some areas, the government reduced the number of laws and regulations to encourage businesses to move there. Businesses were encouraged to set up in the Docklands of London, for example. The Docklands were an **(5)** _____.

> **Over to you**
>
> Write short reports about the issues below. Research them on the internet if necessary.
>
> - How big is the public sector in your country? Do people who work in it have good working conditions compared to those in the private sector?
> - In your country, which of these industries are in the public sector, and which are in the private sector? Which have been privatized?
>
>   bus transport   electricity supply   postal services
>   rail transport   telephone services   water supply

12 Organizations 2

A Self-employed people and partnerships

Oscar is a **freelance** graphic designer – a **freelancer**. He likes the freedom of working for himself. To use the official term, he's a **sole trader**.

People such as designers and journalists are freelancers (see Unit 7), whereas builders and plumbers are normally referred to as being **self-employed**.

Jane and Miranda are architects who have set up their own architecture **partnership**. A lot of professional people like lawyers, accountants, and so on work in partnerships. They are **partners** – there are no shareholders (see Unit 32) in the organization apart from the two of them.

> **Note:** **Sole owner** and **sole proprietor** are both used in BrE and AmE. **Sole trader** is not used in the US.

B Limited liability

Jane and her partners have **limited liability**: if the partnership **goes bankrupt** – runs out of money – the people to whom the partnership owes money can take the company's **assets** to pay the debts, but they can't take personal assets such as the partners' houses or cars. It's a **limited liability partnership (LLP)**.

Jon Robertson is managing director and main shareholder of a small electronics company in Scotland called Advanced Components **Ltd**. 'Ltd' means **limited company**, with limited liability.

Howard Schultz is president of Starbucks **Inc**. 'Inc' stands for **Incorporated**. This shows that it is a **corporation** – used especially in the US for companies with limited liability, and also used in the UK in the names of some big companies.

Some British companies include **PLC** as part of their name. This means that the company is a **public limited company**, and its shares are bought and sold on the stock exchange (see Unit 36).

Howard Schultz

C Mutuals

Some companies like certain **life insurance companies** are **mutuals**. People buying insurance with the company are its **members** and there are no shareholders. Profits are theoretically owned by the members.

In Britain, there are mutuals called **building societies**, which lend money to people who want to buy a house. But a lot of building societies are changing into public limited companies with shareholders: many have **demutualized** in a process of **demutualization** (see Unit 35).

D Non-profit organizations

Organizations with 'social' aims such as helping those who are sick or poor, or encouraging artistic activity, are **non-profit organizations** (BrE) or **not-for-profit organizations** (AmE). They are also called **charities** and form the **voluntary sector**: they rely heavily on **volunteers** – unpaid workers. For example, a charity like Médecins sans Frontières is managed by paid professionals, and together they put a lot of effort into **fundraising** activities. These activities encourage people to give or **donate** money, clothes, food or time to help the organization. These **donations** are essential for the organization to do its work.

Business Vocabulary in Use Intermediate

Exercises

12.1 Look at the words in A and B opposite. Which type of organization is each of these?

1. A group of engineers who work together to provide consultancy and design services. There are no outside shareholders.
2. A large British engineering company with 30,000 employees. Its shares are bought and sold on the stock market.
3. An American engineering company with outside shareholders.
4. An engineer who works by herself by providing consultancy. She works from home and visits clients in their offices. (3 possibilities)
5. An independent British engineering company with 20 employees. It was founded by three engineers, who are shareholders and directors of the company. There are five other shareholders who do not work for the company.

12.2 Complete this newspaper article with expressions from C opposite.

NEWSONLINE

Home | News | World | Business | Food | Technology | Science

Angry scenes as members reject (1) ....

There were angry scenes at the Suffolk (2) .... 's annual meeting as the society's (3) .... rejected by two to one a recommendation from its board that the society be (4) .... Members had travelled from all over the country to attend the meeting in London. The Suffolk's chief executive, Mr Andrew Davies, said, 'This is a sad day for the Suffolk. We need to

(5) .... to bring the society forward into the 21st century. Our own resources are not enough and we need capital from outside shareholders.'
Gwen Armstrong, who has saved with the Suffolk for 32 years, said, 'Keeping (6) .... status is a great victory. Profits should stay with us and not go to outside shareholders.'

Comment Like

12.3 Match the sentence beginnings (1–5) with the correct endings (a–e). The sentences all contain expressions from D opposite.

1. British people donate around £4 a week each on average to charities
2. She organized fundraising
3. Voluntary sector employees earn five to ten per cent
4. Non-profit organizations are not to be confused
5. Research shows that volunteers give the best service

a. with loss-making companies!
b. and many volunteer to give their skills too.
c. parties for the charity.
d. when they are helping people in their own social class.
e. less than they would in the private sector.

Over to you

Which non-profit organizations are well-known in your country? What do they do? How do they raise money?

13 Manufacturing and services

A Manufacturing and services

Here are some of the **manufacturing industries** that make up the **manufacturing sector**.

aerospace	planes and space vehicles
cars (BrE) **automobiles** (AmE)	cars
computer hardware	computers, printers, etc.
construction	buildings
defence (BrE) **defense** (AmE)	weapons
electronics	mobile phones, etc.
food processing	canned, frozen, etc. foods
household goods	washing machines, refrigerators, etc.
pharmaceuticals	medicines
steel	a strong metal used in the manufacturing of machinery and cars
textiles	cloth and clothes

Here are some of the **services** or **service industries** that make up the **service sector**.

call centres (BrE) **call centers** (AmE)	dealing with orders, complaints, etc. from customers by phone
catering	restaurants, bars, etc.
computer software	instructions for computers
financial services	banking, insurance, etc.
healthcare	medical care
leisure	cinemas, sport, etc.
media	books, newspapers, film, television
property (BrE) **real estate** (AmE)	buying, selling and managing buildings
retail	shops
telecommunications	phone, internet services
tourism	travel and holidays

> **Note**
>
> You use all these names in front of **industry** to talk about particular industries. You usually drop the **s** from **cars**, **automobiles**, **pharmaceuticals** and **textiles**: **the automobile industry**, etc.

B Countries and their industries

Industry (uncountable) is the production of materials and goods. An industry is a particular type of business activity. The related adjective is **industrial**. Here is how industry has developed in Brazil.

1950s and 60s	1970–2000	Today
In 1950, Brazil was a relatively poor country, with most people living and working on the land. The government decided to **industrialize**, and one of the new **emerging industries** in the 60s was the building of aircraft.	The Brazilian **economy** developed in many different areas: **growth industries** ranged from **light industries** such as textiles and telecommunications equipment to **heavy industries** like steel production.	Brazil's economy is **diversified**, with many different industries: the service sector makes up 70.8 per cent, industry 24 per cent and agriculture 5.2 per cent.

Business Vocabulary in Use Intermediate

Exercises

13.1 Look at A opposite. Which industry or service is each of these companies in?

1 Microsoft	3 Glaxo Smith Kline	5 Kia	7 Banco Santander
2 Terra	4 Boeing	6 Time Warner	8 Gap

13.2 A company will have to deal with problems that are specific to its industry. Match each problem (1–5) with one of the industries in A opposite.

1 buying a new building and being unable to find people to rent it
2 holidaymakers arriving to find that their hotel is not finished
3 lending to someone who cannot repay the loan
4 selling weapons to governments that people do not approve of
5 making drugs that poor countries cannot afford

13.3 Complete the crossword with the correct form of words from A and B opposite.

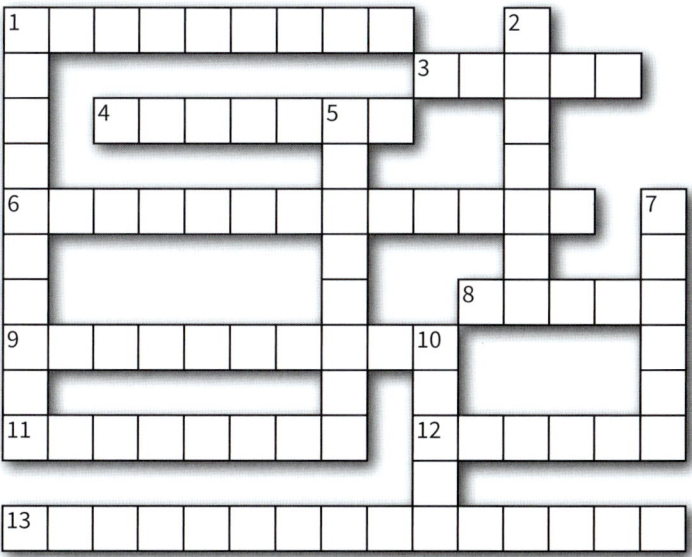

Across
1 plane and rocket industry (9)
3 metal industry (5)
4 an industry that doesn't sell goods (7)
6 making things (13)
8 television, music, the internet (5)
9 related to industry or industries (10)
11 describing a new industry (8)
12 describing an industry that is getting bigger (6)
13 making drugs (15)

Down
1 making cars: the .... industry (10)
2 making weapons (7)
5 serving food and drink, rather than making them (8)
7 keeping people well: .... care (6)
10 making televisions rather than steel: .... industry (5)

```
Over to you
```

- What products are manufactured in your country, and where?
- How diversified is your country's economy?

Business Vocabulary in Use Intermediate 35

14 The development process

A Market research

In designing products and services, **market research** – finding out what people really want – is very important.

There are five ways of carrying out market research:

- **Surveys** are of four types:
    1. **In-person surveys** can show an example or **sample** of a new product, but they are expensive.
    2. **Telephone surveys** are less expensive, but people do not like to be **called up** and asked questions.
    3. **Mail surveys** have **low response rates** because few people send the surveys back; they are inexpensive, however.
    4. **Online surveys** are simple and inexpensive, but usually unpredictable as there is no control over the **pool** or selection of people that **take part in** this kind of survey.
- **Focus groups** usually last 1–2 hours. A **moderator** uses specially prepared questions to ask a group. It takes at least three groups to get accurate results.
- **Personal interviews** usually last about an hour – they are normally recorded. As with focus groups, not doing enough interviews gives inaccurate results.
- **Observations** involve observing consumers in action by videoing them in stores, watching them at work, or observing how they use a product at home.
- **Field trials** involve placing a new product in selected stores to test customer response under real-life selling conditions.

See Unit 15 for more on development and Unit 21 for more on marketing.

In-person survey

Focus group

B Development and launch

- When software **developers** (see Unit 15) have finished the **beta version** – first version – of a program, they **release** this on the internet and users are asked to **try it out** and to identify **bugs** or problems.
- Car **designers** use **CAD/CAM** (computer-assisted design / computer-assisted manufacturing) to help develop and test the first versions or **prototypes** of the new product.
- **Researchers** in **laboratories** may take years to develop new drugs, **testing** or **trialling** them in **trials** to show not only that they are **effective**, but also that they are safe. Drugs need to be made in large numbers on an **industrial scale** before they can be sold.
- **Rollout** is the process of making a product available, perhaps in particular places to test reaction.
- **Product launch** is the moment of truth when a product is officially made available for sale.
- If a **design defect** or **design fault** is found in a product after it has been launched, the company may have to **recall** it, asking those who have bought the product to return it, perhaps so that the defect can be corrected.

> **Note**
>
> **Design defect**, **design fault** and **design flaw** all mean the same thing, but the first of these is the most frequent.
>
> **Testing** and **trialling** (BrE) / **trialing** (AmE) are both used to talk about people trying new products and services. The noun **trial** is used especially to talk about testing the effectiveness of new drugs, for example in the expression **clinical trial**.

Exercises

14.1 Which expression in A opposite does the underlined word refer to in each item (1–6)?

1 <u>It</u> lasts up to two hours and has someone asking specific questions, but just one is not normally considered enough. *focus group*
2 <u>These</u> are useful because you can see how people actually use the product.
3 <u>These</u> can take different forms – some are more efficient than others at getting information about what people want.
4 <u>He or she</u> organizes the discussion in a focus group.
5 <u>These</u> cause problems for one type of survey, which mean that they might not be reliable.
6 With <u>these</u>, you can examine how people react when they see the product on the shelves.

14.2 Three people are talking about their work in product development. Correct the mistakes in the words in italics, using expressions from A and B opposite.

1 '(a) *Market researches* showed that there was a real need for this service on our webpage, but before offering it, we had to test it in a (b) *beta copy* with small groups of users over several months to eliminate all the bugs. Even so, after the (c) *product lunch*, some users said they could get into other people's email accounts!'
2 'Our (d) *searchers* have shown that our new diet drink can make you slimmer and the (e) *focal groups* said they liked the taste, but first we had to prove to the authorities that it was (f) *secure*. Another problem was making the drink on an (g) *industrial level*: at first we could only make it in small quantities in the laboratory, but making it in bigger quantities was impossible.'
3 'At our research centre in Toulouse in France, the (h) *designators* develop the prototypes. People think that my job of flying new aircraft is dangerous, but there is so much (i) *proving* on computer first, that all the danger has been eliminated by the time I fly the plane.
(j) *CAM/CAD* means that all the process of design and manufacture is much quicker than before.'

14.3 Complete this talk by a marketing specialist using these words from A and B opposite.

| consumer | design | groups | launch | market | recall | surveys |

A few years ago a famous car company launched a completely new car. They'd done years of technical research and **(1)** .... research with focus **(2)** .... and **(3)** .... panels, and analysis of responses to questionnaires and **(4)** .... Then came the **(5)** .... Sales of the car were very good until a Swedish newspaper reported the results of its 'elk test'. They found that the car had a tendency to tip over if you turned quickly to avoid an elk. This was due to a **(6)** .... fault in the car, so they had to **(7)** .... all the cars they'd sold in order to correct the fault.

Over to you

- What does a pharmaceutical company need to do before it can release a new drug?
- What kind of surveys have you taken part in?
- What will a company do if they find a problem in a product after the launch? And why might this be a big problem?

15 Innovation and invention

A Innovation and invention

Verb	Noun: concept (uncountable)	Noun: thing (countable)	Noun: person
design – to make plans or drawings for how something is to be made	design	a design	a designer
develop – to make a new idea become successful, for example by making or improving a product	development	a development	a developer
innovate – to think of new ideas, methods, products, etc.	innovation	an innovation	an innovator
invent – to design and make something for the first time	invention	an invention	an inventor

B Research and technology

Google carries out **research and development (R&D)** at its **research centre** in Mountain View, California. Its **laboratories** are some of the most **innovative** in the computer industry.

> **Note**
> BrE: **research centre**
> AmE: **research center**

Google has made many new **breakthroughs** – innovations. Users can try out these products before they are **released** in their final version.

The company is a leader in the **technology** of internet search. They are at the **cutting edge** or **leading edge** of this technology – none of their competitors has better products than them. Everything they do is **state-of-the-art** – using the most advanced techniques available.

Of course, the **hi-tech** products of today become the **low-tech** products of tomorrow. Products that are no longer up-to-date because they use old technology are **obsolete**. Like all companies, Google never wants to get into that situation: they want to develop technology that is **future-proof**.

> **Note**
> **Cutting edge** is used about three times as much as **leading edge**. Both are often used as adjectives, e.g. **cutting-edge products**, **leading-edge technology**.

C Patents and intellectual property

Information or knowledge that belongs to an individual or company is **proprietary**. A product developed using such information may be protected in law by **patents** so that others cannot copy its design.

Other companies may pay to use a design **under licence** in their own products. These payments may be referred to as **royalties**.

> **Note**
> | | Noun | Verb |
> | --- | --- | --- |
> | BrE: | a licence | to license |
> | AmE: | a license | to license |

In publishing, if a text, picture, etc. is **copyright**, it cannot be used by others without permission: this is **copyright infringement**. An example of this is **illegal downloading** of music, films and software from the internet: this is **piracy**.

Another form of piracy is when **fake** products, often luxury products such as Rolex or Chanel, are sold without the permission of the company that owns the **brand name** (see Unit 22) or **trademark** – a recognizable symbol used on the product.

The area of law relating to patents, copyright and trademarks is **intellectual property**.

Business Vocabulary in Use Intermediate

Exercises

15.1 Complete this webpage using these expressions from A and B opposite.

| cutting edge | develop | developed | development | innovation |
| release | state-of-the-art | technologies | technology | |

NEWSONLINE

Home | News | World | Business | Food | Technology | Science

Imagine being able to work on products across all business groups of Microsoft. You can do it here at the Microsoft India Development Center in Hyderabad, a center for true (1) _____ ! MSIDC is located in a 50-acre (2) _____ campus. It is Microsoft's largest product (3) _____ center outside the headquarters in Redmond, and is recognized as an industry leader with teams working at the (4) _____ , developing (5) _____ and products for millions of Microsoft customers worldwide. MSIDC has (6) _____ many core products and technologies for the global market since its inception in 1998. Our teams have end-to-end responsibility for every product or (7) _____ they (8) _____ . They own the strategy, gather customer requirements from across the world, plan different versions, and then design, test and (9) _____ the product for the market.

15.2 Match the expressions (1–10) containing words in C opposite with their meanings (a–j).

1 copyright infringement
2 intellectual property
3 patent application
4 proprietary information
5 royalty payment
6 licensing agreement
7 illegal download
8 piracy
9 trademark
10 brand name

a a payment made to the owner of a design by someone else who uses it, or to an author by a publisher
b an arrangement between the owner of a design and another organization, allowing its use in exchange for payment
c a name or symbol used on a product
d an occasion when an inventor asks the authorities to officially recognize an invention as their property
e designs, ideas, etc. that belong to someone
f a name used on a product
g the whole activity of using designs, text, pictures or copying products without permission
h an occasion when someone makes an illegal copy of music, etc. from an internet site
i the law relating to designs, ideas, etc. that belong to someone
j an occasion when someone uses another's text, pictures, etc. without permission

Over to you

- Name a product that has become obsolete and suggest why that happened.
- How do companies try to prevent illegal downloading of music and films? Will they ever succeed completely?

16 Products and services

A Products

A **product** can be: something natural, e.g. wood, oil, paper; something made to be sold, e.g. cars, computers, clothes; a service, e.g. broadcasting, insurance.

Produce (uncountable) normally refers to agricultural products such as crops or fruit.

Noun: things	Noun: company or country	Verb	Noun: activity
(manufactured) products / goods (see Unit 17)	maker / manufacturer / producer	make / manufacture / produce	manufacture / manufacturing / production
(agricultural) produce / products	producer	produce	manufacture / manufacturing / production
services	provider	provide	provision

B Mass production

Car production started in **workshops** where each car was individually **hand-made**. Producing cars like this was a **craft industry**. It was very **labour-intensive** – it took a lot of work to produce each car.

Then, in 1913, Henry Ford had the idea of an **assembly line** or **production line** at the Ford **manufacturing plant** in Detroit: a team of workers were responsible for each part of the manufacturing process, which meant that the plant could make cars in very large numbers – it could **churn** them **out**.

Today, the same system is used in manufacturing, but with the addition of **industrial robots**. The machines are expensive but very **cost-effective** – they produce a lot in relation to what they cost. These robots are part of the **CAD/CAM** system of **computer-assisted** (or **computer-aided**) **design and manufacturing** (see Unit 14).

> **Note**
>
> BrE: **labour-intensive**; AmE: **labor-intensive**
> A **plant** can also be referred to as a **factory** or a **works**, but **works** is a slightly old-fashioned word.

C Capacity and output

The number or type of things that a company, plant, industry or country produces is its **output**. **Productivity** is a measure of the number of things produced in relation to the number of employees. When there is high output per employee, productivity is high.

The maximum amount that a particular company, plant or industry can produce is its **capacity**. If it is actually producing this amount, it is **working at full capacity**.

> **Note**
>
> There is **overcapacity**, **excess capacity**, **spare capacity** or **surplus capacity** if there is too much capacity in relation to what is required. The expressions are given in their order of frequency. These expressions are also used in service industries.

If too many things are being produced by a particular industry in relation to the number of people who want to buy them, there is **overproduction**. If far too many things are produced, there is a **surplus** or **glut** of these things. If not enough goods are being produced, there is a **shortage**.

Exercises

16.1 Complete the sentences with grammatically correct forms of the words in the table in A opposite. (The number in brackets indicates the number of different possible answers.)

1. A lot of mobile phone .... (3 possibilities) takes place in China, but Nokia still .... (3 possibilities) them in Finland too, so Finland is a .... (3 possibilities) of mobile phones.
2. India is important for call centres, but it is also emerging as a .... of .... of all kinds, including accountancy.
3. Russia is a major oil .... and also important for the .... of gas.
4. The United Kingdom is a big .... of legal and financial services.
5. Brazil is still the world's biggest coffee .... , but coffee is also .... in many other countries, including new ones such as Vietnam.
6. With the increase in medical tourism, Thailand is emerging as an important centre for the .... of healthcare services to people from other countries.

16.2 Look at B opposite. Rearrange these sections of a short presentation about manufacturing into a logical order.

a work. Of course, we still have a large number of assembly-
b plant producing TVs in Singapore. We have two production
c My name's George Chien, and I'm director of a manufacturing
d lines working 24 hours a day. CAD/
e intensive. But with the help of computer-
f line workers, so it's quite labour-
g CAM and robots do some of the assembly
h assisted design and automation, productivity is increasing.

16.3 Match the headlines (1–4), containing words from C opposite, with extracts of the articles they relate to (a–d).

1. FOOD SHORTAGES HIT EASTERN AFRICA
2. TOO MUCH BUILDING LEADS TO GLUT OF OFFICE SPACE
3. AIRLINE REPORTS BIG PRODUCTIVITY RISE
4. LOCAL PLANT AT FULL CAPACITY

a Rainfall has been below average in this part of Africa for the past five years. Not enough food has been grown and now there are food …

b The plant has the capacity to produce 3,000 computers a week, and it's producing 3,000. That's the good news …

c Ryanair is running more flights with fewer pilots and staff. That was the message from Ryanair's CEO Michael O'Leary to shareholders yesterday …

d There has been too much construction in the city centre, and now there is a lot of office space standing empty …

> **Over to you**
>
> Are hand-made products better than mass-produced products?

17 Materials and suppliers

A Inputs

Dyson makes vacuum cleaners. It takes **raw materials** like steel and plastic, and makes some of the **components** – or **parts** – used in its products. (Other components are made by other companies.)

Here are some typical combinations:

| aerospace
automotive
car
computer
electronic | } components |

| replacement
spare | } parts |

Materials and parts are just some of the **inputs**. The others are **labour** – workers and managers – and **capital** – money. **Knowledge** is also important because Dyson is a leader in vacuum technology.

Vacuum cleaners that are in the course of being made are **work-in-progress**. At any one time, Dyson has **goods** (see Unit 16) worth millions of dollars in its factories and warehouses; these are both the materials and components used to make its products, and its **finished goods** – the products that have been made.

Quantities of raw materials, components, work-in-progress and finished goods in a particular place are **stocks**.

> **Note**
>
> BrE: **work-in-progress**; AmE: **work-in-process**
> BrE: **stocks**; AmE: **inventories**
> **Goods** is rarely used in the singular, except in specialized economics contexts.

B Suppliers and outsourcing

Dyson has its own **manufacturing operation**, but it works with its **suppliers** – companies that provide materials and components. Some companies refer to their suppliers as **partners**.

The company uses **subcontracting** – which means using **outside suppliers** to provide components and services. In other words, it uses **outsourcing** rather than doing these activities **in-house** – within the company.

> **Note**
>
> **Outside** is the most frequently occurring adjective in front of **suppliers**.

C Just-in-time

It costs money to keep components and goods available for customers to buy **in stock**. Stocks have to be **financed** – paid for. They also have to be **stored** – kept in special buildings called **warehouses** – and **handled** – moved from one place to another. So Dyson is asking its suppliers to provide components **just-in-time** – when they are needed.

This is part of **lean production** or **lean manufacturing**, in which products are made in the most **efficient** way – doing things as quickly and cheaply as possible, without waste.

A warehouse

> **Note**
>
> **Lean production** is about as frequent as **lean manufacturing**.

42   Business Vocabulary in Use Intermediate

Exercises

17.1 Use words from A opposite to label the diagram.

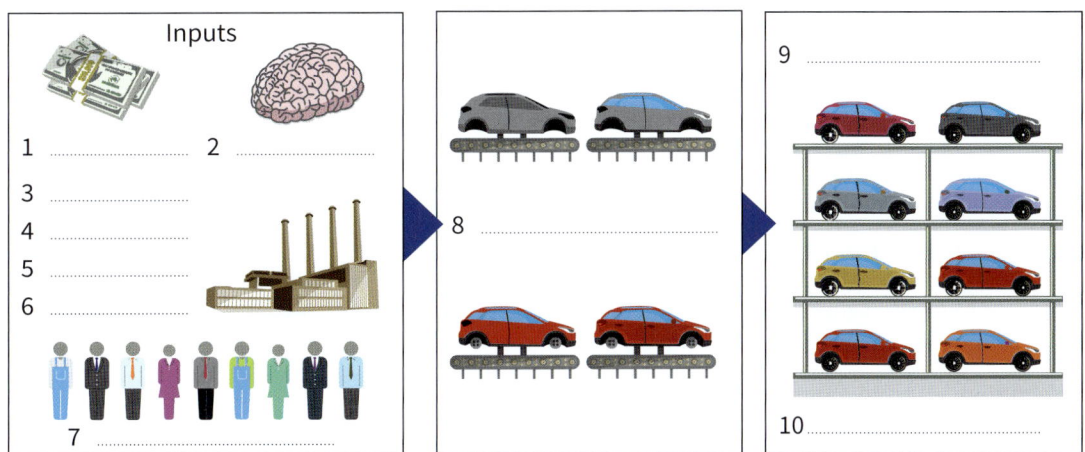

17.2 Match the sentence beginnings (1–6) with the correct endings (a–f) containing expressions from B opposite.

1 The computer manufacturer is cutting back on in-
2 The poor standard of some subcontractors'
3 Retail giants Sharks Ltd have decided to
4 Late deliveries from outside
5 Gruma has manufacturing
6 Lilly and its partners

a maintenance is worrying train operating companies.
b spent $157 million on the Cymbalta advertising campaign.
c house production work in a bid to reduce costs and increase efficiency.
d outsource canteen and cleaning services, to focus better on its buying and selling activities.
e suppliers are causing delays in production, the Azco group claims.
f operations on five continents, and its products are sold in more than 50 countries.

17.3 Replace the words in italics with the correct forms of words from C opposite.

1 Let's get the materials *only when we need them* to keep costs down.

2 It's difficult to find the right *special buildings* to put our finished goods in.

3 You have to decide well in advance how to *pay for* all this.

4 It's very important that we *keep* these components at the right temperature.

5 The company found that using couriers on bicycles was a very *quick and effective* way to deliver documents in big cities.

6 They want to introduce a system of *making things efficiently without waste*.

```
Over to you
```
What are the advantages and disadvantages of the following?
• outsourcing
• asking for components 'just-in-time'

18 Business philosophies

A Mass customization

Production lines (see Unit 16) are good for **mass production** – producing large numbers of similar products. Manufacturers try to make **standard** products, with few variations, that as many people as possible will want to buy. **Standardization** is the most important factor.

Custom-built or **tailor-made** products, where each product is made to meet the **specifications, requirements** or **needs** (see Unit 21) of a particular customer, are more expensive to produce, of course.

Custom-built bicycles

The management thinker Joseph Pine and others talk about the possibilities of **mass customization**, where products are made in large quantities, but each one is made to the specifications of the **buyer** – the person or organization buying it. Dell Computers, where each computer is made for a particular buyer, is the best-known example of this.

B Wikinomics

Wikinomics: How Mass Collaboration Changes Everything is a book by Don Tapscott and Anthony D. Williams. In it, they explain that **Wikinomics** is a form of **mass collaboration**, where companies have large numbers of people working together on the internet to solve problems and develop products. This is totally unlike current business methods and the authors predict that it will be a key to business success in the future. It is like an extreme form of **outsourcing** (see Unit 17). They say that customers who contribute to the design and development of products should be called **prosumers** – they work together to make things in a process of **peer collaboration** and **co-creation**.

C The long tail

Another challenge to mass production is **the long tail**. In *The Long Tail: Why the Future of Business is Selling Less of More,* Chris Anderson says that the mass production **model** – way of doing things – does not apply to many products, such as selling books and music on the internet. In a large **catalogue** of items (see Unit 22), the cost of selling the least popular item is only slightly more than selling the most popular. Amazon has used this model to great advantage, profitably selling small numbers of specialized books, as well as large numbers of popular ones. **Economies of scale** and the **learning curve** (see Unit 28), where the cost of a product comes down in relation to the amount produced, do not apply.

D Benchmarking

Jim is production manager at an electricity power station in Australia. He says, 'We use a system called **benchmarking** to compare our **performance** to performance levels in other power stations. We've recently been to the UK to see how the best power stations operate, to see the **best practice** in the industry, and to copy it. We've managed to **halve** the number of workers, and now our productivity is as good as the best power stations in the UK.'

A power station

Benchmarking can be seen as another form of **collaboration** – people and companies working together. Of course, a company will want to hold on to its **industrial secrets** – prevent competitors from obtaining information about its better performance in a particular area.

Exercises

18.1 Look at A, B, C and D opposite. Which business philosophy is each of these things an example of?

1 A gold mining company makes information about its mines available on the internet. Anyone can analyse the information to suggest where the company may find gold. If gold is found in the place that they suggest, the person gets a prize.
2 A telephone company looks at other telephone companies to see which one issues the lowest number of bills to customers with mistakes in them. It then copies the methods of this company to reduce the number of mistakes in its own bills.
3 An internet site used to stop selling particular products if none were sold for a year. Now it makes all its products available indefinitely.
4 On its website, a bicycle manufacturer allows each buyer to specify exactly what sort of bicycle he or she wants.

18.2 Match the sentence beginnings (1–6) with the correct endings (a–f). The sentences all contain words and expressions from B opposite.

1 Wikinomics describes a scenario where the post-industrial age
2 Students are enthusiastic and positive about their many informal attempts
3 One goal of co-creation is to find a balance between the traditional emphasis on value extraction
4 Linux, Wikipedia, YouTube and Facebook are all examples of mass collaboration.
5 It would be a mistake to think of outsourcing as simply an economic transaction;
6 In the prosumer society we can deduce that all the consumers

a at peer collaboration as a way of coping with a new learning environment.
b Specifically, thousands of programmers contribute to Linux and over 75,000 people are writing and editing articles on Wikipedia.
c will naturally become the producers of the commodities which they want to produce.
d from consumers and the new stress on value creation with consumers.
e is being transformed by allowing more people to put their intellectual muscle to the wheel.
f it is a universal tendency, like gravity, that exerts a pull on everything.

18.3 Complete the sentences with expressions from C and D opposite.

1 Film distributors are working with a business .... that's ten years out-of-date.
2 CEOs might look to unrelated industries for companies with outstanding practices and processes. For example, GE managers carried out .... by studying FedEx, which has exceptional customer service.
3 Some American executives fear that overseas companies seek help from their own governments in stealing US ....
4 Netflix, the largest online film rental website, boasts an endless list of film titles, making millions from the ....
5 The 64-page .... with price list, offers products from 19 manufacturers, and promises 72 hours' delivery for most product lines.

> **Over to you**
>
> In what ways does your company or the place where you study try to improve efficiency?

19 Buyers, sellers and the market

A Customers and clients

People who buy IBM's products and services are IBM's **customers** or **clients**.

Foster and Partners, a big architectural firm, has clients, rather than customers. **Client** often refers to people and organizations who buy the services of professionals such as accountants, lawyers, etc.

IBM's customers considered as a group make up its **customer base**. Foster and Partners' clients considered as a group form a **client base**. These are slightly technical expressions, used for example in business journalism.

People who buy a company's or a professional's products or services, especially expensive or exclusive ones, are its **clientele**.

A Foster and Partners' project

> Note: **Clientele** is rarely used in the plural.

You can also talk about the **users** of a product or service who may not be the organizations who actually buy it. The expression **end-users** refers especially to people who use products, particularly computer equipment and other technology. These expressions are often used in contrast to the producers and distributors (see Unit 24) of a product. For example, IBM sells products through various channels, but the end-users are the employees of the companies that buy its products.

People who buy products or services for their own use are **consumers**, especially when considered as members of large groups of people buying things in advanced economies.

B Buyers, sellers and vendors

A person or organization that buys something is a **buyer** or **purchaser**. But these terms are also used to talk about someone in a company or shop responsible for buying goods that it uses or sells. These people are also **buying managers** or **purchasing managers**. An **industrial buyer** is an organization that buys things for use in producing its own goods or services.

A person or organization that sells something is a **seller**. In some contexts, for example selling property, they are referred to as the **vendor**. (Business journalists and lawyers may also refer to people selling products, rather than services, as vendors.) People selling things in the street are **street vendors**. A **vending machine** is a machine from which you can buy coffee, cigarettes, etc.

C The market

The market, **the free market** and **market economy** are used to talk about an economic system where prices, jobs, wages, etc. depend on what people want to buy, how much they are willing to pay, etc., rather than being controlled by a government. In this sense, **market** is often used in these combinations:

market	forces / pressures	used to talk about the way that a market economy makes sellers produce what people want to buy, at prices they are willing to pay
	-place	producers and buyers in a particular market economy, the way they behave, etc.
	prices	prices that people are willing to pay, rather than ones fixed by a government
	reforms	changes to an economy made by a government so that it becomes more like a market economy

> Note: **Market pressures** occurs more frequently in the context of financial markets such as stock markets.

Business Vocabulary in Use Intermediate

Exercises

19.1 Match each beginning (1–6) with its continuation to make true statements containing expressions from A opposite.

1 The Richard Rogers partnership has some prestigious clients –
2 Louis Vuitton luggage appeals to
3 Telefónica's client base grew 15 per cent,
4 Microsoft sells Vista to end-users
5 BSkyB said 92,000 new customers had signed up for its products in the last quarter,
6 Centrica, owner of British Gas, angered consumers by announcing pre-tax profits of almost £1 billion

a one day after increasing its customers' gas bills by a record 35 per cent.
b Spanish Airports Authority, for example.
c an upmarket clientele.
d bringing its customer base to 8.98 million.
e and also to major manufacturers, such as Dell and HP.
f to 245.1m, from the end of June last year to the same time this year.

19.2 Find appropriate forms of expressions in A and B opposite that refer to the following.

1 someone who buys food in a supermarket (4 expressions)
2 all the people who buy food from a particular supermarket chain, from the point of view of the chain
3 someone who buys the services of a private detective agency
4 all the people who buy the services of the agency, seen as a group (2 expressions)
5 someone who sells goods or services
6 someone selling a house (2 expressions)
7 someone buying a house (2 expressions)
8 someone who sells hamburgers to tourists outside the Tower of London
9 someone whose job is buying tyres for a car company (4 expressions)
10 someone who uses a computer, even if they have not bought it themself, but their company has (2 expressions)

19.3 Complete the TV reporter's commentary with expressions from C opposite containing 'market'.

'In China, all economic activity used to be controlled by the state. Prices were fixed by the government, not by buyers and sellers in the **(1)** .... But in the last 20 years there has been a series of **(2)** .... that have allowed people to go into business and start their own companies. **(3)** .... are determined by what buyers are willing to pay, no longer by the state. There are still state-owned companies that lose a lot of money. Until recently, they have been protected from **(4)** .... (2 possibilities), but **(5)** .... (2 possibilities) will eventually mean that they close down. Of course, the **(6)** .... has its losers – those without work, and victims of crime, which used to be very rare.'

> Over to you
>
> • What companies in your country have a large customer base?
> • What is the purchasing manager responsible for buying in a large office?

Business Vocabulary in Use Intermediate   47

20 Markets and competitors

A Companies and markets

The **market** for a particular product is the people/organizations that buy it, or might buy it.

Buyers and sellers of goods or services in a particular place form a **market**.

If a company	enters	a market,	it starts selling there for the first time.
	penetrates		it starts selling, or sells more and more, there.
	abandons / gets out of / leaves / withdraws from		it stops selling there.
	dominates		it is the most important company selling there.
	corners		it becomes the main company selling there.
	monopolizes		it is the only company selling there.
	drives another company out of		it makes the other company leave the market, perhaps because it can no longer compete.

B More word combinations with 'market'

Market is often used in these combinations:

market	growth	There has been huge **market growth** in the sales of digital music, with Apple in particular seeing a massive increase in the number of people buying songs from iTunes.
	segment	Regional airlines are important customers for the Embraer ERJ–145. They are a big **market segment** for Embraer.
	segmentation	Microsoft divides the software market into large companies, small companies, home office users, and leisure users. This is how it does its **market segmentation**.
	share	In the US, Japanese carmakers have been gaining **market share** – they are selling a bigger percentage of cars sold, and US manufacturers are selling a smaller percentage.
	leader	Tesco is the biggest supermarket chain in the UK and is therefore the **market leader**.

C Competitors and competition

Companies or products in the same market are **competitors** or **rivals**. Competitors **compete** with each other to sell more, be more successful, etc.

The most important companies in a particular market are often referred to, especially by journalists, as **key players**.

Competition is used to talk about the activity of trying to sell more, be more successful, etc. When competition is strong, you can say that it is **intense**, **stiff**, **fierce** or **tough**. If competition isn't strong, it may be described as **low-key**.

The **competition** refers to all the products, businesses, etc. competing in a particular situation, seen as a group.

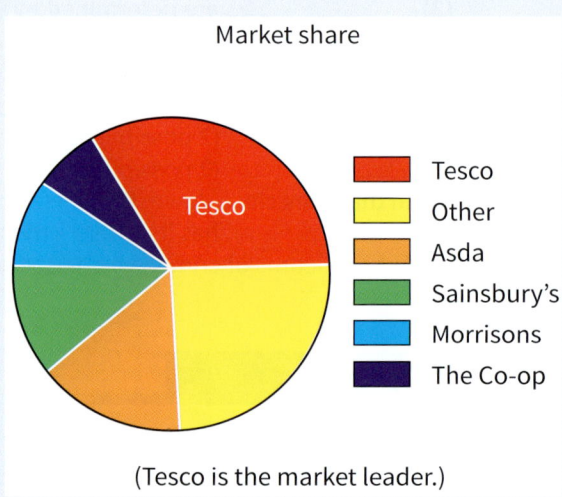

(Tesco is the market leader.)

Business Vocabulary in Use Intermediate

Exercises

20.1 Choose the correct verb from A opposite to complete the sentences and write its correct grammatical form.

1 Houston, Texas is conveniently located in the southern US and our objective is to make it the gateway for Latin American technology companies that want to .... (abandon / withdraw from / penetrate) the US market by opening an office there.
2 Las Vegas has .... (enter / corner / get out of) the market on US tourists looking for a wild escape for adults.
3 Foreign pharmaceutical firms are .... (enter / leave / monopolize) the market for the first time to target the country's growing and increasingly health-conscious middle class.
4 Listeners now have numerous stations to choose from, whereas in the past the market was .... (monopolize / dominate / withdraw) by All-India Radio network.
5 As Swiss bankers .... (penetrate / leave / get out of) markets abroad, they are facing like-minded competitors from elsewhere in the world.

20.2 Replace the underlined expressions with expressions from B opposite. You may need to add a verb in the correct form.

I'm Olinka and I'm marketing manager for a soft drink company in the Czech Republic. In this market, we **(1)** sell more drinks than any other company. In fact, we **(2)** have 55 per cent of the market. **(3)** Sales are increasing at seven to eight per cent per year. There are two main **(4)** groups of consumers: those who drink them in cafés, bars and restaurants, and those who buy them to drink at home. Of course, many consumers belong to both groups, but this is our **(5)** way of dividing our consumers.

20.3 Read this description of a language training market. Answer the questions.

> In Paris, 500 organizations offer language training to companies. However, 90 per cent of sales are made by the top five language training organizations. The market is not growing in size overall. Organization A has 35 per cent of the market, and faces stiff competition from B which has about 25 per cent of the market and from C, D and E who have 10 per cent each, but who are trying to grow by charging less for their courses.

1 How many competitors are there in this market?
2 Is competition in the market strong?
3 Who is the market leader?
4 Who are the two key players?
5 Who mainly takes up the competition, from the market leader's point of view?
6 If one competitor increases its market share, can the others keep their market share at the same level?

Over to you

Talk about the competitors in a particular market and their market shares. (You could talk about the market that your company, or a company you would like to work for, is in.)

21 Marketing and market orientation

A Marketing

Marketing is the process of

- **planning** – identifying future needs for –
- **designing** – developing and making –
- **pricing** – deciding the price for –
- **promoting** – informing customers about –
- **distributing** – making available –

goods/services in order to satisfy customer needs profitably.

The **marketing concept** should be shared by everyone in an organization – all managers and employees, not just those in the **marketing department**, should think in these terms of profitability through satisfying customer needs.

Companies point out how the special **features** – important characteristics and qualities – of their products and services possess particular **benefits** – advantages – in relation to the needs of the people who buy them.

Non-profit organizations have other goals, such as persuading people to give money to help people in poor countries, but these organizations also use the techniques of marketing. This is **social marketing**.

In some places, even totally different organizations such as government departments think about – or at least talk about – their activities in terms of the marketing concept.

B The four Ps

The four Ps are:

- **product** – deciding what to sell
- **price** – deciding what prices to charge
- **place** – deciding how the product will be distributed and where people will buy it
- **promotion** – deciding how the product will be supported with advertising, special activities, etc.

A fifth P which is sometimes added is **packaging** – the materials used to protect and present a product before it is sold.

The four Ps are a useful summary of the **marketing mix** – the activities that you have to combine successfully in order to sell. The next four units look at these activities in detail.

To **market** a product is to make a plan based on a particular marketing mix and put it into action. The **marketing plan** for a new product or service shows how this can be realized.

A **marketer** or **marketeer** is someone who works in this area.

Marketer can also be used to describe an organization that sells particular goods or services.

> **Note**
> **Marketeer** is also used in expressions such as **free marketeer** – someone who believes in the benefits of the market economy (see Unit 19) and **black marketeer** – someone who makes money by selling goods illegally in a place where they are not normally available.

C The market orientation

Marketers often talk about **market orientation** – the fact that everything they do is designed to meet the needs of the market. They, their organizations and the products they sell may be described as **market-driven**, **market-led** or **market-oriented**.

Business Vocabulary in Use Intermediate

Exercises

21.1 Read this conversation from a marketing meeting. Replace the underlined expressions with expressions from A and B opposite. The first one has been done as an example.

Annika: There's a real customer need out there. We really want a **(1)** coherent set of ideas on how we're successfully going to design and sell the product.
marketing plan

Baltazar: Yes, and we've got to decide on the product's **(2)** important characteristics and qualities and **(3)** advantages.

Annika: We've got to work out **(4)** what we're going to sell, **(5)** how we're going to communicate this, **(6)** where we're going to sell it and **(7)** what people are going to have to pay for it.

Baltazar: That's right, the **(8)** whole combination. And we mustn't forget about **(9)** how we're going to protect the product and make it look attractive.

Annika: Yes, we're first-class **(10)** specialists in this area (2 possibilities).

21.2 Match the sentence beginnings (1–7) with the correct endings (a–g). The sentences all contain expressions from C opposite.

1 There are now more efficient and market-oriented
2 Since the 1990s, China has had a much more market-led
3 Many of today's best market-led growth businesses – General Electric, Microsoft, Virgin and Sony – are
4 Lack of investment and poor market orientation
5 For 50 years, American television has been a market-driven industry,
6 Deng decentralized control over the economy
7 Communities of actors, writers, directors and technicians

a in several markets at once.
b and replaced state planning with a market-oriented system.
c – where a common spirit improves the work – are not easy to make or keep going in our market-driven society.
d approach to economics.
e left the companies with falling sales and profits.
f farms with less dependence on government money.
g and the audience has decided the direction it takes.

Over to you

Think of an organization that is famous for being market-oriented. What factors are important?

22 Products and brands

A Word combinations with 'product'

product		
	catalogue (BrE) / catalog (AmE)	a list of a company's products (see Unit 18)
	mix / portfolio	a company's products considered together and in relation to one another
	line / range	a company's products of a particular type
	lifecycle	the stages in the life of a product and the number of people who buy it at each stage
	positioning	how a product is seen, or how a company would like it to be seen, in relation to its other products and/or to competing products
	placement	when a company pays for its products to be used or seen in films and TV programmes

B Goods

Goods are the materials and components used to make products, or the products that are made. **Raw materials** are basic materials from which other things are made.

Finished goods are products ready to be sold.

Industrial goods are bought by other companies for use in their activities and products. **Consumer goods** are bought by individuals for their own use.

Consumer goods that last a long time, such as cars and washing machines, are **consumer durables**. Consumer goods such as food products that sell in large quantities are **fast-moving consumer goods** (**FMCG**).

Raw materials

Finished goods

C Brands and branding

A company gives a **brand** or **brand name** to its products so that they can be easily recognized. This may be the name of the company itself: in this case, you can talk about the **make** of the product, for example LG. For many products, you refer to the make and **model** – the Ford (make) Ka (model), the Sony Vaio or the Canon EOS.

Some brand names become names for the whole **product category** – for example Hoover for vacuum cleaners or Biro for pens.

Brand awareness or **brand recognition** is the degree to which people know a particular brand. All the ideas that people have about a particular brand are its **brand image**. A **brand manager** is in charge of the marketing of goods or services with a particular brand.

Branding is creating brands and keeping them in customers' minds through advertising, product and package design, and so on. A brand should have a clear **brand identity** so that people think of it in a particular, hopefully positive, way in relation to other brands.

Products that are not **branded** – those that do not have a manufacturer's **brand name** – are **generic products** or **generics**.

A product sold by a retailer with its own name rather than the name of its manufacturer is an **own-brand product** (BrE), or **own-label product** or **store brand** (AmE).

Exercises

22.1 Choose the correct expression from A opposite to complete each gap.

1. Unlike traditional product .... (line / mix / placement), under which companies provided goods at no cost in exchange for the exposure, TV advertisers will pay a lot of money for their products to get worked into the actual storyline.
2. At this food shop, the product .... (lifecycle / mix / positioning) includes local produce as well as nuts shipped from California, wine from France and olive oil from Italy.
3. The new product .... (lines / range / placement) are Mr Ballmer's answer to the most difficult questions about Microsoft's future: Where will it find new growth as the Windows and Office businesses continue to mature?
4. There needs to be a tough cost-control policy throughout the different stages of the product .... (catalogue / lifecycle / mix) in order to keep costs down.
5. The firm must define its markets, position ranges of brands and identify gaps which offer opportunities for expansion or new product .... (line / mix / positioning).
6. Ford's CEO Mark Fields wants to streamline the company's product .... (lifecycle / portfolio / positioning) so more cars and trucks are produced in fewer plants.

22.2 Which group or groups in B opposite does each of these products belong to?

1 microwave ovens   2 cotton   3 cars   4 hamburgers   5 soap powder

22.3 Match the sentence beginnings (1–8) with the correct endings. The sentences all contain expressions from C opposite.

1. A new breakfast food marketed under the brand
2. The supermarket group says there is evidence of customers opting for cheaper store
3. It has been a leader in its product
4. The law sought to increase the availability of cheaper generic
5. The commodity of energy is only beginning to form a brand
6. The range of careers within the fashion industry includes: buyer, brand
7. Ads are obviously used to increase brand
8. Many shoppers have now realised budget own-label

a. brand packaged food.
b. identity in terms of green or non-green energy.
c. name of Slub would stand little chance of success.
d. manager, retail manager, and advertising planner.
e. awareness, so as media habits change, advertising approaches need to evolve too.
f. products are cheap for a reason.
g. category for more than 30 years.
h. products while providing incentives for drug companies to discover new products.

> **Over to you**
>
> - What are typical product placements in a particular film or TV show that you know?
> - What are the most famous brands of chocolate, soft drinks, breakfast cereal and fast food in your country?

23 Price

A Pricing

The owner of Allmart Stores talks about its prices:

'As you know, our goods are **low-priced** and this permanently **low pricing** means we **charge** low prices all the time. Our competitors say their goods are more **expensive** because they provide customer service. But we believe that our customers are interested in **cheap** goods and don't want to pay extra for service.

'It is true that we have **loss-leaders** – these are cheap items which are there to attract customers. We have a policy of selling our goods below the 'official' **list price** or **recommended retail price**. This policy of **discounting** – selling at a **discount** to the list price – has been very successful.'

The owner of Luxmart says:

'Allmart's goods are **cheap** – low-priced but not of high quality. Our top-quality goods are **high-priced**, I agree, but we have high levels of customer service. In fact, most of our goods are **mid-priced** – not cheap and not expensive. But Allmart are **undercutting** us on some products – selling the same ones at lower prices than us.'

B Word combinations with 'price'

price		
	boom	when prices are rising quickly, to the benefit of sellers
	controls	government efforts to limit the amount by which prices increase
	cut	a reduction
	hike	an increase, especially one not wanted by the buyer; used by journalists
	war	when competing companies reduce prices in response to each other
	tag	a label attached to goods, showing the price; also means 'price'

C Upmarket and downmarket

Products exist in different **models**. Take skis for example. Some are **basic** and others more **sophisticated** and **exclusive**. The cheapest skis are **low-end** or **bottom-end**. The most expensive ones are **high-end**, **top-end** or **premium** products – designed for very experienced users (or people with a lot of money!). The cheapest **entry-level** skis are intended for beginners who have never bought skis before. Those in between are **mid-range**. When you buy more sophisticated skis to replace basic ones, you **trade up** and **move upmarket**.

If you buy cheaper skis after buying more expensive ones, you **trade down** and **move downmarket**.

To say that something is **downmarket** often shows disapproval. For example, if a publisher **takes** a newspaper **downmarket**, they make it more popular, less cultural, etc. in an attempt to increase the number of readers.

> Note: BrE/AmE: **upmarket**, **downmarket**
> AmE: **upscale**, **downscale**

D Mass markets and niches

Mass market is used to talk about goods that sell in large quantities and the people who buy them, for example family cars. A **niche** is a group of buyers with specific requirements that is relatively small but that may be profitable for companies that sell to it, for example sports cars.

Business Vocabulary in Use Intermediate

Exercises

23.1
Look at A opposite and the table below. Then say if the statements (1–6) are true or false.

Model	List price (£)	Our price	Average price of similar competing products
Small off-road 4×4	30,600	29,500	29,100
Medium off-road 4×4	31,095	28,999	29,000
Large off-road 4×4	59,700	58,999	58,600

1. The retailer has a pricing policy where the prices are below list prices.
2. The small off-road 4x4 model is low-priced, and cheap in relation to competing products.
3. This retailer charges £59,700 for the large off-road 4x4 model.
4. The large off-road 4x4 model is the highest-priced model.
5. The large off-road 4x4 model is cheap in relation to competing products.
6. All the models are sold at a discount to their list price.

23.2
Complete the sentences with the appropriate form of words in B opposite.

1. A standard tank with enough helium gas to fill 400 average-size balloons cost $40 five years ago but $88 today, Kaufman said. And there will be another 50 per cent price .... before Christmas.
2. Share prices of firms related to the corn industry have closely followed the recent corn price ...., which has been largely fuelled by an increase in ethanol production.
3. The price .... have made the televisions, which are manufactured in Asia and Mexico, affordable to many more families.
4. Government price .... make Alcon's pharmaceutical products less profitable.

23.3
Look at C and D opposite. Then read an article from 2008 and answer the questions.

STARBUCKS IN TROUBLE

From the beginning, the key to Starbucks' success was its upmarket image. That the coffee itself was rather expensive only added to its appeal. If you wanted cheap coffee, then go to a diner.

For a long while Starbucks managed to keep ahead of the game, expanding very fast, buying competitors and launching new products. Premium coffee remained the basic product – and one others could easily copy. Now McDonald's offers premium coffee, not only cheaper than Starbucks' but of a quality that won first place in a survey in March by Consumer Report.

As a result, Starbucks finds itself caught in a new, unwelcome 'third place', pressed from below by the fast-food chains that until recently had been considered more downmarket, and from above by a new generation of more upmarket, exclusive and sophisticated coffee houses.

1. What sort of image did Starbucks have when it was launched?
2. Was the fact that it was expensive a problem?
3. Did Starbucks grow just by opening new coffee shops?
4. How has McDonald's coffee changed in the last few years?
5. Is Starbucks in a good competitive position? Why? / Why not?

Over to you

- Which companies in your country offer the lowest prices?
    - for family cars   – for home furniture   – in supermarkets
- What are the advantages and disadvantages for a company with an upmarket image trying to increase its sales by offering cheap products?

24 Place

A Distribution: wholesalers, retailers and customers

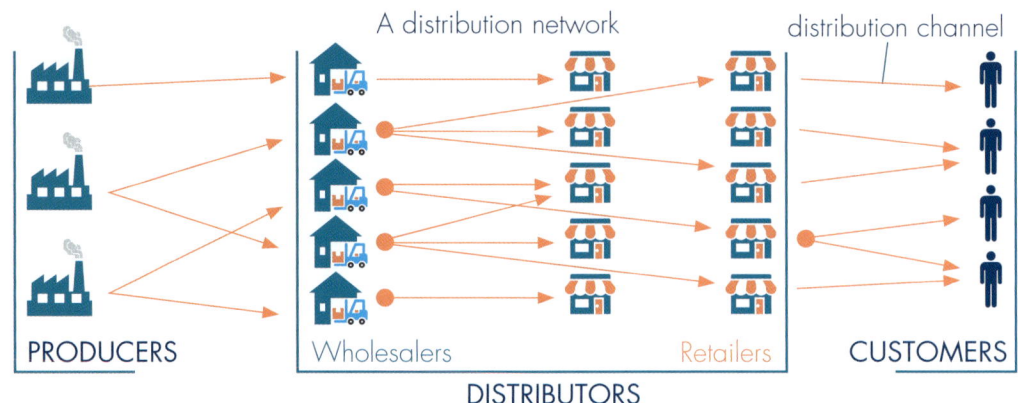

A wholesaler or retailer selling a particular type of product, for example cars, is a **dealer**, or, especially in the case of computer equipment or telecommunications services, a **reseller**.

Wholesalers and retailers are **distributors**. Distributors may be referred to, sometimes disapprovingly, as **middlemen**. If someone buys something directly from a producer, instead of from a distributor, in order to save money, they might say that they are **cutting out the middleman**.

B Shops

A **shop** (BrE) or **store** (AmE) may be referred to technically, for example by a maker of goods, as a **retail outlet** or **sales outlet**. Here are some types of shop:

- **chain store** – a shop that is part of a group of shops, all with the same name
- **convenience store** – a shop in a town that is open long hours
- **discounter** – a wholesaler or retailer with very low prices
- **department store** – a very large shop, usually in a town centre
- **hypermarket** – a very large shop with a wide variety of goods, usually outside a town
- **supermarket** – a very large shop, selling mainly food

In Britain, a **shopping centre** is an area or building with a number of shops. There are **malls** or **shopping malls** where it is easy to park, especially on the edge of towns.

Franchises are owned by **franchisees** – the people that run them – but they only sell the goods of a particular company. The **franchisor** – the company – provides the goods and organizes advertising centrally and in return takes a percentage of the profits of each franchisee. Other types of business, such as restaurants, can also be run in this way.

C Direct marketing

'Hi, I'm Beatrice and I work in a **direct marketing** company in Brussels. We organize **mailings**, sending information by post for everything from magazines to vacations. We call this **direct mail**, but the people who dislike receiving it sometimes call it **junk mail**. Of course, we **target** our mailing lists very carefully – choose who to send them to. There's no point in sending **mailshots** for garden tools to people who live in apartments!

'We also do **telemarketing** – selling by telephone from our **call centres**. The most difficult thing is making **cold calls** to people who have had no contact with us before.'

> Note
> BrE: **call centre**
> AmE: **call center**

Business Vocabulary in Use Intermediate

Exercises

24.1 Use expressions from A opposite to complete this presentation.

Michael Dell started out in the PC business in the 1980s when he tried to buy a PC. There was a complicated **(1)** d................ c................ between the manufacturer and the customer: **(2)** w................, **(3)** r................ and **(4)** r................ all added to the costs, but at that time they didn't add much value from the point of the **(5)** c................ . So until recently, Dell manufactured every PC to order and delivered straight to the buyer. This allowed them to reduce costs, and thanks to this they have become the biggest manufacturer of PCs. Now they are in this strong position, they have started to sell their computers through **(6)** r................ (2 possibilities) as well.

24.2 Look at B opposite and say where you go if you want to do the following.

1. park easily and visit a number of different shops without having to go to the town centre
2. visit different shops grouped together in a British town centre
3. buy a packet of sugar if all the supermarkets are closed
4. buy food and some other products extremely cheaply
5. buy clothes in a town centre without going to a specialized clothes shop
6. buy clothes, a computer and products for doing repairs on your house all in one shop, outside the town centre

24.3 Which expression in C opposite does 'it' in each sentence refer to?

1. I really hate <u>it</u>, all that stuff coming through my letter box.
2. <u>It</u>'s a terrible place to work. We have to make 30 calls an hour, and the manager is always checking up on us.
3. 300,000 well-targeted letters to cat-lovers? We can organize <u>it</u>, no problem.
4. I have to do <u>it</u>. I've never spoken to them before, and they may be in the middle of lunch, but I've got no choice.
5. The two main activities that make <u>it</u> up are mailings and telemarketing.
6. People who come home to ten answerphone messages, all selling things, tend to hate <u>it</u>.

```
Over to you
```

- Do you prefer shopping in the city centre or out of town? Why?
- Which companies in your country often advertise by direct mail?
- What do you think of telemarketing?

25 Promotion

A Advertising

Each photo shows a different advertising **medium**.

Neon signs

Open-air hoardings (BrE) / Billboards (AmE)

Classified advertisements

Special displays

TV commercial

A series of advertisements for a particular company, product, etc. is an **advertising campaign**. A television advertisement is also called a **commercial**.

A person or business that **advertises** is an **advertiser**. An organization that designs and manages advertising is an **advertising agency**.

Another form of advertising is **sponsorship**, where companies **sponsor** events like concerts and sports events, by paying some of their costs or paying for their products to be displayed.

> Note
> BrE: ad, <u>ad</u>vert, ad<u>ver</u>tisement
> AmE: ad, adver<u>tise</u>ment

B The sales force

A company's **salespeople** – its **salesmen** and **saleswomen** – visit or phone customers and persuade them to buy its products. Each member of this **sales force** has his or her own **sales area** or **sales territory** – they may be responsible for a particular region. The head of the sales force is the **sales manager**.

C Promotional activities

Promotion (uncountable) can refer to all the activities designed to support the sale of a product, including advertising. **A promotion** (countable) can describe:

- a **special offer** such as a **discount** or reduced price (see Unit 23)
- a **free sample** – a small amount of the product to try or taste
- a **free gift** given away with the product
- a **competition** with **prizes**

Supermarkets, chain stores and airlines also offer **loyalty cards** – the more you spend, the more points you get, and you can exchange these points for free goods or flights.

A **cross-promotion** is where you buy one product, and you are recommended to buy another product, for example a washing machine with a recommendation for a particular brand of washing powder.

Advertisements where famous people recommend the product are **product endorsements**.

Product placement is when a company pays for its products to be used or seen in films and TV programmes (see Unit 22).

Business Vocabulary in Use Intermediate

Exercises

25.1 Complete the crossword with the correct form of words from A, B and C opposite.

Across

4 particular offers, competitions, etc. (10)
6 You find these at exhibitions: special .... (8)
7 They give you direct experience of a product. (7)
10 You win these in competitions. (6)
11 an organization that plans and designs campaigns: advertising .... (6)
14 all the sales people: sales .... (5)
15 given away with a product (5)
16 organizations that advertise (11)
17 The sales force is made up of salesmen and sales............... . (5)

Down

1 BrE for 'billboard' (8)
2 can encourage customers to revisit the same store: .... cards (7)
3 TV advertisements (11)
5 One salesperson takes care of this. (9)
7 not necessarily neon (4)
8 head of the sales force: sales .... (7)
9 male salespeople (8)
12 TV is an example of a .... (6)
13 One salesperson takes care of this. (4)

25.2 Match the sentences (1–5) with the correct expressions (a–e) from C opposite.

| a free gift | b loyalty card | c product placement | d promotions | e special offer |

1 Many supermarkets run competitions and offers to encourage people to buy from them. ☐
2 Yesterday, I bought two kilos of oranges for half the usual price. ☐
3 I bought some coffee that came with a free mug. ☐
4 Cars in Bond films have ranged from an Aston Martin to a BMW. ☐
5 I sometimes forget to take it when I go shopping, but you can add the points later. ☐

Over to you

- Describe a sponsorship deal in sport that you know of.
- Which companies offer loyalty cards in your country?

Business Vocabulary in Use Intermediate

26 E-commerce

A B2C, B2B and B2G

Selling to the public on the internet is **business-to-consumer** or **B2C e-commerce**. **Business-to-business** e-commerce or **B2B**, with firms communicating with and ordering from their suppliers over the internet, is **e-procurement**.

The internet is also changing the way that citizens deal with their governments. In some places you can already communicate with government departments, apply for government contracts and pay taxes using the internet. Businesses doing this are using the internet for **business-to-government** or **B2G** purposes.

B Web 2.0

The first phase of selling over the internet ended with the **dot-com bust** of 2001, when many **internet sellers** went out of business.

We are now in a more stable phase of **internet selling**, dominated by a few big websites such as Amazon and eBay. This second phase is sometimes referred to as **Web 2.0**.

Web 2.0 is also used to refer to the increasing importance of **social-networking** sites such as Facebook, **video-sharing** sites such as YouTube, **blogs** – online diaries – and **collaborative sites** where people work together on particular projects. The best known is Wikipedia, the online encyclopaedia entirely written by users.

C E-commerce companies

Amazon was founded in 1994, and launched online in 1995 by Jeff Bezos. It started by selling books but now sells everything from jewellery to electronics. It also **hosts** other sellers on its site – other sellers can offer their goods – and takes a **commission** – percentage of money from sales – from them on products sold through the site.

eBay was founded in 1995 by Pierre Omidyar. It's an **auction site** linking buyers and sellers, a method of selling where buyers put in **bids** – increasing offers – for goods: the **highest bidder** – person offering the most – wins, and eBay takes a commission on each sale.

> **Note**
> **Online** is also spelled **on-line**. **Online** is ten times more frequent than **on-line**.

D Word combinations with 'online'

Online selling is only one form of e-commerce. Here are some others.

With **online**		
	banking	you can check the state of your bank account.
	dating	you can find a partner.
	gambling / gaming	you can make (and lose!) money in games of chance.
	brokerage	you can buy and sell shares, etc.
	travel	you can make bookings for flights, etc.
	fundraising	non-profit organizations (see Unit 12) can raise money.

Exercises

26.1 Look at A opposite and say whether each of these uses of the internet is B2B, B2C or B2G.

1 Private individuals can rent a car without phoning the car rental company.
2 The city is looking for construction companies to build a new airport. There are hundreds of pages of specifications you can obtain from the city authorities.
3 Car companies are getting together to buy components from suppliers in greater quantities, reducing prices.
4 Businesses can get information about taxes from a government website.
5 Members of the public can buy legal advice from law firms.

26.2 Look at B and C opposite. Read the article and answer the questions.

SOCIAL SHOPPING

Stephanie Rahlfs is a keen follower of the latest fashion trends. She reads a dozen fashion magazines. She writes a blog called Adventures in the Stiletto Jungle, an online source for fashion product reviews. Rahlfs, a 30-year-old former lawyer in Santa Clara, also is one of the style-setters helping to power the next generation of online shopping sites. On ThisNext, Rahlfs recommends must-have clothes and accessories, from a Marc Jacobs bracelet to a Juicy Couture sweater. Her suggestions feed into an engine that lets other shoppers – not just her friends and readers of her blog – find products online.

Called social-shopping sites, ThisNext, Kaboodle, Stylehive, StyleFeeder and others are incorporating the community features of Web 2.0 into online shopping. They represent the latest tool for online shoppers this holiday season, using the power and expertise of friends and others online to help locate the perfect gift.

"I'm a really good shopper in fashion and beauty, but I don't know anything about shopping for gadgets or kids," said Rahlfs. "The great thing is I can share my expertise and I can pull from the expertise of others and find out what other people would buy."

Online Christmas holiday shopping is expected to grow this year, despite fears that the economic crisis could discourage people from spending too much money. A report by the Forrester research firm predicts that online shoppers will spend about $33 billion this season, 21 per cent more than last year.

"The online shopping population is more affluent and less price-sensitive," said Sucharita Mulpuru, an analyst with Forrester. "They're busy and time-starved and looking for solutions on the Web."

1 What is Stephanie Rahlfs's blog about?
2 Can you buy products on her blog?
3 Are social-shopping websites like ordinary e-commerce sites?
4 What is the advantage of social-shopping websites for Stephanie Rahlfs?
5 Why is it surprising if online Christmas shopping grows by 21 per cent this year?
6 According to Sucharita Mulpuru, are online shoppers a) richer than average, and b) less worried about paying higher prices than most other people?

26.3 Complete each sentence with an expression from D opposite.

1 Thirty-five per cent of US adults don't take all of the vacation days they receive, according to a survey done by the online .... service Expedia.
2 With debit cards and online ...., how much cheque-writing do you still do?
3 Médecins sans Frontières has used online .... to successfully raise money and show the world the projects it is working on.
4 Investors are advised to consider costs beyond advertised rates in selecting an online ....
5 We didn't have a problem before the casino opened, but in the past few years more and more of my clients have become addicted to online ....

Over to you

What are the potential problems of shopping online?

27 Sales and costs

A Sales

The goods and services that a business sells, and the money it receives for them from customers, are its **sales**. Denise van Beek of Nordsee Marine **works in sales**. In fact, she is **sales director**, in charge of the **sales department**. Denise is talking to her **sales team** at a **sales meeting**.

'Our **sales figures** last year were good and **revenue** or **turnover** – money from sales – was €14.5 million, on **sales volume** or **unit sales** of 49 boats. This was above our **target** for the year of €13 million. We estimate our **sales growth** next year at 10 per cent as the world economy looks good and there is demand for our products, so my **sales forecast** for next year is nearly €16 million.'

A sales meeting

> **Note**
> **Sale** and **sales** are nouns. **Sell** (**sold**, **sold**) is a verb. In shops, **the sales** are a period when goods are sold more cheaply than at other times. BrE/AmE: **sales revenue**; BrE only: **sales turnover**

B Costs

The amounts of money that a business spends are its **costs**:

- **direct costs** are directly related to providing the product, e.g. salaries
- **fixed costs** do not change when production goes up or down, e.g. rent, heating, etc.
- **variable costs** change when production goes up or down, e.g. materials
- **cost of goods sold (COGS)** are the variable costs in making particular goods
- **overheads**, **overhead costs** or **indirect costs** are not directly related to production, e.g. administration

Some costs, especially indirect ones, are also called **expenses** or **operating expenses.**

Costing is the activity of calculating costs. Amounts calculated for particular things are **costings**.

> **Note**
> **Overheads** is much more commonly used than **overhead costs**, and **indirect costs** is the least frequently used.
> BrE and AmE: **overheads** (plural noun); mainly AmE: **overhead** (uncountable noun)

C Margins and mark-ups

Here are the calculations for one of Nordsee's small boats.

- **selling price** = €50,000
- **direct production costs** (= costs of raw materials, labour, etc.) = €35,000
- selling price – direct production costs = **gross margin** = €15,000
- **total costs** = €40,000
- selling price – total costs = **net margin, profit margin** or **mark-up** = €10,000

The net margin or profit margin is usually given as a percentage of the selling price, in this case 20 per cent.

The mark-up is usually given as a percentage of the total costs, in this case 25 per cent.

62 Business Vocabulary in Use Intermediate

Exercises

27.1 Match the expressions (1–7) from A opposite with their definitions (a–f). Two expressions have the same definition.

1 sales figures
2 sales forecasts
3 sales growth
4 sales revenue
5 sales target
6 sales turnover
7 sales volume

a the money received from sales (2 expressions)
b sales hoped for in a particular period
c the amount of sales, either in terms of money or the number of things sold
d increase in sales
e statistics showing the amount sold, perhaps over time
f sales expected in a particular period

27.2 Complete the sentences with the correct expressions from A or B opposite.

1 Can your four cleaners clean 30 hotel rooms in five hours at 45 minutes per room? Your answer to this will affect your .... (unit sales / costings)
2 The bank's CEO said operating .... (expenses / sales) rose due to a new wages agreement and higher staff numbers in Australia.
3 Last Christmas, many people realized they could get far better value if they waited until .... (the sales / sales forecast) in January to buy their presents.
4 Our .... (costings / sales) department specializes in organizing holidays and conferences tailored to individual group requirements.
5 The costs for external consultants are .... (fixed / variable) as they change with the number of consulting days. The costs for internal consultancy, by contrast, comprise a large proportion of .... (fixed / variable) costs because setting up the internal consultancy – hiring permanent staff, renting offices, etc. – and maintaining it involves .... (fixed / variable) costs.
6 Pricing your cheese sandwich at £3 when the variable costs of making it are £2.80 does not mean that you have made 20p profit. If your .... (overheads / unit sales) are £40,000 per year, you will have to sell 200,000 cheese sandwiches just to cover them.

27.3 Choose the correct expression from B opposite to describe Ford Motor's costs.

1 the salary of an office receptionist (direct cost / indirect cost)
2 heating and lighting of the building where cars are made (fixed cost / variable cost)
3 the materials used in the cars, and the salaries of production workers (overhead cost / COGS)
4 running the office (overhead cost / direct cost)
5 metal used in making the cars (fixed cost / variable cost)
6 the salary of a worker building the cars (direct cost / indirect cost)

27.4 Look at C opposite. Then read what this company owner says and answer the questions.

'I'm Vaclav and I own a small company in Slovakia that makes furniture for IKEA. For example, we make a very popular line of wooden chairs. They cost €36 each to make, including materials and production costs. We estimate overheads, including administration and marketing costs, for each chair at €4, and we sell them to IKEA at €50.'

1 What is the gross margin for each chair?
2 What is the net margin for each chair?
3 What is the mark-up for each chair as a percentage of total costs?
4 What is the profit margin for each chair as a percentage of the selling price?

> **Over to you**
>
> Think of the company you work for or one you would like to work for. Which of its products or services has the highest sales? What are its biggest costs?

28 Profitability and unprofitability

A Profitable and unprofitable products

A supermarket manager talks about the costs and prices for some of its products.

Product	Cost per unit (euros)	Sale price per unit (euros)	Result
A	10	12	We **make a profit**: the product is **profitable** or **profit-making**.
B	15	15	We **break even**: we **reach break-even point**.
C	8	7	We **make a loss**. The product is **loss-making**, but we use Product C as a **loss-leader** (see Unit 23) to attract people to the store, knowing they will then also buy profitable products.
D	12	22	Product D is very profitable and we sell a lot of it. It's one of our **money spinners** or **cash cows** – products that have very good profitability.

B Budgets and expenditure

Here are some graphs about the marketing activities that Nordsee and Vaclav's firm (see Unit 27) **budgeted for** – the money that they planned to spend on each one.

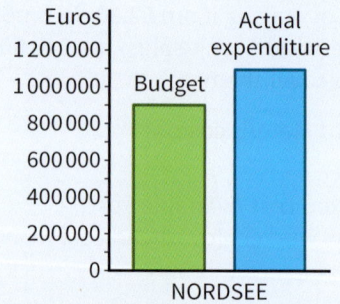 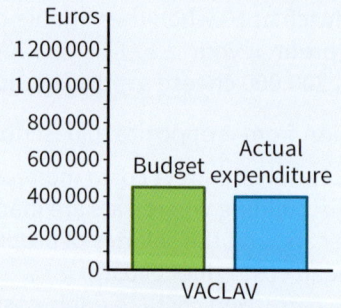 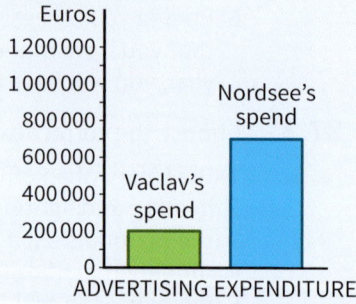

Nordsee went **over budget** and **overspent** by 200,000 euros.

Vaclav **underspent** by 50,000 euros. He was **under budget**.

On advertising, Vaclav's **expenditure** or **spend** was only 200,000 euros, while Nordsee's advertising spend was 700,000.

 Note: **Spend** is usually a verb, but can be used as a noun, as in **advertising spend**.

C Economies of scale and the learning curve

Big manufacturing companies such as Ford benefit from **economies of scale**. For example, the costs of developing a new car are enormous, but the company can spread them over a large number of cars produced and sold. However, there are limits to this. After a point, a given increase in production actually causes **diseconomies of scale** – an even bigger increase in production costs.

The company also benefits from the **experience curve** or **learning curve** – as it produces more, it learns how to do things more and more quickly and efficiently. This brings down the cost of each thing produced, and the more they produce, the cheaper it gets.

Business Vocabulary in Use Intermediate

Exercises

28.1 Look at this information about Vaclav's firm's products and answer the questions.

	Unit production cost (€)	Overheads per unit (€)	Selling price (€)	Number of units sold per year
Chairs	18	2	19.50	70,000
Armchairs	36	4	50	50,000
Coffee tables	55	5	60	30,000
Sofas	70	7	80	20,000
Dining tables	250	30	300	15,000

1 Which products make a profit?
2 Which product has the highest level of profitability as a percentage of its selling price?
3 Which loses money?
4 Which just breaks even?
5 Which is the biggest money spinner or cash cow, in terms of overall profit?

28.2 Complete the sentences using correct forms of expressions from B opposite.

1 She felt the organization was .... on entertainment and luxury travel, which was a waste of money.
2 Dallas–Fort Worth airport's expenses were running $10.9 million .... at $343.3 million, with lower maintenance costs providing the majority of the savings.
3 In planning the concert, they found they had forgotten to .... the singers, and only had money to pay the orchestra.
4 The Chinese government has poured large amounts of money into innovation, doubling its .... (2 possibilities) on research and development.
5 The film *Are We There Yet?* with Ice Cube earned $82 million in ticket sales on a .... of $32 million.

28.3 Look at C opposite. Then read this article and answer the questions.

1 Which of Nokia's markets does the article refer to?
2 What is the main difference in these markets, compared to a few years ago?
3 Do global economic problems mean that the markets will grow more slowly?
4 What percentage of its phones does Nokia sell in these markets?
5 Which one of the concepts in C opposite does the article relate to?

Churning out nearly 40 per cent of the world's phones, Nokia has said it anticipates replacement phone unit sales in new growth markets to exceed first-time unit sales this year. Nokia dominates low-end phone sales in emerging markets.
  "The name of the game is changing," Alex Lambed, Nokia's Vice President, Entry, told Dow Jones Newswires. "It is changing from simply a first-time user, voice-driven market, to a replacement market where we see an opportunity for providing additional services."

Lambed, who oversees Nokia's efforts in emerging markets, said he still sees "very strong underlying growth" in these markets, despite broader economic weakness in global financial markets.
  Thanks to its massive size, Nokia is a powerful force in these high-growth regions with its ability to produce large numbers of low-end handsets at ever lower cost. Nokia says emerging markets made up 60 per cent of the industry's device volumes last year, up from 55 per cent in the previous year.

```
Over to you
```

- What kind of products are money spinners in your country?
- What kind of companies have very large advertising spends in your country?
- How do companies benefit from economies of scale?

Business Vocabulary in Use Intermediate

29 Getting paid

A Shipping and billing

When you ask to buy something, you **order** it or **place an order** for it. When the goods are ready, they are **dispatched** or **shipped** to you.

An **invoice** is a document asking for payment for something and showing the amount to pay. The activity of producing invoices and sending them to customers is **invoicing** or **billing**. If a supplier **chases an invoice**, they ask for payment because it has not been paid on time. If you **settle an invoice**, you pay it.

 Note: **Billing** is much more frequent than **invoicing**, especially in the US.

B Trade credit

Vaclav talks about his furniture business.

'Of course, we don't expect our business customers to pay immediately: they are given **trade credit** – a period of time, usually 30 or 60 days, before they have to pay. If a customer orders a large quantity or pays within a particular time, we give them a **discount** – a reduction in the amount they have to pay.

'But we ask some customers, especially ones we haven't dealt with before, to pay **upfront** – before they receive the goods. Like all businesses, we have a **credit policy**, with **payment terms** – rules on when and how customers should pay. This is part of controlling **cashflow** – the timing of payments coming into and going out of the business.'

C Accounts

Jennifer and Kathleen are businesswomen. Jennifer has her company in Britain and Kathleen owns one in the US.

These businesses are our customers or **accounts**. The most important ones are **key accounts**.

I'm waiting for these customers to pay me. They're my **debtors** (BrE).

I must pay these suppliers and other organizations. They're my **creditors** (BrE).

I'm waiting for these customers to pay me. They're my **accounts receivable** (AmE) or **receivables** (AmE).

I must pay these suppliers and other organizations. They're my **accounts payable** (AmE) or **payables** (AmE).

Some businesses that owe me money will probably never pay. These are **bad debts** and I've **written them off**.

Jennifer

Kathleen

Exercises

29.1 Look at A opposite and rearrange these events involving two companies into a logical order.

a Superinc eventually settled the invoice.
b Superinc ordered goods from Messco, which dispatched them to Superinc.
c Superinc then received the invoice but did not pay it on time.
d Two weeks later, Superinc had still not received an invoice from Messco and began to think that Messco's invoicing was not very efficient.
e Someone in the accounts department at Messco chased the invoice by phoning the accounts department at Superinc.
f After the goods were shipped, someone in the accounts department at Superinc noticed that they had not received an invoice for them and asked Messco to issue one.

29.2 Complete these extracts using expressions from B opposite. Use each expression once.

1 .... is a constant problem. I'm getting my materials from different suppliers on a 30-day payment basis and supplying large companies who pay me on a 60-day payment term.
2 With some new wines, you can pay a special price .... and wait for it to be delivered in about ten months' time.
3 Small businesses often complain that larger companies abuse .... by paying invoices more and more slowly.
4 We offer a 2 per cent .... for payment within ten days.
5 We have a very strict .... – our .... are that everyone pays within 30 days.

29.3 Replace the underlined parts of what Saleem says with expressions from C opposite, using British English.

'My name's Saleem and I own a clothing company. Our **(1)** <u>most important customers</u> are department stores. Getting paid on time is very important and we have an employee whose job is to chase **(2)** <u>people who owe us money</u>. Of course, we pay
(3) <u>suppliers and other people we owe money to</u> as late as possible! Luckily, I haven't had much of a problem with
(4) <u>people who don't pay at all</u>, so we haven't had to **(5)** <u>decide not to chase them any more</u>.'

Over to you

- Once you have ordered a book online, how long would you expect to wait for the book to arrive after it had been dispatched to you?
- What kinds of companies offer discounts, and why?

30 Assets, liabilities and the balance sheet

A Assets

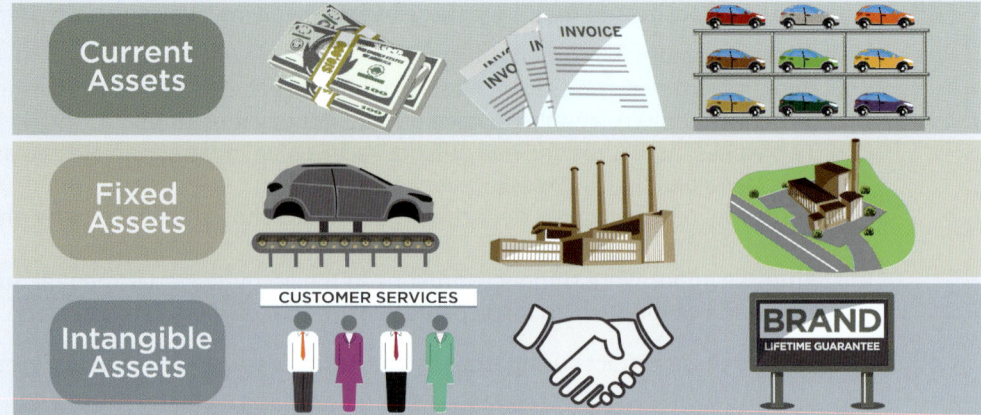

Something that has value or the power to earn money for a business is an **asset**. These include:

- **current assets** – money in the bank, investments (see Unit 36) that can easily be turned into money, money that customers owe, stocks of goods that are going to be sold
- **fixed assets** – equipment, machinery, buildings, land
- **intangible assets**: **goodwill** – the value that a company has through its reputation with existing customers – and **brands** (see Unit 22), because an established brand allows its owner to earn money from it, rather than having to build up a brand from nothing

If a company is sold as a **going concern**, it is sold as a functioning operation.

B Depreciation

Joanna Cassidy is an accountant in a publishing company:

'Assets, such as machinery and equipment, lose their value over time because they wear out, or are no longer up to date. Amounts relating to this are **depreciation** or **amortization** (AmE mainly). For example, when we buy new computers, we **depreciate** them or **amortize** (AmE mainly) them **over** a very short period, usually three years. A **charge** for this is shown in the financial records: the value of the equipment is reduced or **written down** each year over that period. It is then **written off** completely – shown as having no value at all – at the end (see Unit 29). This is a **write-off**.

'The value of an asset at a particular time as shown in a company's accounts is its **book value**. This may or may not be the amount that it could be sold for. For example, land may be worth more than shown, because it has increased in value. But our computers could probably only be sold for less than book value.'

C Liabilities

A company's **liabilities** are its debts to suppliers, lenders, the tax authorities, etc. Debts that have to be paid within a year are **current liabilities**; those payable in more than a year are **long-term liabilities** – for example long-term bank loans.

D Balance sheet

A company's **balance sheet** gives a picture of its assets and liabilities at a particular time. This is usually at the end of the 12-month period of its **financial year** (see Unit 31).

Exercises

30.1 Look at A opposite. Which three of these items are not assets? What kind of assets are the other five items?

1. Vans owned by a delivery company, and which it uses to deliver goods.
2. Vans for sale in a showroom.
3. A showroom owned by a company that sells vans.
4. A showroom rented by a company that sells cars.
5. Money owed by customers that will definitely be paid in the next two months.
6. Money owed by a bankrupt customer that will certainly never be paid.
7. The client list of a successful training company, all of which are successful businesses.
8. The client list of a training company, with names of clients that have all gone bankrupt.

30.2 Use correct forms of expressions from B and C opposite to complete the sentences (1–6). The first one has been done as an example.

1. A bank lent money to people who did not repay the loans, and decided to show that they would never be repaid: it ____wrote____ them ____off____.
2. An oil company reported a reduction of $118 million in the value of its oil reserves: it showed an amount for _____ in its accounts, which meant an equivalent reduction in the _____ _____ of its oil reserves.
3. A firm owes €550,000 to the tax authorities, payable at the end of this month. These are one of its _____.
4. A manufacturing company bought a machine and decreased the value shown in its accounts by 20 per cent per year for five years: it _____ (2 possibilities) the machine's value over five years.
5. A company showed a charge of $1.5 million in the value of its spare parts inventory in its accounts, reducing its estimated value from $6 million to $4.5 million: it _____ _____ the value of this inventory.
6. A company pays pensions to retired employees and will have to go on doing so indefinitely: these are _____-_____ _____.

30.3 Look at C and D opposite, and say if these statements are true or false.

1. Money that a company has to pay to a supplier in less than a year is a long-term liability.
2. A loan that a company has to repay to a bank over a period of seven years is a long-term liability.
3. Looking at the balance sheet for a company for just one financial year tells you how much money the company has made during the year.
4. A company's financial year can run from 1 May to 30 April.
5. Money that a company keeps in one of its bank accounts is a liability.

> **Over to you**
>
> Obtain a copy of your company's balance sheet or a copy of the balance sheet of a company that you are interested in. What are its main assets and liabilities?

31 The bottom line

A Accounts

'Hi, I'm Fiona and I'm an **accountant**. I work in Edinburgh for one of the big **accountancy firms**. We look at the financial records or **accounts** of a lot of companies. We work with the accountants of those companies and the **book-keepers** – the people who work under them. Sometimes we act as **auditors** – specialist outside accountants who check a business's accounts at the end of a particular period to see if they give a **true and fair view** – in other words, that they are accurate and complete.

'When a company's results are presented in a way that makes them look better than they really are, it may be accused of **creative accounting** or **window dressing**. Of course, one of our jobs is to spot this and to prevent it happening!

'**Audits** are only part of what accountants do, but it's a very important part.'

> The profession is called **accountancy** (BrE) or **accounting** (AmE).
> The activity is called **accounting** in both BrE and AmE.

B Results

A firm **reports** its performance for a particular period in its **results**. In Britain, results for a particular year are shown in the company's **annual report**. This contains, among other things, a **profit and loss account**; in the US, they call this the **income statement**.

In theory, if a company makes more money than it spends, it **makes a profit**. If it makes less than it spends, it **makes a loss**. But it's possible for a company to show a profit for a particular period because of the way it presents its activities under the **accounting standards** or **accounting rules** of one country, and a loss under the rules of another.

A **pre-tax profit** or a **pre-tax loss** is one before tax is calculated. An **exceptional profit** or **loss** is for something that is not normally repeated, for example the sale of a subsidiary company or for the costs of restructuring (see Unit 34). A company's **gross profit** is before charges like these are taken away; its **net profit** afterwards. Profits are also referred to as **earnings**. The final figure for profit or loss is what people call informally the **bottom line**. If a company makes a profit, it is **in the black**. If it makes a loss, commentators may say that it is **in the red**. They may also use expressions with **red ink**, saying, for example, that a company is **bleeding red ink**.

> BrE: **profit and loss account**; BrE/AmE: **profit** AmE: **income statement**; AmE only: **income**

> **Accountancy standards** is about twice as frequent as **accountancy rules**.

C Financial reporting

A company's **financial results** – its balance sheet (see Unit 30), profit and loss account, and a lot of other information – is given in its **annual report** for a particular **business year** or **financial year** (not necessarily January to December). US companies also refer to this as their **fiscal year**. UK companies **report their results** every six months, and refer to **first-half results** and **second-half results**. US companies report their results every **quarter** – every three months. Information given by a company about its financial results is **financial reporting**.

70 Business Vocabulary in Use Intermediate

Exercises

31.1 Complete the crossword with the correct form of words from A and B opposite.

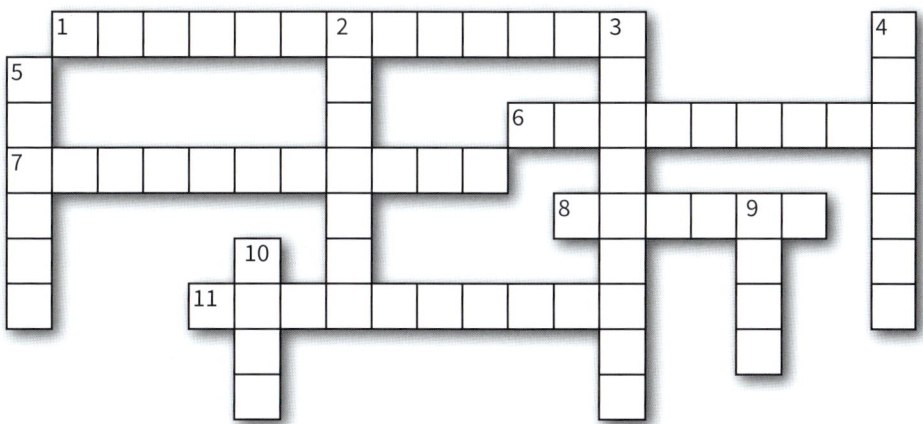

Across

1 and 2 down what the British call the income statement (6, 3, 4, 7)
6 what accounts have to follow (9)
7 not occurring regularly (11)
8 what companies do when they announce results: they .... them (6)
11 the final figure for profit or loss (6, 4)

Down

2 see 1 across
3 what Americans call the profit and loss account: income .... (9)
4 Companies publish their financial .... in their annual report. (7)
5 before tax is taken away (6)
9 another name for 'standard' (4)
10 not a profit (4)

31.2 The article below contains expressions in B and C opposite. Read the article and say if the statements are true or false.

FORTH PORTS ANNOUNCES RESULTS

Charles Hammond, chief executive of Edinburgh-based Forth Ports, announced first-half results that showed increased pre-tax profits at its ports division of £18.6 million, on revenue of £89.4 million. The figures contributed to overall pre-tax profits – including the group's property division – that fell from £12 million to £9 million on revenue of £90.1 million. The pre-tax figure was hit by an £8.3 million loss from Forth's property investments, mainly a result of Forth's £7.5 million writedown in value of the company's Ocean Terminal development in Leith, on Edinburgh's waterfront.

1 The company's results are for a full financial year.
2 The company made an overall pre-tax loss for the period.
3 All its activities made a profit.
4 Revenue in its port activities was about £90 million.
5 Overall pre-tax profit was only about half of that for its port activities alone, because of losses in another activity.
6 Profit in its property activities was badly affected by the reduction in value of one of its developments.

Over to you

- What industries are likely to bleed red ink if the price of oil rises?
- What happens to companies if they are involved in creative accounting in your country?

32 Share capital and debt

A Capital

Capital is the money that a company uses to operate and develop. There are two main ways in which a company can **raise capital** – find the money it needs: it can either use **share capital** or **loan capital** from **investors**. These are people or organizations who put money in, hoping to make more money from their **investment** or **stake** in the company (see Unit 36).

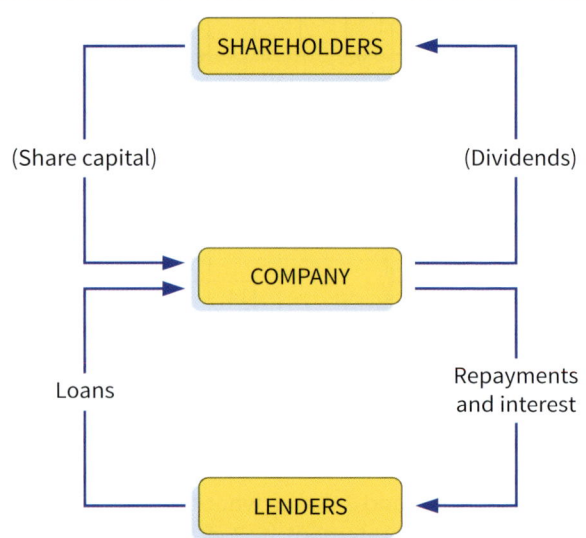

B Share capital

Share capital is contributed by **shareholders**. They are individuals or organizations that have provided or **put up money** to buy **shares** or **stock** in the company. Each share represents a part of the ownership of the company. If you **hold shares** in a company, you may receive **dividends** periodically, usually based on the company's **earnings** – profit – in the relevant period, if any. But some companies do not pay dividends, and investors make a profit as the company grows and the value of its shares increases. Capital in the form of shares is also called **equity**.

C Loan capital

A company can also obtain capital in the form of money lent by investors who do not then have part of the ownership of the company. This is **loan capital**; an investor or a financial institution providing money in this way is a **lender**, and this money is referred to by them as **lending**.

The company borrowing money is the **borrower** and refers to the money as **borrowing** or **debt**. A company's total debt is its level of **indebtedness**.

The sum of money borrowed is the **principal**. The company has to pay **interest** – a percentage of the amount it has borrowed – on its debt whether it has made a profit in the relevant period or not.

D Security

Borrowing by companies and other organizations is often in the form of **bonds** or **debentures** that they **issue** – make available and sell to lenders. Different types of bonds and debentures have particular technical conditions.

One of these conditions is whether there is **collateral** or **security** for the loan – if the borrower cannot repay the loan, the lender has the right to take equipment, property, etc. from the borrower and to sell it in order to get their money back. This equipment or property may be an asset that was bought with the loan (see Unit 30).

E Leverage

The amount of loan capital that a company has in relation to its share capital is its **leverage**. A company with a lot of borrowing in relation to its share capital is **highly leveraged**. A company that has difficulty in making payments on its debt is **overleveraged**.

> Note
> BrE/AmE: **leverage, highly leveraged**
> BrE only: **gearing, highly geared**

72   Business Vocabulary in Use Intermediate

Exercises

32.1 Look at A and B opposite. Then read the article and match the figures with the things to which they refer.

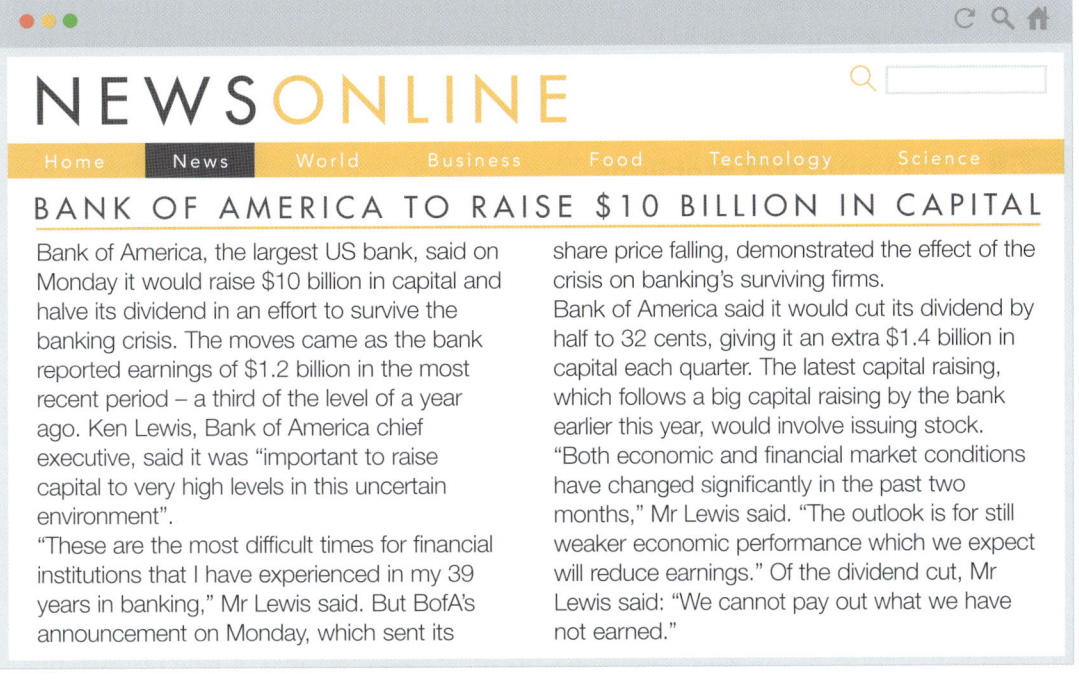

BANK OF AMERICA TO RAISE $10 BILLION IN CAPITAL

Bank of America, the largest US bank, said on Monday it would raise $10 billion in capital and halve its dividend in an effort to survive the banking crisis. The moves came as the bank reported earnings of $1.2 billion in the most recent period – a third of the level of a year ago. Ken Lewis, Bank of America chief executive, said it was "important to raise capital to very high levels in this uncertain environment".

"These are the most difficult times for financial institutions that I have experienced in my 39 years in banking," Mr Lewis said. But BofA's announcement on Monday, which sent its share price falling, demonstrated the effect of the crisis on banking's surviving firms.

Bank of America said it would cut its dividend by half to 32 cents, giving it an extra $1.4 billion in capital each quarter. The latest capital raising, which follows a big capital raising by the bank earlier this year, would involve issuing stock. "Both economic and financial market conditions have changed significantly in the past two months," Mr Lewis said. "The outlook is for still weaker economic performance which we expect will reduce earnings." Of the dividend cut, Mr Lewis said: "We cannot pay out what we have not earned."

1 $10 billion
2 $1.2 billion
3 39
4 $1.4 billion
5 32 cents

a BofA's profit in the latest period
b the amount of capital that BofA wants to raise
c the amount per share of its latest dividend
d the number of years that BofA's CEO has worked in the banking industry
e the amount of extra capital that BofA will have in each three-month period following the reduction in its dividend

32.2 Answer these questions, using expressions from C, D and E opposite.

1 You want to raise money for your company, but you do not want to sell shares. What can you use instead? (2 expressions)
2 You want to raise money and you want to reassure lenders that they will get their money back if your company cannot repay. What would you offer them? (2 expressions)
3 You are interviewed by a financial journalist who wants to know why you are borrowing money. What do you tell them that you want to increase? (2 expressions)
4 The financial journalist writes an article saying that your company has a lot of debt in relation to its share capital. Which two expressions might she use in her article?
5 A few months later the financial journalist writes an article saying that your company has too much debt in relation to its ability to pay. Which expression might she use in her article?

Over to you

- Have you ever thought of starting your own business? What sort of business would it be? Where would you get the capital?
- Where do existing companies in your country normally get capital? Describe two methods of doing this, and give some of the advantages and disadvantages of each.

Business Vocabulary in Use Intermediate

33 Success and failure

A Cash mountains

Microsoft is an extremely profitable company. Over the years, it has paid or **distributed** some of its profits or **earnings** (see Unit 31) to shareholders, but it has also kept profits in the form of **retained earnings** and **built up** – increased – its **reserves**. Commentators may say that it is sitting on a **cash pile** or **cash mountain**. These reserves can be used for investment or to **make acquisitions** – to buy other companies (see Unit 34).

B Debt and debt problems

Debt often occurs in these combinations. These expressions are also used to talk about a country's foreign debts.

Debt		
	repayment / servicing	is when a company repays its debt and/or interest on it. 'Debt repayments' refers to particular amounts repaid.
	burden	is when a company has difficulty repaying its debt.
	crisis	is when a company can no longer pay its debt as planned.
	rescheduling / restructuring	is when a company arranges with lenders to put its debt into new forms, with new repayment dates, etc.
	default	is when a company cannot make payments on its debt.

Note

to reschedule / restructure a debt
to repay / default on / service a debt

Note

Debt repayment and **debt servicing** are equally common. **Debt restructuring** is used three times more than **debt rescheduling**.

C Turnarounds and bailouts

When the Northern Rock bank was in financial trouble, journalists described it as **sick**, **ailing** or **troubled**. The UK government called in Ron Sandler, a **company doctor** – an expert in **turning round** companies like this. At first, he looked for another company to buy Northern Rock and **bail it out** so as to **rescue** it. Eventually, the government itself gave the bank money, hoping it would **recover** – improve its situation. The government said it would not allow the bank to **collapse** completely and to **go out of business**.

Note

bail a company out (verb); **bailout** (noun)
recover (verb); **recovery** (noun)

D Bankruptcy

A company in serious financial difficulty has to take some legal steps.

In the US, it may ask a court to give it time to reorganize by **filing for bankruptcy protection** from creditors. This means that the company doesn't have to pay back its debts immediately.

In Britain, a company that is **insolvent** and unable to pay its debts may **go into administration** under the management of an outside specialist called an **administrator**.

If the company cannot be saved, it **goes into liquidation** or **into receivership**. **Receivers** are specialists who **wind up** the company – they sell the company's assets and pay out what they can to **creditors** (see Unit 29). When a company is **wound up** like this and it **ceases trading**, it stops functioning and no longer exists.

When a company is in difficulty and cannot be saved, it **goes bankrupt** or (more informally) it **goes bust**.

Business Vocabulary in Use Intermediate

Exercises

33.1 Match the sentence beginnings (1–6) with the correct endings (a–f). The sentences all contain expressions from A opposite.

1 Warren Buffett's Berkshire–Hathaway is sitting on a cash
2 Surgut, Russia's fourth-largest oil producer, has been building up its cash
3 Large cash
4 If an organization fails to make a profit, dividends may still be paid out of previous retained
5 AstraZeneca's $15.6 billion acquisition
6 Sunoco Logistics has grown rapidly, extending a pipeline-and-terminal network, and its annual growth in distribution of

a pile for several years, without making any additional investments either in refining or production.
b mountain of $36 billion, and he has chosen to place more than one-third of the cash in foreign currencies.
c earnings is 12.6 per cent.
d of MedImmune Inc., the biotechnology company, makes AstraZeneca a clear leader in the industry.
e earnings, but ultimately these will become exhausted and the business will become bankrupt.
f reserves have been a competitive advantage in the tech industry, where companies often need to make rapid investments.

33.2 Complete the sentences with expressions from B and C opposite.

1 Now the economy threatens to c _ _ _ _ _ _ _ under the country's huge debt b _ _ _ _ _ – more than $100 billion is owed to foreign investors and banks alone.
2 We were a little bit surprised by the size of Temple-Inland's debt r _ _ _ _ _ _ _ _, as we had been expecting all of the profit to be returned to shareholders.
3 Ms Keller is an auto industry analyst and author of *Rude Awakening: The Rise, Fall, and Struggle for R _ _ _ _ _ _ _ of General Motors.*
4 The International Monetary Fund's b _ _ _ _ _ _ might not be enough to pull the country back from debt c _ _ _ _ _.
5 Gordon Owen, the chairman of Energis, is to receive a bonus of nearly £900,000 in recognition of his work in t _ _ _ _ _ _ round the a _ _ _ _ _ company.

33.3 Rachel is an accountant. Look at D opposite and correct what she says.

'I work with the corporate recovery department of a London accountancy firm, with companies that are in financial difficulty. They may be in **(1)** *administer*, and we try to find ways of keeping them in operation. We may sell parts of the company and this, of course, means that people will be laid off.

'Our US office works with a system where companies in difficulty can get **(2)** *protectors* from **(3)** *credit*, giving it time to reorganize and pay off some of its debts.

'If the company can't continue as a going concern, it **(4)** *goes into receivers*: we **(5)** *wind off* the company and it **(6)** *ends business*. We sell all the assets and divide the money up among the creditors in a process of **(7)** *liquification*.'

> **Over to you**
>
> - What happens when a company defaults on its debt repayments?
> - Are there famous companies in your country that are in danger of going bankrupt?
> - Should governments bail out ailing companies to save people from being laid off?

34 Mergers, takeovers and sell-offs

A Stakes and joint ventures

a stake / an interest / a holding	in a company	the shares that an investor has in a company
a majority	stake / interest / holding	when more than half of a company's shares are owned by one investor, giving them control over how the company is run
a minority	stake / interest / holding	when fewer than half of a company's shares are owned by one investor

Two companies may work together in a particular area by forming an **alliance** or **joint venture** – they may remain separate companies, or form a new company in which they both have a stake.

B Mergers and takeovers

Delta Air Lines and Northwest Airlines are to **merge**[1] in a deal that will create the world's biggest carrier. The **merger**[2] could well bring about further **consolidation**[3] in the US airline industry.

Yahoo on Wednesday rejected allegations by Carl Icahn, the investor, that it had damaged the chances of any **acquisition**[8] by Microsoft with an expensive worker compensation plan. The internet company said Mr Icahn's reference to its employee plan as a **poison pill**[9] 'could not be further from the truth'.

Commerzbank, until not long ago seen as a poor fourth in German banking – and seemingly inevitable **prey**[4] for a **takeover**[5] – has become a **predator**[6], and is about to **acquire**[7] its rival, Allianz.

Continental has potential investors which could act as **white knights**[10] as the German motor supplier seeks to **fend off**[11] an €11.3 billion ($17.6 billion) **hostile bid**[12] from Schaeffler, its privately owned rival. Continental is in talks with five strategic and financial investors that are prepared to pay a higher price than Schaeffler's **takeover bid**[13] launched last week.

[1] join
[2] combination
[3] reduction in the number of companies
[4] company that might be bought
[5] purchase
[6] possible buyer
[7] buy
[8] taking control by buying most or all of its shares
[9] something that makes a company less attractive to buy
[10] companies which can save another from being bought against their will
[11] resist
[12] unwanted attempt to buy it (opposite = **friendly bid**)
[13] attempt to buy it

C Conglomerates

1909 Lonrho began operating in Africa.
1961 Tiny Rowland started to transform the company into a worldwide **conglomerate**[1].
1995 Lonrho's African non-mining businesses had expanded, with the **parent company**[2] controlling approximately 90 **subsidiaries**[3] that had **diversified into**[4] a wide range of business activities.
1995 Lonrho decided to **restructure**[5] these African non-mining businesses into five **core activities**[6]: motors, agribusiness, distribution, hotels and property, and construction.
1998 These businesses were **demerged**[7] in a process of **divestment**[8] and a new company was created.
2000 Lonrho began to **refocus**[9] and to follow a strategy of **divesting**[10] its **non-core assets**[11] in order to pay off its debt.
2005 Most of Lonrho's assets had been sold and the **disposal**[12] programme completed.
2006 Lonrho starts to rebuild an African conglomerate.

[1] large group of companies
[2] main company
[3] smaller companies
[4] become involved in
[5] reorganize
[6] main activities
[7] separated
[8] selling unwanted companies
[9] change its activities
[10] selling
[11] non-essential property, etc.
[12] sales

Exercises

34.1 Match the two parts of these sentences containing expressions from A and B opposite.

1 The Canadian government decided to sell up to 45 per cent of Air Canada to the public ☐
2 The BBC has a minority ☐
3 Russia's second biggest airline is trying to buy a stake ☐
4 China signed an agreement with Airbus to develop jointly a regional jet. The programme will be managed through a joint ☐
5 New Tribune shares will be issued to company employees over time, and they will eventually gain a majority ☐

a venture company in which China will have a 46 per cent stake, Airbus 39 per cent and Singapore Technologies 15 per cent.
b and keep a 55 per cent controlling stake.
c interest in the successful satellite channel UK Gold.
d holding of the company's common shares.
e in a US airline so that they can work out a marketing alliance.

34.2 Which expressions from A and B opposite do the underlined words in these headlines refer to?

1 GERMAN TRUCKMAKER MAN IN FRIENDLY APPROACH TO SWEDISH RIVAL SCANIA

2 FORD TO BREAK UP ITS EUROPEAN LUXURY DIVISION TO RAISE CASH

3 Midwest rejects airtran's 'inadequate' offer of $11.25 per share

4 UK COMPANIES UP FOR SALE TO FOREIGN BUYERS

5 Conoco in combined operation with origin energy in canadian natural gas

6 MFI IN POSSIBLE COMBINATION WITH HOMEFORM

34.3 Use correct forms of expressions from C opposite to complete what a journalist says about conglomerates.

If a large company that has previously **(1)** d................ i................ a wide range of activities then finds that some of these are becoming less profitable, it may decide to sell those **(2)** s................ that do not fit in with its overall strategy. The board of the **(3)** p................ c................ may talk about **(4)** d................ these activities and **(5)** r................ so that they can get out of particular businesses. In this case, the group makes **(6)** d................ of its **(7)** n................-c................ a................ and uses the money from these **(8)** d................ to invest in and concentrate on its **(9)** c................ activities.

> **Over to you**
>
> - Why do companies form joint ventures?
> - Describe a recent merger in your country or elsewhere. Why did the companies merge?
> - What is the core activity of your country's biggest company?

35 Personal finance

A Traditional banking

'I'm Elizabeth. I have an **account** at the local **branch** of one of the big **banks**. I have a **current account** which I use to write cheques, make bill payments, and so on. It's a **joint account** with my husband. Normally, we're **in the black**, but sometimes we spend more money than there is in the account and we **go into the red** and have an **overdraft**. We have an **overdraft facility** – an agreement with the bank to be in this situation as long as the overdraft stays within a certain amount. There are **charges** that are taken from the account if we **go overdrawn**. And of course we pay **interest** (see Unit 32) on the overdraft. The **interest rate** is quite high.

> **Note**
> BrE: **current account, cheque account**
> AmE: **checking account**
> BrE: **cheque**; AmE **check**

'I also have a **deposit account** or **savings account** for keeping money for the longer term. This account pays us **interest** but not very much, especially after tax!

'We have a **credit card** with the same bank too, plus other cards with other **credit card companies**. Paying with **plastic** is very convenient. But we **pay off** the total amounts we've spent every month, so we don't pay interest on these, luckily.

'We also have a **mortgage** – a loan to buy a house. This is with a type of bank called a **building society**. Luckily, we were not affected by the **credit crunch**, when banks were much more hesitant to lend than before, or **negative equity**, when house prices fell and left some buyers owing more on their mortgage than their house was worth.'

B Internet banking

'In the old days, there was always a queue when I went to my bank, but now they offer **internet banking**. Through my computer at home, I can check my **account balances** – the amount I have in each account – and **transactions** – money going in and coming out. I can even **apply for a personal loan** online. If there's a problem, I can always phone the bank's **call centre** (see Unit 24).'

C Personal investing

'We have some **unit trusts** – shares in **investment companies** that put money from **small investors** like me into a range of companies. One type of unit trust here in the UK is in the form of an **ISA** – an **individual savings account** – but there are many other **financial products** available for **savers**.

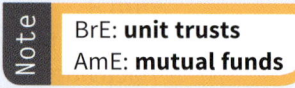

> **Note**
> BrE: **unit trusts**
> AmE: **mutual funds**

'My husband and I have **life insurance** which would **pay out** if either of us dies. This is just one of the **insurance policies** that we have.

'I pay **contributions** into a **private pension**, which will give me a regular income for my **retirement** when I stop working (see Unit 7). I've never joined a **company pension scheme** and the government **state pension** is very small!

'I'm lucky: I recently received a **windfall**, an unexpected one-off increase in the value of my **pension fund**, when my pension company was **demutualized** (see Unit 12).

'Some **financial institutions** now offer all these **financial products**.'

78   Business Vocabulary in Use Intermediate

Exercises

35.1 Look at A opposite and say if these statements are true or false.
1. You talk about the local 'agency' of a bank.
2. Americans refer to current accounts as cheque accounts.
3. A joint account is held by more than one person.
4. If you put €10,000 into a new account and spend €11,000, you are overdrawn by €1,000.
5. An account for saving money is called a safe account.
6. An account that pays a lot of interest has a high interest rate.

35.2 Lisa is looking at her bank's internet site. Look at B opposite. What does she click on if she wants to do the following?

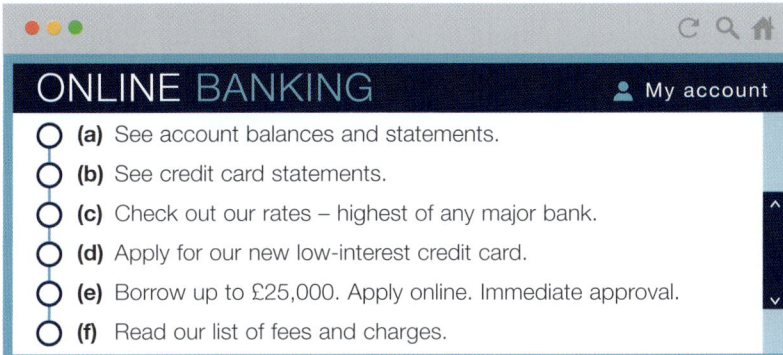

ONLINE BANKING — My account
(a) See account balances and statements.
(b) See credit card statements.
(c) Check out our rates – highest of any major bank.
(d) Apply for our new low-interest credit card.
(e) Borrow up to £25,000. Apply online. Immediate approval.
(f) Read our list of fees and charges.

1. see what rate of interest she is getting on her savings account
2. see if she is in the red on her current account
3. see how much she owes on her existing credit card
4. obtain a new credit card
5. understand why she has been charged for something she thought was free
6. apply for a personal loan

35.3 Read the article and answer the questions relating to expressions from A, B and C opposite.

COMPLAINTS ABOUT FINANCIAL PRODUCTS REACH RECORD LEVELS

Complaints about financial products and services leapt by 30 per cent last year to hit a record, underlining growing dissatisfaction with banks and insurers. The Financial Ombudsman Service (FOS) said the sharp rise was fuelled by "sudden surges" in complaints about unauthorized overdraft charges and loan payment protection insurance (PPI), driven largely by media and internet campaigns.
The FOS said that during the year, it referred 123,089 new cases for more detailed dispute-resolution work. A spokesman said it had seen the number of mortgage and banking disputes more than triple, while insurance complaints had doubled.

There was a tenfold increase in complaints about charges on current accounts, and a sixfold increase in complaints about PPI, which has been heavily criticized amid claims that it is overpriced and is mis-sold to people who would never be able to make a claim. Meanwhile, the number of disputes relating to travel and health insurance fell during the period. Sir Christopher Kelly, chairman of the FOS, said: "This time last year we had hoped we were starting to see a downward trend in complaint numbers for the first time. But instead, events during the year have led to the service receiving record numbers of new cases."

1. Which of these financial institutions are mentioned specifically?
   a) banks   b) insurance companies   c) building societies
2. Which of these financial products do the problems mentioned relate to?
   a) pensions   b) current accounts   c) loan payment protection insurance
   d) life insurance policies
3. Which other financial products are mentioned?
4. For which products has the number of complaints increased? For which ones has it decreased?

Over to you

- Think of one advantage and one disadvantage of online banking.
- What is the biggest bank in your country? Is it a national or international bank?

36 Financial centres

A Financial centres

Financial centres are places where there are many banks and other **financial institutions**. The financial centre of London is called **the City** or **the Square Mile**, and in New York it is called **Wall Street**.

Financial centres bring together **investors** (see Unit 32) and businesses that need their investment in order to function and develop. A **speculator** is an investor who wants to make a quick profit, rather than one who wants to invest over a longer period of time.

Brokers, **dealers** and **traders** buy and sell on behalf of these investors and, in some cases, for themselves or the organizations they work for.

Traders in Wall Street

> Note
> BrE: **financial centre**
> AmE: **financial center**

B Stock markets

The chief executive of Advanced Computers went through this process:
1 'We needed to **raise capital** (see Unit 32) to develop and expand, so we decided to **float** the company – in other words to **go public**.
2 'Our **shares** were **issued** and **listed** for the first time on a **stock market** that specializes in small companies.
3 'Our shares were **oversubscribed** – there weren't enough shares for all the investors who wanted them!
4 'The shares rose by 10 per cent on their first day. The **flotation** was a big success.'

> Note
> BrE: **stock** (countable) list/quote shares on a stock market flotation
> AmE: **stock** (uncountable) list shares on a stock market initial public offering (IPO)
> **Stock markets** outside the main English-speaking countries may be referred to as **bourses**.

C Other financial markets

Products that are bought and sold on other **financial markets** include:
- **commercial paper** – short-term lending to businesses (less than a year)
- **bonds** – longer-term lending to businesses and the government (over several years)
- **currencies** (**foreign exchange** or **forex**) – buying and selling the money of particular countries
- **commodities** – oil, metals and farm products, for example cereals

These are traded directly between dealers over the telephone and computer networks. Some commodities are traded in a central building called a **commodities exchange**. Shares, bonds and commercial paper are **securities**, and the financial institutions that deal in them are **securities houses**. Securities markets are also called **capital markets**.

D Derivatives

A **futures contract** is an agreement giving an obligation to sell a fixed amount of a security or commodity at a particular price on a particular future date.

An **options contract** is an agreement giving the right, but not the obligation, to buy or sell a security or commodity at a particular price at a particular future time, or in a period of future time.

These contracts are **derivatives**. Dealers guess how the price of the related **underlying shares** – the shares that the derivatives relate to – is going to change in the future, and use derivatives to try to buy them more cheaply than they could otherwise.

80 Business Vocabulary in Use Intermediate

Exercises

36.1 A financial journalist talks about the importance of financial centres. Complete the gaps with expressions from A opposite.

Now that a lot of buying and selling can be done over computer networks, **(1)** b_ _ _ _ _s and **(2)** t_ _ _ _ _s do not need to be in one place, and **(3)** s_ _ _ _ _ _ _ _ _s can make money by dealing over the internet from a computer in their living room.

In New York, the area around **(4)** W_ _ _ _ _ _ _ _ _ is home to many **(5)** f_ _ _ _ _ _ _ _ i_ _ _ _ _ _ _ _ _ _s such as the New York Stock Exchange.

London is one of Europe's most important financial **(6)** c_ _ _ _ _s: over 500 foreign banks have offices in London. But more and more of these financial institutions are not actually based in the traditional area of the **(7)** C_ _ _ or **(8)** S_ _ _ _ _ _ _ _ _, as it's often referred to. As in New York, they are moving to areas where property is cheaper.

Wall Street

36.2 Complete the sentences using appropriate forms of expressions from B opposite. Use British English.

1 A lot of companies that went bankrupt in the crash should never have .... in the first place.
2 All three technology firms have announced plans to .... more than £900 million through stock market ....
3 The shares were .... and we will see other companies in this field coming to the market this year.
4 The new law would prohibit oil companies that invest in that country from .... on US stock markets.
5 Around the world, businesses are being judged by .... according to their ability to earn profits.
6 The airline expects to make a small profit next year, its first since it .... on the bourses. (2 possibilities)

36.3 Use expressions from C and D opposite to describe the following.

1 a bank that makes companies' shares available
2 a contract to buy 500 tons of wheat for delivery in three months
3 coffee and copper
4 dollars, euros and yen
5 lending to a company for less than a year
6 lending to a local government authority in the form of ten-year investment certificates
7 shares, bonds, etc. but not currencies or commodities
8 the London Metals Exchange
9 the right to buy shares in a company in one month's time at $1.50 per share

Over to you

- What is your country's main financial centre?
- What commodities are most commonly traded in your country?

37 Trading

A Market indexes

If there is **demand** for shares in a company, for example because it is doing well, its **share price** goes up. The overall value of shares traded on a stock market is shown by an **index** (plural **indexes** or **indices**). Here are some of the most important indexes:

1. London: FTSE: the Financial Times Stock Exchange index – pronounced 'Footsie'
2. New York: Dow Jones Industrial Average – specializes in shares of long-established companies
3. New York: Nasdaq – specializes in shares of hi-tech companies
4. Paris: CAC 40
5. Frankfurt: DAX
6. Tokyo: Nikkei
7. Hong Kong: Hang Seng
8. Shanghai: SSE

B Market activity: good times ...

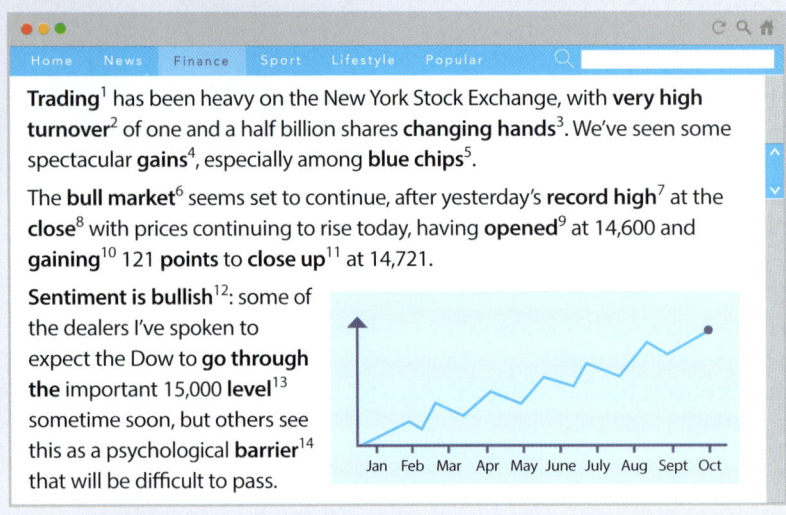

Trading[1] has been heavy on the New York Stock Exchange, with **very high turnover**[2] of one and a half billion shares **changing hands**[3]. We've seen some spectacular **gains**[4], especially among **blue chips**[5].

The **bull market**[6] seems set to continue, after yesterday's **record high**[7] at the **close**[8] with prices continuing to rise today, having **opened**[9] at 14,600 and **gaining**[10] 121 **points** to **close up**[11] at 14,721.

Sentiment is bullish[12]: some of the dealers I've spoken to expect the Dow to **go through the** important 15,000 **level**[13] sometime soon, but others see this as a psychological **barrier**[14] that will be difficult to pass.

[1] buying and selling of shares
[2] a large number
[3] being bought and sold
[4] big increases in value
[5] famous companies that are profitable in good times and bad
[6] rising level of prices
[7] highest level ever
[8] end of the working day
[9] started the day
[10] increasing by
[11] ending the day higher
[12] feelings are optimistic
[13] to pass the 'round' number of …
[14] an important level, but one that is not easy to get through

C ... and bad

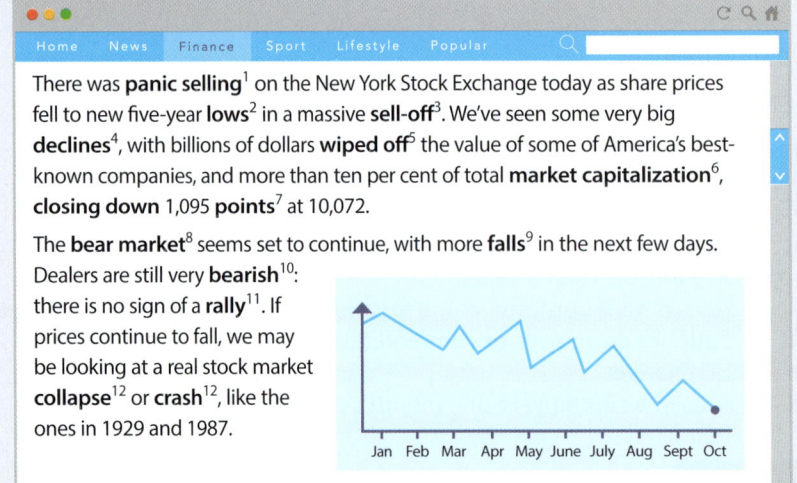

There was **panic selling**[1] on the New York Stock Exchange today as share prices fell to new five-year **lows**[2] in a massive **sell-off**[3]. We've seen some very big **declines**[4], with billions of dollars **wiped off**[5] the value of some of America's best-known companies, and more than ten per cent of total **market capitalization**[6], **closing down** 1,095 **points**[7] at 10,072.

The **bear market**[8] seems set to continue, with more **falls**[9] in the next few days. Dealers are still very **bearish**[10]: there is no sign of a **rally**[11]. If prices continue to fall, we may be looking at a real stock market **collapse**[12] or **crash**[12], like the ones in 1929 and 1987.

[1] selling shares at any price
[2] lowest level for five years
[3] selling
[4] decreases
[5] taken off
[6] the total value of shares on the market
[7] ending the day lower
[8] falling level of prices
[9] decreases
[10] pessimistic
[11] prices starting to rise again
[12] very serious drop in the value of shares, with very serious consequences

Business Vocabulary in Use Intermediate

Exercises

37.1 Complete the article using information from A opposite.

Yesterday in Asia, in **(1)** .... , the Hang Seng closed 1.6 per cent up at 15657 exactly. In Tokyo, the **(2)** .... was also up, at 15747.20. In New York last night, the **(3)** .... closed 1.8 per cent higher at 10824 exactly, and the hi-tech **(4)** .... index was 3.3 per cent up at 3778.32. Turning now to Europe, in early trading in **(5)** .... the FTSE 100 is 0.1 per cent down at 6292.80. The French **(6)** .... index is also slightly down at 6536.85. The DAX in **(7)** .... , however, is 0.1 per cent higher at 6862.85.

37.2 Use expressions in B opposite to answer these questions.

1. What are shares in companies like IBM, Shell, and Procter & Gamble called?
2. What is the activity of buying and selling of shares on a stock market?
3. How do you describe the situation on a day with twice as many shares sold as usual on a particular stock market?
4. How do you describe dealers who think shares in general will gain ten per cent in one day?
5. What is the name for a period when the stock market index has gone from 20,000 to 25,000?
6. How do you describe dealers who think that prices will fall?
7. How do they refer to the idea that 30,000 on a particular stock market index is important but not easy to get through?

37.3 Match the headlines (1–4) containing expressions from C opposite with the graphs (a–d).

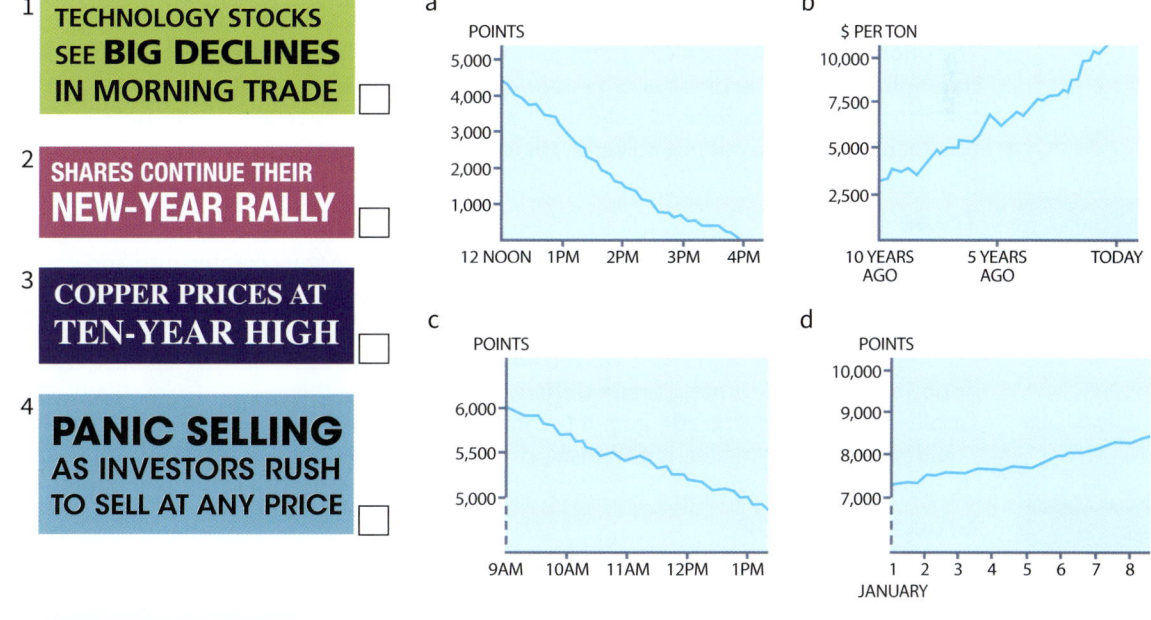

> **Over to you**
>
> - Which company would you buy shares in today, and why?
> - What might start panic selling on the stock market?
> - What is the difference between a bull market and a bear market?

38 Indicators 1

A Finance and economics

Finance is:
- money provided or lent for a particular purpose.
- the management of money by countries, organizations or people.
- the study of money management.

A company with money problems has **financial problems**.

High finance involves very large amounts of money used by governments and large companies. A person's or organization's **finances** are the money they have and how it is managed, etc. The related adjective is **financial**.

Economics is:
- the study of the way in which money works and how it is used.
- calculations of whether a particular business activity will be profitable or not. A profitable activity is **economic** and an unprofitable one is **uneconomic**.

A government with money problems has **economic problems**.

Do not confuse 'economic' with **economical**. If something is economical, it is cheap to buy, to use or to do. If not, it is **uneconomical**.

Economic indicators (see below) are figures relating to how well a country's **economy** – system of money, production, etc. – is working.

> Note: You don't say 'I'm studying economy' but 'I'm studying economics.'

B Inflation and unemployment

Inflation is rising prices, and the rate at which they are rising is the **inflation rate**. The related adjective is **inflationary**.

The **unemployed** are people without jobs in a particular area, country, etc. The level of **unemployment** is the number of people without a job. Unemployed people are **out of work**, and are also referred to as **jobless** (adjective) or **the jobless**, especially by journalists. When there are not enough people available to work, there are **labour shortages**.

C Trade

The **balance of payments** is the difference between the money coming into and going out of a country. The **trade balance** is the difference between payments for **imports** – goods and services from abroad – and payments for **exports** – products and services sold abroad. When a country exports more than it imports, it has a **trade surplus**. When the opposite is the case, it has a **trade deficit**. The amount of this surplus or deficit is the **trade gap**. If the trade gap gets bigger, it **widens**; if it gets smaller, it **narrows**.

> Note: Nouns: **export, import**
> Verbs: **export, import**

D Growth and GDP

Economic output is the value of goods and services produced in a country or area.

Gross domestic product or **GDP** is the value of all the goods and services produced in a particular country. **GDP per capita** is the total output of a particular country divided by the number of people living there.

The size of an economy is also sometimes measured in terms of **gross national product** or **GNP**. This also includes payments from abroad, for example from investments.

Growth is when output in the economy increases. The **growth rate** is the speed at which a country's economy **grows** and gets bigger.

Business Vocabulary in Use Intermediate

Exercises

38.1 Read the definitions (1–9) and write words from A opposite. The first one has been done as an example.

1 A country's system of money, work, etc.: economy
2 The study of this subject in schools, universities, etc.: ....
3 Adjective used to talk about profitable activities: ....
4 The opposite of 3: ....
5 Adjective meaning 'cheap': ....
6 The opposite of 5: ....
7 How money is used, and the study of this: ....
8 An organization's money and how it is managed: its ....
9 Adjective related to 8: ....

38.2 An economics reporter is talking about the economic situation in China. Complete what she says with expressions from B, C and D opposite.

'China's economic indicators show that growth is likely to continue at its current level, with a (1) .... of about 4 per cent per year over the next few years. Unemployment is not a problem, with very few people (2) .... In fact, there are (3) .... , for example in agriculture. As far as the (4) .... is concerned, China (5) .... more than it imports, but the (6) .... will narrow as the cost of its manufactured goods increases. China will continue to import more services than it exports, so the (7) .... in this area will continue to (8) ....'

38.3 Look at D opposite and complete the bar graph and the pie charts using the information.

The growth rate in China for the first ten years remained stable at around 4 per cent per year. After that the economy took off and a period of very fast growth followed, with 10 per cent growth per year, dipping to 8 per cent nine years later. Growth then picked up – at 10 per cent per year for the following nine years, but reaching 12 per cent this year.

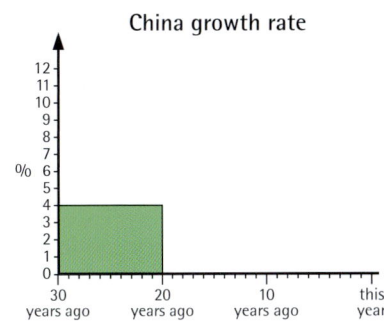

Thirty years ago, 75 per cent of GDP in China came from agriculture, 20 per cent from industry and 5 per cent from services. At that time, GDP was US$1,000 per person in today's terms. Today, GDP per person is US$5,500, 45 per cent coming from industry, 45 per cent from agriculture and 10 per cent from services.

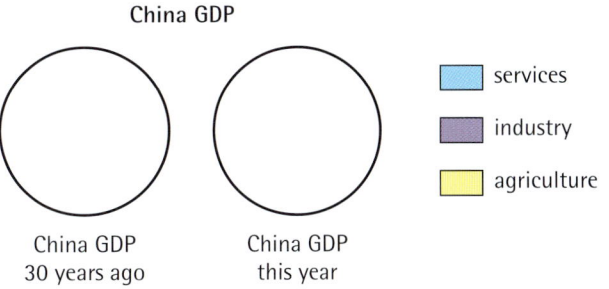

> Over to you
>
> • What is the difference between a trade surplus and a trade deficit?
> • What is the inflation rate at the moment in your country? Is it rising or falling?
> • Which three countries currently have the highest GDP?

39 Indicators 2

A Going up

Journalists in particular use these verbs to describe amounts or figures that are going up.

1. **BT SHARES ADVANCE IN ACTIVE TRADING** — Shares in BT increased in value, and a lot of them were bought and sold.
2. **TRADE SURPLUS JUMPS TO RECORD LEVEL** — The value of exports over imports is higher than ever.
3. **FUEL PRICES SET TO SKYROCKET** — Prices for fuel are going to rise by a large amount.
4. **UNEMPLOYMENT LEAPS TO TEN-YEAR HIGH** — The number of people without work is now higher than it has been for ten years.
5. **GOOGLE SOARS AS INTERNET GROWTH CONTINUES** — Shares in Google have increased greatly in value due to continued growth in internet use.
6. **VW PROFITS UP AS CAR SALES CONTINUE TO SURGE** — Profits in VW have increased thanks to rapidly rising car sales.

B Going down

The verbs here are used to talk about amounts, figures, etc. that are going down.

7. **1,000 JOBS AXED AS DEFENCE PLANT CLOSES** — A defence company has told 1,000 factory employees that they are to lose their jobs.
8. **EUROPEAN CENTRAL BANK CUTS RATE IN SURPRISE MOVE** — The ECB has reduced interest rates when this was not expected.
9. **SIEMENS EASES ON PROFITS WARNING** — Siemen's share price has gone down slightly after they said that profits would be lower than expected.
10. **SEPTEMBER RETAIL SALES PLUMMET** — Sales in shops have fallen a long way in September.
11. **GOVERNMENT SLASHES INCOME TAX TO TEN PER CENT** — The government has reduced income tax by a large amount to 10 per cent.
12. **EURO DIVES TO NEW LOWS** — The euro is worth less in relation to other currencies than it has ever been.

C Peaks and troughs

If a series of figures rises to a level and then stops rising, it **levels off** or **levels out** and remains **steady** or **stable**, perhaps before going down again. If it reaches a **peak** – its highest level – and then goes down, it **peaks at** that level. If it reaches a **trough** – its lowest level – and then **bottoms out**, it stops falling.

D Boom and bust

Demand is the amount of goods and services that people want in a particular period. A **boom** is when there is rising demand, fast economic growth, falling unemployment, etc.

Stagnation is when the economy is growing slowly, or not at all. **Stagflation** is when there is slow growth, but prices are increasing fast.

A **recession** is a period when there is **negative growth** – a period when the economy is getting smaller because it is producing less. A **slump** is a very bad recession. A **depression** is a very bad slump. **Boom and bust** is a period of growth and rising company profits followed by one with falling growth and losses. (See also **go bust** – Unit 33.)

Business Vocabulary in Use Intermediate

Exercises

39.1 Look at these headlines containing words from A and B opposite and say whether the statements about them are true or false.

1. **ELECTRIC CAR SALES LEAP** — Sales have risen by a small amount.

2. **Sterling Plummets As US Dollar Falls Slightly** — The British pound has fallen a lot in value, but the US dollar has fallen less.

3. **POLES AIM TO SLASH NEXT YEAR'S BUDGET DEFICIT** — The Polish government wants to reduce the difference between what it spends and what it receives in taxes.

4. **Brazilian President Axes Finance Minister** — The president of Brazil has asked the minister to stay in his job.

5. **ZIMBABWE INFLATION SKYROCKETS** — Prices in Zimbabwe have risen sharply.

6. **ELI LILLY SURGES ON HOPES FOR DRUG APPROVAL** — EL's share price has increased because it appears that a new drug it has developed will be approved for use.

7. **AMB JUMPS 13% ON BID HOPES** — Shares in AMB have fallen because it may be a takeover target.

39.2 Complete the crossword with expressions from C and D opposite.

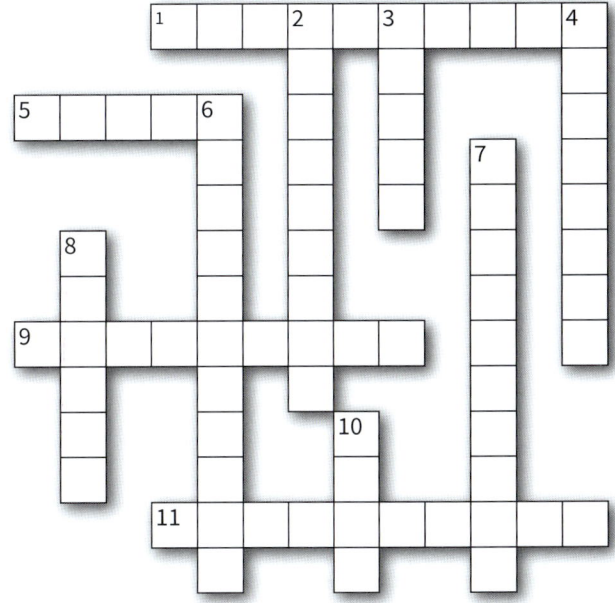

Across
1. the worst economic situation (10)
5. Inflation .... when it reaches its highest level. (5)
9. When a figure goes up to a level and stays there, it .... (6, 3)
11. When output starts rising from its lowest level, it .... (7, 3)

Down
2. a period when the economy is not healthy (9)
3. worse than 2 down, but not as bad as 1 across (5)
4. If the economy gets smaller, there is .... growth. (8)
6. rising prices without rising growth (11)
7. a very slow economy (10)
8. If inflation doesn't change, it remains .... (6)
10. a very positive economic situation (4)

Over to you

- Have banks in your country cut interest rates this year – or have they increased them?
- What is the difference between stagnation and stagflation?

Business Vocabulary in Use Intermediate

40 Wrongdoing and corruption

A Wrongdoing

FINANCIAL SERVICES AUTHORITY

We **regulate** the financial services industry in this country. Our job is to prevent **market abuse** and other financial **wrongdoing**, and punish the **wrongdoers**.

- **Insider dealing** or **insider trading** is when someone buys or sells securities using information that is not publicly available, for example because they have been involved with the company in some way. **Chinese walls** are measures that financial institutions take in order to stop knowledge in one department being used by another department to buy or sell shares, etc. at an advantage.
- **Price fixing** is when a group of companies in the same market secretly agree to set prices at a certain level so that they do not have to compete with each other.
- **Market rigging** is when a group of investors work together to stop a financial market functioning as it should, to gain an advantage for themselves.

People who commit **financial crimes** can be **banned** or **barred** – prevented from continuing in their jobs. They can also be **fined** – made to pay a sum of money – or even sent to **prison**.

B Bribery and corruption

An illegal payment to persuade someone to do something is a **bribe**, or more informally, a **kickback**, **sweetener** or **backhander** (BrE only). Making an illegal payment is **bribery**. People are **corrupt** and involved in **corruption** if they make or accept illegal payments. The more informal word **sleaze** is used especially in connection with politicians who receive payments in this way.

C Fraud and embezzlement

'My name's Samuel Woo. I've been a detective in the **fraud squad** for 20 years.

'Once, a gang **counterfeited** millions of banknotes in a garage. We found the equivalent of US$10 million in **counterfeit notes**. Very good quality they were! **Counterfeiting** or **forgery** of banknotes and financial certificates used to be a problem, but now all the forgers are in jail!

'Until recently, **faking** luxury goods like Rolex watches was also a problem, but we're working hard to close workshops where **fakes** are made.

> **Note**
> You can **forge** cheques, letters, statements, documents, signatures, banknotes, invoices.
> You can **fake** credentials, documents, records.
> You can **counterfeit** goods, drugs/medicines, banknotes, cigarettes, products.

'There are many cases of **fraud**. For example, some borrowers lie about their ability or intention to repay loans. A new form of fraud is **identity theft** – where the criminal uses another person's details, for example their credit card, to make purchases.

'And then there's **embezzlement**. This is a type of fraud where someone illegally gets money from their employer. One accountant sent false invoices from non-existent companies to the company she was working for. She paid out money into bank accounts of the companies she had 'created'. She **embezzled** $2 million – quite a **scam**!

'There are **rackets** – illegal activities for making money. For example, there used to be a lot of **racketeers** demanding 'protection money' from business and shop owners. If they didn't pay, their businesses were burnt down!

'**Money laundering** – hiding the illegal origin of money – is a problem, as gangsters are buying property with money from drugs. When they sell the property, the money becomes 'legal'. But banks must now tell us when someone makes a large deposit in cash.'

Exercises

40.1 Answer the questions using expressions from A and B opposite.

1. Ferry company managers from three ferry companies on the same route have been found guilty of meeting in secret in order to decide the prices they will charge next summer.

   What are they guilty of?

2. A company has been making secret payments to investors who buy its shares.

   What are the company and the investors guilty of?

3. The case involved a rich businessman who lent $1 million to a politician so that he could buy a house. The politician was paying no interest on the loan and did not mention it when asked to give a complete account of his finances.

   Which word, used especially about politicians, do people use to talk about this?

4. It was revealed that specialists in one department of the financial institution are advising Company X on a merger with another company. In another department of the financial institution, traders heard about this and bought large numbers of Company X's shares.

   What are the traders guilty of? (2 expressions) What should the financial institution use to prevent this?

5. A company selling weapons to a foreign government has been making secret payments to politicians who make decisions on which companies to buy arms from.

   What could these payments be called? (4 expressions) What are the company and the government guilty of? (3 expressions)

6. The man was charged with stealing data with the personal details of 150 people in order to make purchases with fake credit cards so that he could have a millionaire lifestyle.

   What was he accused of?

40.2 Complete this table, using information from C opposite. The first row has been done for you.

Noun: crime	Noun: criminal	Verb: what the criminal does (He/She …)	Noun: thing made or done in the crime	Related adjective
counterfeiting	counterfeiter	counterfeits	a counterfeit	counterfeit
	embezzler			
		fakes		
			a forgery	
	money launderer		–	–
racketeering		–		–

Over to you

- What do you think should happen to someone who is guilty of bribing a politician? What should happen to the politician?
- What kind of wrongdoing is common on the internet?

41 Business ethics

A Professional behaviour

Some professions have a **code of ethics** or **code of conduct** – rules or **professional guidelines** that control the way they behave. Behaviour may be described as **ethical** or **unethical**. It may also be described as **professional** or **unprofessional**.

> **Note:** **Code of conduct** is more frequent than **code of ethics**.

> **Note:** BrE: **behaviour** AmE: **behavior**

If there are **breaches** in the rules and they are broken, those responsible are guilty of **unprofessional conduct**.

Companies also have codes of conduct, of course, but talk increasingly about **corporate social responsibility (CSR)**. With CSR, companies are establishing systematic rules for their behaviour on **moral**, **social** and **environmental issues**.

B Social issues

Investors are increasingly concerned about **ethical investing** – where their money is invested. They want companies in which they have **stakes** or **holdings** – investments – to be **socially responsible**. For example, they want firms that they invest in to protect **human rights** – the ways of treating people fairly and with justice. They don't want them to employ **child labour** – children who work. Investors check that the firms don't **exploit** workers by using **sweatshop labour** – employees working very long hours for very low wages.

Sweatshop labour

They may want to know if the companies have **affirmative action programs** to prevent **discrimination**:

- to stop people from **ethnic minorities** – particular racial groups – being treated unfairly (see Unit 8).
- to stop women being treated unfairly in relation to men.

> **Note:** BrE: **labour** AmE: **labor**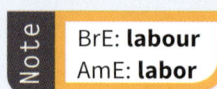

If investors do not approve of a company's activities, they may **sell their stake** or **holding** in it.

Investors are one group of **stakeholders** in a company. Other stakeholders include employees, customers, suppliers and taxpayers.

C Environmental issues

Climate change

Environmental or **green issues** are of course very important. The most important of these is **carbon emissions**, the amount of carbon dioxide produced by industry that contributes to **global warming** or **climate change** – the way that the atmosphere is getting hotter and causing warmer temperatures, more storms, etc. Businesses are trying to reduce their **carbon footprint** – the level of these emissions – to show that they are **carbon-neutral**, so that emissions that they do produce are compensated for by reductions elsewhere: this is known as **carbon offset**.

Business Vocabulary in Use Intermediate

Exercises

41.1 Complete the crossword with the correct form of words from A, B and C opposite.

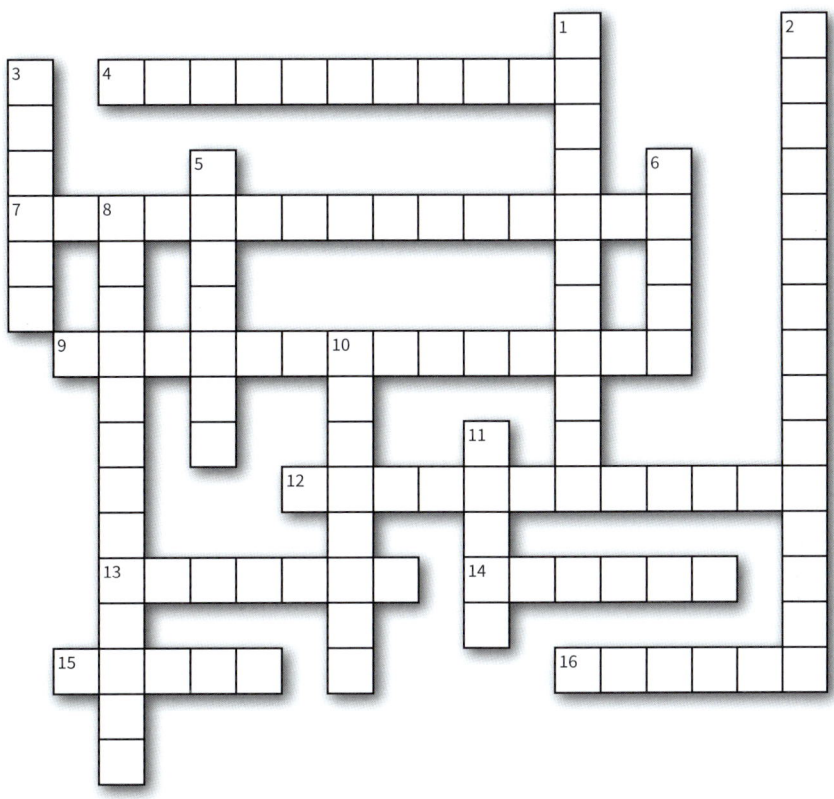

Across

4 and 14 measures taken to prevent discrimination: _____ _____ programs (11, 6)
7 when manual workers are employed in very bad conditions with very low pay (9, 6)
9 when one group of people is unfairly treated in relation to another (14)
12 a written set of rules of behaviour (4, 2, 6)
13 If companies pay very low wages for very long hours, they _____ their workers. (7)
15 another word for 'holding' (5)
16 See 6 down.

Down

1 If you behave in ways that do not harm people, the environment, etc., you are socially _____. (11)
2 gases produced by industry, transport, etc. (6, 9)
3 actions taken to compensate for 2 down (6)
5 the adjective related to 'ethics' (7)
6 another word for the adjective in 8 down (5)
8 and 16 across   problems relating to the land, air, water, etc. (13, 6)
10 a particular racial group: ethnic _____ (8)
11 one aspect of CSR: _____ issues (5)

> **Over to you**
>
> - Think of a company that has a good reputation for social responsibility. Describe some of the ways in which it has gained this reputation.
> - Do companies in your country have affirmative action programs? What do they consist of?

42 Time and time management

A Timeframes and schedules

'**Time** is money,' says the famous phrase. The **timescale** or **timeframe** is the overall period during which something should happen or be completed. The **lead time** for something is the period of time it takes to prepare and complete or deliver all or part of something.

The times or dates when things in a plan should happen are its **schedule** or **timetable**. If a project is completed at the planned time, the project is **on schedule**; completion before the planned time is **ahead of schedule** and later is **behind schedule**. If something happens later than planned, it is **delayed**: there is a **delay**. If you then try to go faster, you try to **make up time**. But things can **take longer than planned**!

A period when a machine or computer cannot be used because it is not working is **downtime**.

> **Note**
> **Schedule** is far more frequent than **timetable**, **timeframe** or **timescale**.
> **Schedule** is also more used in expressions like **ahead of schedule**, etc.

B Projects and project management

A **project** is a carefully planned piece of work to produce something new.

Look at this **Gantt chart** for building a new supermarket.

Building a new supermarket

stages
phases
steps
tasks

	Jun	Jul	Aug	Sep	Oct	Nov	Dec	Jan	Feb	Mar	Apr	May
Prepare site												
Build walls												
Build roof												
Fitting out												
Finish site												
Recruit employees												
Opening												

These stages **overlap** – the second one starts before the first finishes.

These stages are **simultaneous**: they **run in parallel** – they happen at the same time.

Project management is managing these stages. Big projects often include **bonus payments** for **completion** early or on time, and **penalties** for late completion.

C Time tips

Everyone complains that they never have enough time to do things. Lots of company employees go on **time-management** courses – looking for guidance on how they should organize their time. Here are some tips for time management:

- Use a **diary** (BrE) or **calendar** (AmE) to plan your day, week, etc., also known as **personal organizers**. The most modern form are smartphone apps which can display messages and help you organize your **events** and even make **notes** about them.
- Plan your day in advance. Make a **realistic plan** (not just a list) of the things you have to do and **prioritize** them – put them in order of importance. Work on the things that have the highest **priority** and leave the others until later.
- Avoid **interruptions** and **distractions** – things which stop you doing what you had planned.
- Do jobs to a realistic level of quality in the time available, and only to a level that is really necessary. Don't always aim for **perfectionism**. Try to balance **time**, **cost** and **quality**.

Business Vocabulary in Use Intermediate

Exercises

42.1 This is what actually happened in the building of the supermarket in B opposite. Use appropriate forms of expressions from A and B opposite to complete the text.

	J	J	A	S	O	N	D	J	F	M	A	M	J	J	A	S	O
Prepare site																	
Build walls																	
Build roof																	
Fitting out																	
Finish site																	
Recruit employees																	
Opening																	

'The overall **(1)** .... (2 expressions) was originally 12 months, but the project took 17 months. The project started on **(2)** .... in June, but site preparation took **(3)** .... because of very bad weather in the autumn. Site preparation and building the walls should have **(4)** ...., but the walls were started in January. We were able to **(5)** .... a bit of time on the roof: it took two months instead of three, but we were still **(6)** .... schedule. The next **(7)** .... (4 expressions) was fitting out the supermarket, but there was a series of strikes by the electricians, so there were **(8)** .... here too. The store opened in October, but now there's a lot of **(9)** ...., when the computers don't work. Everyone seems to have had bad luck with this project!'

42.2 Harry is a magazine journalist. Give him advice based on the ideas in C opposite. The first one has been done for you.

1. Harry started the day by making a list of all the things he had to do.
   You should make a realistic plan and prioritize the things you have to do, not just make a list.
2. He started writing an article, but after five minutes a young colleague came over and asked him for help on an article he was writing. Harry helped his colleague for half an hour and then they chatted about last night's television.
3. He started work again on his article, but he heard police cars outside and went to the window to look.
4. He wanted to make the article look as good as possible on the page, so he spent a lot of time adjusting the spacing of the lines, changing the characters of the text, etc., even though an editor would do this later.
5. At 6 pm he realized that he hadn't started on the other article he had to write, but he went home. On the train home, he realized that he had arranged to have lunch with an important contact, but had completely forgotten.
6. Harry decided he needed some training to change his behaviour.

Over to you

- What can a company do if it is behind schedule on a project? Is it always a good idea to increase the number of people working on it?
- What is your best personal tip on time management?

43 Stress and stress management

A When work is stimulating

'My name's Patricia and I'm a university lecturer. I chose this profession because I wanted to do something **rewarding** – something that gave me satisfaction. Ten years ago, when I started in this job, I had lots to do, but I enjoyed it: preparing and giving lectures, discussing students' work with them and marking it. I felt **stretched** – I had the feeling that work could sometimes be difficult, but that it was **stimulating**, it interested me and made me feel good. It was certainly **challenging** – difficult, but in an interesting and enjoyable way.'

B When stimulation turns to stress

'In the last few years there has been more and more administrative work, with no time for reading or research. I felt **pressure** building up. I began to feel **overwhelmed** by work – I felt as if I wasn't able to do it because the pressure and my employer's **demands** – what they wanted – were too high. On Monday mornings I began to feel so worried about the week ahead that I felt quite ill. I'm sure this feeling was caused by **stress**. My doctor agreed and said that it was **stress-induced**.

'Luckily, I was able to deal with this by starting to work part-time. I was luckier than one of my colleagues, who was also continually **under stress**. He **became** so **stressed out** because of **overwork** that he had a **breakdown**. He's completely **burned out** – so stressed and tired by his work that he will never be able to work again.'

C Downshifting

'More and more people want to escape the **rat race** and get off the **treadmill** – the feeling that work is too competitive – and are looking for **lifestyles** that are less **stressful** or completely **unstressful**.

'Some people choose to work from home so as to be nearer their families. People are looking for a better **quality of life** – a more relaxed way of living, perhaps in the country. Or perhaps they are looking for more **quality time** with their children – more than just preparing meals for them, taking them to school, etc. All this is part of **work–life balance** – a better balance between the demands of their job and the need for relaxation time with family, friends, etc.

'Choosing to work in less stressful ways is known as **downshifting** or **rebalancing**, and people who do this are **downshifters**.'

Exercises

43.1 Rearrange these sentences containing expressions from A and B opposite into a logical order.

a and stimulating. I felt pleasantly stretched. But then the pressure got to be too much and I felt overworked

b and under a lot of stress: I found the travelling very tiring and stressful. I had the feeling of being overwhelmed by my work. I started getting very bad headaches, and I'm sure they were stress-induced.

c challenging to change professions in this way, but now I can feel the stress building up again! I must do something to avoid complete breakdown and burnout.

d Hi, my name's Piet. I'm an engineer, at least I was. For twenty years I worked for a Dutch multinational. I was based here in Holland, but my work involved a lot of travelling, visiting our factories, and at first I liked my job: technically it was very rewarding

e So, when I was 45, I made a big change. I started a little wine shop in Amsterdam, working on my own. But now, after five years, I have 15 employees. At first it was

43.2 The underlined expressions below refer to different aspects of stress. Complete what the speakers say with appropriate words and expressions from B and C opposite.

1 I don't like <u>all this competition towards objectives that are not that worthwhile</u> – I don't like the .... and I want to get off the ....

2 I'm ok now, but I had <u>these feelings</u> of being unable to do what I was supposed to do – I was totally .... and ....

3 My partner and I decided to make a <u>change for the better</u> by going to live in the country – we wanted to .... and ....

4 Another <u>good thing</u> you get by living there is a better ....

5 I think my illness was caused by <u>feeling tense and irritable all the time</u> because of work – I'm sure it was ....

6 We spent a lot of time arguing with our children over basic things and we wanted <u>to spend more time doing interesting activities</u> with them – we wanted more ....

7 <u>It felt</u> like there was a great weight pressing down on me. But my colleagues told me that it was probably because of my work – all that .... and ....

8 <u>The things</u> my employer was asking me to do were impossible – I just couldn't face their ....

9 <u>Seventy hours a week</u> is not normal – no one should be asked to accept this level of ....

10 It's <u>a feeling</u> you hear but never think will happen to you. I retired at the age of 51 because I couldn't face work any more and I knew I would never go back – I was completely ....

> **Over to you**
>
> - Do you sometimes get stressed at work or college? What do you do about it?
> - What are some of the symptoms of stress?
> - What are the possible disadvantages of downshifting?

44 Leadership and management styles

A Leadership

Ken Manners is an expert on leadership and management styles.

Can leadership be taught?

'Traditionally, the model for **leadership** in business has been the army. Managers and army officers give orders and their **subordinates** – people working under them – carry them out in a system of **command and control**. Managers, like army officers, may be sent on leadership courses to develop their **leadership skills**. But I think they must have a basic talent for leadership to benefit from this. Some people say that the only real leaders are **born leaders**.'

Developing leadership skills

What makes a great leader?

'The greatest leaders have **charisma** – an attractive quality that makes other people admire them and want to follow them. A **charismatic** leader like this may be described as **visionary** – having the power to see clearly how things are going to develop in the future. (Someone like this is **a visionary** and is said to have **vision**.) Leaders are often described as having the following: **drive** – planned effort to achieve something; **dynamism** – a lot of ideas and enthusiasm; and **energy** – the power to be physically and mentally active.'

B Modern management styles

How have management styles changed in the last few years?

'Before, leaders were **distant** and **remote** – not easy to get to know or communicate with. But now managers are more **accessible** and **approachable** – easy to meet and to talk to. This is a completely different **management style**. They want to involve employees in a process of **consultation** – getting everyone to participate in making decisions that will affect them. This is management by **consensus** – a situation where most people agree with the decisions taken. The old style was to **impose** decisions in a **top-down** approach – forcing people to accept ideas that they did not agree with.'

Do you think this trend will continue?

'Yes. There are more women managers now. I would say that they are more **consensual** – more able to build consensus than traditional **authoritarian** male managers.'

C Empowerment

What, exactly, is empowerment?

'Encouraging employees to use their own **initiative** to take decisions on their own without asking managers first. This is **empowerment**. **Decision-making** becomes more **decentralized** and less **bureaucratic** – less dependent on managers and management systems. This is often necessary where the number of management levels is reduced.

'This is related to the ability of managers to **delegate** – to give other people responsibility for work rather than doing it all themselves. Of course, with empowerment and **delegation**, the problem is keeping control of your operations, one of the key issues of modern management style.'

Business Vocabulary in Use Intermediate

Exercises

44.1 Which expressions in A opposite do the underlined words relate to?

1 <u>These qualities</u> enabled Margaret Thatcher to work incredibly long hours and survive on three hours' sleep per night. (3 expressions)
2 Tim Berners-Lee had <u>it</u>, and foresaw a time when computers all over the world would communicate with each other.
3 <u>These people</u> often just have to obey instructions and do what they are told.
4 Many people think <u>these</u> cannot be learned – either you have them or you don't.
5 <u>This system</u> does not require individuals to think for themselves.

44.2 Complete the crossword with the correct form of words from B and C opposite.

Across

1 and 7 down what managers do, with or without talking to employees (8, 6)
5 leading without consultation (13)
8 not easy to talk to (7)
9 See 12 across.
11 what the boss in 5 across does not do (7)
12 and 9 Managers deciding without talking to employees is a ....-down .... (3, 8)
13 If managers ask employees to take on responsibility, they .... (8)
14 If all the decisions are not made in a company's head office, the firm is .... (13)

Down

2 to allow employees to decide things for themselves (7)
3 An organization where there are a lot of rules and procedures is .... (12)
4 If you decide without asking a manager, you use .... (10)
6 the adjective relating to 'consensus' (10)
10 If decisions are not arrived at by consensus, they are .... from above. (7)

Over to you

- Who is the most charismatic business leader you have seen?
- What happens during a process of consultation?
- What kind of management styles are common in your country?

45 Business across cultures 1

A Cultures and culture

Culture is the 'way we do things round here'. 'Here' might mean a country, an area, a social class or an organization such as a company or school. It includes **values** – things that people think are important – and **beliefs** – things that people believe in.

For example, you talk about:

business		the way that companies in general behave, the way business is done, etc. in a particular place
company or **corporate**	culture	the way a particular company works and the things that its employees believe are important
long-hours		where people are expected to work a long time each day
macho		the values typically associated with men – strength, etc.
sales		when selling is seen as the most important thing in an organization, rather than other activities
learning		when learning and innovation are seen as important

See also **enterprise culture**, Unit 11.

But you must be careful of **stereotypes** – fixed ideas that may not be true.

B Power and distance

A company's culture depends to a large extent on the country it is based in. Geert Hofstede is a world-famous expert on **cultural differences**. **Power–distance** is one of the important **cultural dimensions** that he identified.

Sweden is a **low power–distance culture**. Managers are **accessible** and **approachable** (see Unit 44) and there is a tradition of employees being involved in **decision-making** as part of a **team of equals** – everyone's opinion is treated equally.

France is a **high power–distance culture**. Managers are usually more **distant** and **remote**. Employees may feel quite distant from their managers and show a lot of **deference** – respect – to them, following decisions but not participating in them.

Now have a look at these organigrams:

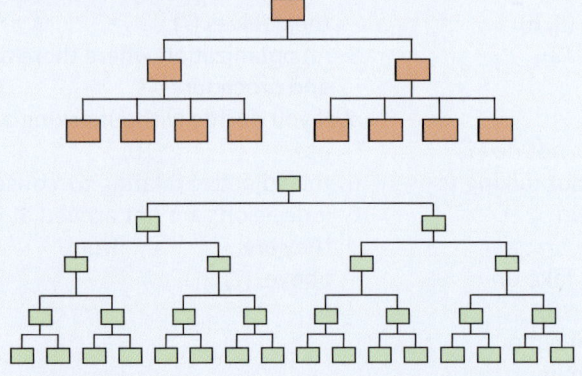

This Swedish company is not very **hierarchical**, with only three **management layers** – different levels.

French companies are on the whole more **hierarchical** than Swedish ones, with more **management layers.**

Deference and distance may be shown in language. Some languages have many **forms of address** that you use to indicate how **familiar** you are with someone. In English, whether first names or surnames are used can show distance.

See Unit 7 for more on hierarchy and **delayering** – reducing the number of management layers – and Unit 44 for more on management styles.

Business Vocabulary in Use Intermediate

Exercises

45.1 Look at A opposite. Which word combination with 'culture' relates to each of the following?

1. The men really dominate in this company – they don't make life easy for women at all. All they talk about is football.

2. They say that if you go home at 5.30, you can't be doing your job properly. But I'm going anyway.

3. We're all encouraged to go on courses and to keep up our specialist knowledge.

4. There was a time when managers could only wear white shirts in this particular company – things are a bit less formal now. (2 expressions)

5. In this country, it's easy to do business and there's very little bureaucracy.

6. All the chief executives in the company's history have had a background in selling.

45.2 Read this information about two very different companies and answer the questions.

The Associated Box Company (ABC) and the Superior Box Company (SBC) both make cardboard boxes.

At ABC, there are three different levels of management between the CEO and the people who actually make the boxes. At SBC, there is only one level.

Managers at ABC are very distant. They rarely leave their offices, they have their own executive restaurant and the employees hardly ever see them. Employees are never consulted in decision-making. At SBC, managers share the same canteen with employees. Managers have long meetings with employees before taking important decisions.

Managers and the CEO of SBC have an open-door policy where employees can come to see them about any complaint they might have. At ABC, employees must sort out problems with the manager immediately above them.

At ABC, employees call their managers 'Sir'. At SBC, everyone uses first names.

1. Which company is … ?
   a more hierarchical
   b more informal in the way people talk to each other

2. In which company are managers … ?
   a more approachable
   b more remote

3. In which company are employees … ?
   a more deferential
   b on more equal terms with their bosses

> **Over to you**
>
> Look again at the issues in 45.2 above. What is the power–distance culture in your country in general? Think of the distance between teachers and students in your school, or between managers and subordinates.

Business Vocabulary in Use Intermediate

46 Business across cultures 2

A Individualism

Individualism and **collectivism** relate to the way individuals form and behave in groups. This affects how companies operate.

In **individualist** societies, such as in the United States, the **connections** between individuals and the company are unique. Every employee is viewed as an **independent entity** and has a high level of personal responsibility.

In **collectivist** societies, such as in China, employees are part of strong groups, which protect them in exchange for their **loyalty** – feeling that they will do nothing to harm the group. The relationship between employer and employee or business partners is based on **trust** and **harmony**.

B Time

Attitudes towards **time** can vary enormously. Look at this information about France.

a **Working hours**
People start work at 8.30 or 9 and officially finish at 6, though many managers start later and stay at work much longer. Among some managers there is a culture of **presenteeism** – being at work when you don't really need to be.

b **Holidays**
Employees take five weeks' **holiday** a year and often take four of them in August. Many companies close down completely that month. There are a lot of **bank holidays** or **public holidays** (about 15) during the year.

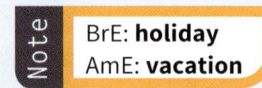
Note: BrE: **holiday** AmE: **vacation**

c **Meals and entertaining**
The **lunch break** is important and a lot of business is done over restaurant lunches. There are no snacks between meals, just coffee. Lunch, more than dinner, is important for discussing business. The **working breakfast** is rare.

d **Punctuality**
If you arrive five minutes after the time given for meetings, nobody minds, or even comments on it. If you are invited to someone's house (which is unusual in business), arrive between 15 to 30 minutes after the time given.

e **Boundaries** – limits – **between work and private life**
Don't **phone** people at home about work, and don't phone them at all after 9 pm.

C Cross-cultural communication

Here are some more areas for potential cultural misunderstandings.

a **distance** when talking to people – What is comfortable?
b **eye contact** – How much of the time do people look directly at each other?
c **gesture** – Do people make a lot of facial gestures? How much do they move their arms and hands?
d **greetings/goodbyes** – Do people shake hands every time? Are there fixed phrases to say?
e **humour** – Is this a good way of relaxing people? Or is it out of place in some contexts?
f **physical contact** – How much do people touch each other?
g **presents** – When should you give them? When should you open them? What should you say when you receive one?
h **rules of conversation** and the **role of silence** – How long can people be silent before they feel uncomfortable? Is it acceptable to interrupt when others are speaking?

Note: BrE: **humour** AmE: **humor**

Exercises

46.1 Complete the sentences using appropriate forms of words and expressions from A opposite.

1 Those from .... cultures are more likely to describe themselves as part of a social group with statements such as "I am a student, from Oxfordshire, part of a private flying club," whereas people from .... cultures will present more personal information like characteristics and preferences: "I am shy, I want to be a doctor, I like pizza."
2 He is a man with a strong sense of moral responsibility and a commitment to .... between individuals and communities.
3 It was a difficult decision the business partners had to make, but because they have the .... of the employees, it was quickly accepted.
4 This department must show a high level of group .... and expect high performance levels to be achieved by each team member.
5 Isn't there any middle ground between .... and the selfless call for .... ? Why must it be one or the other?
6 It's not easy for this team to work together; they all think of themselves as ....

46.2 Insert each heading (a–e) from B opposite at an appropriate place in this description of Swedish business culture.

(1) .... There is high consumption of coffee and snacks during the day. Lunch is not that important. Evenings can be spent with clients in the capital's restaurants, but there is not much night life outside the capital. In other cities, business hotels are good for entertaining.
(2) .... It's OK to phone people at home about work-related issues until about 9.30 pm.
(3) .... There are not that many public holidays and many people own houses in the country where they relax when they have days off or longer holidays.
(4) .... People finish work earlier each day in summer in order to benefit from the long summer evenings – this is part of a culture of work–life balance, which is very important. Even so, some managers don't see much of their families during the week.
(5) .... If you are invited to dinner at 8 pm, it's not a problem to arrive at 8 on the dot!

46.3 Match one of the items of advice (1–8) relating to different cultures with each point (a–h) in C opposite.

1 Don't start speaking immediately after the other person finishes – it shows you're considering what they said. ☐
2 It's probably best not to tell jokes at all – avoid the danger of your humour not being appreciated! ☐
3 When you receive a gift, open it immediately and thank the person at length. ☐
4 Don't touch people's heads – adults or children. ☐
5 Remember to shake hands each time you say goodbye. ☐
6 Stand about a metre and a half away – people feel more comfortable at this distance. ☐
7 Feel free to underline your points using your hand and arm, but don't overdo it! ☐
8 Look the other person in the eye for about half the time. ☐

```
Over to you
```
Write a description for your own country like the one in B opposite.

47 Telephoning 1: phones and numbers

A Telephones and beyond

- **landline** – a 'traditional' phone plugged into the wall
- public **telephone** / **payphone** – a phone in a public place operated with coins or a **phone card**
- **mobile phone** (BrE) / **cellphone** (AmE) – a phone you can carry with you. Callers can **leave a voice message** on **voicemail**, or send you a written **text message** or **text**.
- **smartphone** – a mobile phone that can be used as a small computer and that connects to the internet
- With **3G** mobile phone networks you can use your smartphone to connect to the internet and with a **4G** signal the internet connection is faster.
- **extension** – one of a number of phones on the same **line**, in a home or office
- **cordless phone** or **cordless** – a phone extension not attached by a wire that you can use when you are walking around the house, outside in the garden, etc.
- **VoIP** (voice over internet protocol) – uses the internet for phone calls, such as on **Skype**, so you don't pay the normal phone charges
- **webcam and microphone** – a camera attached to a computer so that two people connected over the internet can see each other and talk to each other using the microphone
- **videoconferencing** allows several people in one place to see people in another location and hold a meeting together. This is normally used to refer to companies who have their own systems, but videoconferencing can now also be done with participants each using their individual webcam over the internet.

B 'Phone', 'call' and 'ring'

to { call / phone / telephone } someone

to give someone a call

Note

In BrE you can say:			In AmE you can say:		
to	ring / ring up	someone	to	call up	someone
to	ring	someone up	to	call	someone up
In BrE, you can also say:			In informal BrE, you can also say:		
to	give	someone a ring	to	give	someone a bell / a buzz

C Numbers

When saying numbers, use rising intonation for each group, except for the last group, when you should use a falling tone. This shows you have reached the end of the number.

	country code	area code	number	
00 ↗	44 ↗	1746 ↗	845 ↗	921 ↘
Double oh (BrE)	double four	one seven four six	eight four five	nine two one
Zero zero (AmE)	four four			

D Doing things over the phone

Phone numbers for particular purposes include:

- **helpline/information line** – you can find out about a company's products or services
- **hotline** – often used by companies as a more exciting alternative to 'helpline'
- **booking/reservations line** – make bookings for events, travel and hotels

Note
People who answer and deal with calls like these work in **call centres** (BrE); **call centers** (AmE).
BrE/AmE: **reservations**; BrE only: **booking**
A number that you can call free of charge is:
an 0800 number or **a freephone number** (BrE);
a 1–800 number or **a toll-free number** (AmE).

Exercises

47.1 Which type of phone or service in A opposite would each of these people use?

1 Two people in different countries who want to talk without paying for an international call.
2 Five company managers in different countries who want to talk and see each other using a special system set up by their company.
3 A building contractor who works in lots of different places.
4 Someone who wants to stay in touch when they're in their garden.
5 A teenager who has gone out without her mobile and wants to tell her parents where she is. (2 expressions)
6 A manager who phones a colleague and finds that their mobile is switched off. (2 expressions)
7 Two ordinary people – not company managers – each sitting in their own bedroom in their respective homes, without access to a special system, who use the internet to see and talk to each other.

47.2 Look at B opposite and decide which of these items are grammatical. Correct the ungrammatical ones.

1 It would be good to see Anna soon. I'll phone to her and see when she's free.
2 I gave Brian a call yesterday and we had a long chat.
3 Why you don't ring to Pizza Palace and order some takeaway pizza?
4 I rang them five minutes ago but there was no answer.
5 Call up me next time you're in New York.
6 Give me a ring when you're next in London.
7 I'll give the bell to her and we'll go out for a meal.
8 When you get some news, make me a call.

47.3 Look at C opposite. You phone the Cross-Channel Ferry Company and you hear this:

'Welcome to the Cross-Channel Ferry Company's freephone hotline. If you'd like to receive a brochure, press 1. For today's sailing times and weather conditions, press 2. If you'd like to make a reservation, press 3. If you'd like to change an existing reservation, press 4. If you want to book a package holiday, press 5. If you want to hear this list again, press 6.'

Which number do you press in these situations?

a You have a reservation on the 15.00 ferry and you want to take the 18.00 instead.
b You want to book a return trip.
c You are confused about the different choices.
d You often get seasick and want to check how rough the sea will be today.
e You want a ferry crossing and an organized trip to the Loire Chateaux.

```
Over to you
```

- Do you like using call centres, or do you prefer to look for information, make bookings, etc. on the internet?
- When was the last time you called an organization? What happened? Were you happy with the way the call was dealt with?

48 Telephoning 2: trying to get through

A Asking to speak to someone

Mike Barr wants to speak to Jane Owen.

Primo Plastics, **good morning**.

Hello. **Can you put me through to** Jane Owen **in** Sales, **please?**[1]

One moment, please.[2] **I'm afraid the line's busy. Do you want to hold or would you like to call back later?**

I'll call again later. What's her **direct line?**[3]

Her direct line is 7942 8321.

7942 8321. **Thanks. Goodbye.**

You can also say:

[1] Extension 123, **please.**
[2] **I'm putting you through.**
[3] **I'll try again later. Could you give me the number for** her **direct line?**

B Voicemail 1

Later, Mike Barr calls again, and this time he **gets through** to Jane's **voicemail**. This is her **greeting**:

'You're **through to the voicemail** of Jane Owen. I'm **away** at a conference **until** Monday the 5th, but **I'll be picking up my voicemail on my mobile**. If you leave a message, **I'll get back to you**. For anything urgent, **please call** my PA, Ros Brown, **on extension** 8325.'

'**Please leave a message after the tone**.'

After leaving a message, you may hear this:

'**To listen to your message**, press 1.'

After listening to your message, you will probably hear this:

'**If you'd like to change your message,** press 2. **If you'd like to delete your message**, press 4. Otherwise, **please hang up**.'

C Voicemail 2

Mike leaves this message:

'Hello, **this is** Mike Barr **from** Smartauto. **It's about** our order for specialized plastic components. There have been some last-minute changes in the specifications. I hope your manufacturing people haven't started making them yet! **Would it be possible to** call me back **at** my office **on** 0117 893 4522? Otherwise, you could call me **on my mobile** on 07974 522 742 during the weekend, or **first thing** on Monday. It's very urgent. Bye for now.'

Exercises

48.1 Arabella Ford is trying to phone John Quinn in Primo's finance department. Complete the gaps with expressions from A opposite. Be careful to use the alternative expressions where necessary.

Receptionist: Primo Plastics, good morning.
Arabella: Hello. Can (1) .... to John Quinn in Finance, please?
Receptionist: (2) ...., please. I'm (3) .... I'm afraid (4) .... Do you (5) .... or would you like to (6) .... ?
Arabella: I'll (7) ...., ...

(One minute later.)

Receptionist: The line's still (8) ...., I'm afraid.
Arabella: I'll try (9) .... Could you give me (10) .... his direct line?
Receptionist: His (11) .... is 7942 ...
Arabella: 7942 ...
Receptionist: ... 8339.
Arabella: 8339. Thanks. Goodbye.
Receptionist: Goodbye.

48.2 Write voicemail greetings for other Primo employees, based on this information, using expressions from B opposite.

1 Steve Fox – on holiday until Mon 12th – will not be picking up messages – will respond when he gets back – anything urgent, contact colleague Rob Timmins – extension 8359. If you have message – leave it after tone.
2 Sue Leighton – away on business trip until Thursday – will pick up messages – leave a message after the tone – get back to you as soon as possible.
3 Rod Baxter – on training course until 20 Jan. Not picking up voicemail – can leave message and will respond when he gets back. Urgent queries – PA Jill Salford – direct line 8466.
4 Tina Preston – in meetings all day today, Friday. Leave a message – will get back Monday morning. Urgent matters – colleague Keith Samson – extension 8521.

48.3 Another caller leaves a message on Jane Owen's voicemail. Complete the message using the correct words from C opposite.

'Hello, this (1) .... Jenny Robin (2) .... Quirky Furniture Ltd. It's very urgent. Would it be possible (3) .... call me back (4) .... my office (5) .... 020 8945 8333 first thing on Tuesday? Otherwise, you could call me this afternoon (6) .... my mobile (7) .... 07962 290 821. It's about our order for plastic furniture components. We still haven't received them! Bye for now.'

> **Over to you**
>
> - What are some of the difficulties in using the phone in English?
> - Write a voicemail greeting in English for yourself of a kind you use when not at your office.
> - Do you leave messages on people's voicemail? Or do you prefer email?

49 Telephoning 3: getting through

A Getting through

Mike phones again and gets through to Jane Owen's PA – her personal assistant.

PA: Jane Owen's **office**, **good morning**.
MB: **Hello. Can I speak to** Jane Owen, **please? Is** she **available?**
PA: **I'm afraid** Ms Owen**'s not available** – she**'s with** a customer **right now.**
MB: **Oh, right. Can I leave a message for** her, **please?**
PA: **Who's calling, please?**
MB: **It's** Mike Barr **here, from** Smartauto Cars.

B Giving and taking messages

The personal assistant can also say:

- Can/May I take a message?
- Would you like to leave a message?
- I wonder if you could call back later?
- Can I ask who's calling?
- Could you give me your name?
- Which company are you calling from?
- Can/May I ask what it's about?
- I'll ask her to call you (when she gets back / when she's free).
- I'll give her your message.

The caller could say:

- Could I leave a message?
- Could you tell her that … ?
- I'm calling about …
- I want / I'd like to talk about …
- I'm calling to confirm that …
- Could you ask her to call me back? My number's …

 Note: When you answer the phone, you do not say 'I am X.'

C Spelling names

If you want to spell a name, you can say, for example, 'A for Alpha, B for Bravo', etc.

Alpha	Bravo	Charlie	Delta	Echo	Foxtrot	Golf
Hotel	India	Juliet	Kilo	Lima	Mike	November
Oscar	Papa	Quebec	Romeo	Sierra	Tango	Uniform
Victor	Whiskey	X-ray	Yankee	Zulu		

You may also need these expressions:

| capital A | small a | all one word | new word/line | dash (–) or hyphen (-) |
| slash (/) | dot (.) | at @ | colon (:) | com (as in internet addresses) |

Spell email addresses like this: jane-smith@aol.com = jane hyphen smith at a–o–l dot com.

D Taking messages: checking information

a **I'm sorry, I didn't catch** your name. Could you spell it, please?
b **Is that with** a D **at the end** – D for David?
c **Did you say** your number is 624 426?
d **Is that with** B for Bravo **or** V for Victor?
e **Where did you say** you're calling from?
f **Is that with** one M **in the middle** or two?
g The code for Sweden is 49, **right**?
h **Is that** Milan **like** the city?

Exercises

49.1 Look at A and B opposite. Change the underlined expressions in these conversations so that they are correct and more polite.

1 A: <u>I want</u> to speak to Ms Sangster.
   B: <u>She's busy.</u>
   A: <u>I'm</u> Sven Nyman <u>talking</u>.
   B: <u>Why are you calling?</u>
   A: <u>I want to discuss</u> her order.
   B: I'll <u>tell</u> her to call you when she's free.

2 A: Hello. Is Jack Bronson <u>able to speak on the phone?</u>
   B: <u>No. Who are you? What company do you work for?</u>
   A: Rosario Gonzalez. <u>Excelsior Media Services. Take a message for him. Tell him that I've received his cheque.</u>
   B: <u>He will get the message.</u>

49.2 Spell the following as you would spell them on the phone. Use the table in C opposite to help you. The first one has been done as an example.

1 **Maeght:** M for Mike, A for Alpha, E for Echo, G for Golf, H for Hotel, T for Tango.

2 • Valladolid

3 WEBER

4 http://www.britishcouncil.org/courses

5 PETER HOUSE

6 Macpherson

7 TO: john-smith@cambridge.ac.uk
   SUBJECT:

49.3 Match the responses (1–8) with the questions (a–h) in D opposite.

1 No, actually it's 46.
2 It's Valladolid with a V at the beginning, V for Victor.
3 No, it's Schmidt with a T at the end, T for Tango.
4 Two. T–I–double M–E–R–M–A–N.
5 No, 642 246.
6 Springer Verlag in Hamburg.
7 Krieslovski. K–R–I–E–S–L–O–V–S–K–I.
8 No, it's with two Ls in the middle and a D at the end.

Over to you

- Practise spelling words you have to give on the phone using the alphabet in C opposite.
- Practise giving your own email address and the address of your company's website.

50 Telephoning 4: arrangements and ending calls

A Phoning again

Mike phones again and gets through to Jane Owen.

MB: Hello. **Can I speak to** Jane Owen, **please?**
JO: **Speaking.**
MB: **It's** Mike Barr **here. I tried to phone you** last week. **It's about** our order.
JO: **Right. I got your message. I was about to call you.**
MB: **Yes, we need to** talk more about the technical specifications for the plastic.

B Making arrangements

You get through to the person you want to speak to and fix a meeting.

- Can we fix a meeting?
  Shall we arrange an appointment?
  Would it be useful to meet up soon?

- How about tomorrow?
  What about Tuesday?
  Would Wednesday be suitable?
  Would Thursday suit you?
  Shall we say Friday?

- I'll (just) get/check my diary.

- That's fine.

- I can't / won't be able to make Thursday.

C Closing the conversation

Here are some ways of finishing a conversation without sounding rude.

- See you on Friday then.
- I'm going to have to go now.
  I've got to go to a meeting.
  I have to go and see someone.
- Nice talking to you.
  (It's been) good talking to you.
  Good to talk to you.
- Talk to you soon, no doubt.
  Thanks for phoning.
  We'll be (back) in touch soon.
  Look forward to hearing from you soon.

- Yes, I'll look forward to seeing you then.

- Nice talking to you.

- Thanks for calling.

D Changing arrangements

Jane Owen and Mike Barr are continuing their conversation.

a JO: **I can't make** Tuesday. **Something has come up. I've got to** go over to Berlin to see a client. **How about** Wednesday morning?
b MB: I can't make Wednesday morning, I'm afraid. **Can you make** the afternoon instead?
c JO: **I think that's OK.** Just let me check my diary ... I'm afraid that's **not going to be possible**. I'd completely forgotten we have a departmental meeting that day. Can we **put it off** till the 22nd?
d MB: I'm afraid the 22nd **won't be possible**. I'm going to be very busy that day. Could we **put it back** until the following week?
e JO: **I'm completely snowed under** the following week. **Can we leave it open? I'll get back in touch** when I'm less busy.
   MB: Yes, but we need to make a decision soon!

Exercises

50.1 Annelise Schmidt (AS) phones James Cassidy (JC) and arranges to meet him. Reorder their conversation, which contains expressions from A and B opposite.

a AS: Fine thanks. I'm going to be in London on Tuesday and Wednesday next week. How about meeting up to discuss how Penguin and Sprenger might work together?
b AS: Hello. This is Annelise Schmidt. You remember we met at the Frankfurt Book Fair last month?
c AS: Look forward to seeing you then. Bye.
d AS: Sounds good. Shall I meet you at your office? I've got the address.
e AS: Yes, that's fine.
f JC: James Cassidy speaking.
g JC: Goodbye.
h JC: I'll just check my diary. I won't be able to make Tuesday. I've got to go to Manchester. Would Wednesday suit you? How about lunch?
i JC: OK. See you on Wednesday at 12.30, then.
j JC: Yes, how are you?
k JC: Yes. Why don't you come round here at about 12.30? Ask for me at reception and I'll come down.

50.2 Look at B and C opposite. Which of these exchanges are natural, and which are illogical?

1 A: Nice talking to you. See you on Wednesday.
   B: See you Wednesday. Thanks for calling. Bye.

2 A: I'll look forward to seeing you tomorrow, then.
   B: Talk to you soon, no doubt. Bye.

3 A: It's been good talking to you. I'm going to have to go. I've got to go to a meeting.
   B: Nice talking to you. I'll be in touch soon.

4 A: See you this afternoon at 4, then.
   B: Yes, we'll be back in touch soon.

5 A: I've got to get on with some work. I'm going to have to go.
   B: Talk to you soon, no doubt. Bye.

50.3 Match these possible replies (1–5) with what the speakers say in D opposite.

1 I suppose so: it would have been good to meet. Look forward to hearing from you when you're less busy.
2 The 22nd … I'm going to be on holiday. What about the 29th?
3 The afternoon would be no problem. How about at 3?
4 Wednesday's going to be difficult. Can you make the next day?
5 Yes, the same day the following week would be fine.

> **Over to you**
>
> - Do you make arrangements on the phone at work – or do you prefer to use email?
> - Do you find it difficult to end phone calls in English and also in your own language?

51 Business communication 1: staying in touch

A Business cards 1

Business cards are an important source of information about your **business contacts** – people you meet doing business. Business cards may help you understand the **hierarchy** (see Unit 45) of the company you are dealing with. In some places, especially in Asia, it's important to **follow the etiquette** – rules – for their use. In Asia, when someone hands over their card, take it with both hands, look at it carefully and treat it with care and respect. Do not write or make notes on it. Store it carefully. Hand over your card in return, ensuring that you always have a supply with you.

B Business cards 2

*Chartered Institute of Marketing

[1] **first name**
[2] **middle initial** – some people use an initial to show the first letter of their middle name
[3] **family name**, **surname** – in the Western world, the family name comes last (in China and some other places it comes first)
[4] **job title** – the official name of someone's job
[5] **qualifications** – some people show their **academic qualifications**
[6] **membership of professional organizations**
[7] **contact details** – **phone numbers**, **email address**, **postal address**, etc.

C Staying in touch

Gunilla Madsen is speaking to Wu Lee.

GM: Thanks for your card. Wu is your family name, right?
WL: Yes, but please call me Lee.
GM: OK. Yes, I think you'll be very interested in our latest equipment – the technical specifications have only just been finalized.
WL: **Could you email** the specs to me when you get back, Gunilla? My **email address** is on my card.
GM: Sure. I'll **attach** the specs to the email. It's going to be quite a **large attachment**! There are about ten pages of specs. And I'll send some brochures **by courier** – we use DHL.
WL: No problem.
GM: **Please get back to me** if you have any questions, of course. Email is probably easiest.
WL: Especially with the time difference between Shanghai and Oslo!
GM: Yes, but **don't hesitate to give me a call** if you'd like to discuss anything. People don't use the phone enough these days!
WL: No, they don't. So, **we'll be in touch** soon … **by email** or **by phone**.
GM: Absolutely, it was very nice meeting you, Lee.
WL: Likewise!

Exercises

51.1 George was representing his company, Primo Plastics, on their stand at a trade fair in Tokyo. Look at A opposite and identify five mistakes that he made in relation to card etiquette.

A Japanese businessman, Bunzo Watanabe, came to the stand and said that Primo Plastics was the sort of special plastics company that his company might like to work with. He handed over his card, and George took it with one hand. He wrote 'Tokyo trade fair' on the back to remind him where he had met Mr Watanabe. He did not read the card carefully, but put it casually in his pocket. When Mr Watanabe asked for George's card, George said, 'Sorry, but I've run out. I'll write my details on a sheet of paper.'

51.2 Look at B opposite. Then identify the items below (1–7) on each card. Write the numbers next to the items.

 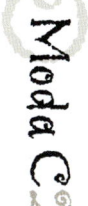

1 first name
2 middle initial
3 family name / surname
4 job title

5 qualifications
6 membership of professional organizations
7 contact details, including email address

51.3 Complete the conversation between the people in 51.2 using expressions from C opposite.

WS: OK. Yes, I think you'll be very interested in the latest technical developments – we can offer consultancy services that will help you choose the right textile supplier.
FR: Could you email me something when you get back, Wolfgang? My **(1)** .... is on my card.
WS: Of course, but it's going to be quite a large **(2)** .... ! Our electronic 'brochure' is about 15 pages long.
FR: No problem.
WS: Please don't hesitate to **(3)** .... if you have any questions, of course. Email is probably easiest …
FR: Even if there's no time difference between Frankfurt and Milan!
WS: Yes, please feel free **(4)** .... It's sometimes easier to talk over the phone rather than by email.
FR: Yes, you're right.
WS: And I can always send textile samples **(5)** .... : we use FedEx.
FR: Good. In our business it's always good to be able to see and touch the fabric.
WS: Absolutely. Well, it was very nice meeting you, Francesca.
FR: Likewise! We'll be in touch soon, no doubt.

Over to you

You meet someone at a conference and promise to send them more information about your school or organization. Write an email to them.

52 Business communication 2: email

A Email

Most email programs on computers have **icons** with abbreviations like these:

- **inbox** contains email waiting for you to read
- **subject** – what the email is about
- **cc** – copy this email to …
- **bcc** – blind copy this email to … (so that the other people you're sending the email to don't know you're sending this copy)
- **fwd** allows you to **forward** an email – to send an email you have received to someone else
- **delete** allows you to get rid of an email you don't want to keep
- **reply** allows you to send an answer back to the person who sent the email
- **reply to all** allows you to send the answer to the person who sent the email, plus all those who received copies of it
- **attach** allows you to send an **attachment** – a document that you **attach to** and send with an email
- **contact information** can be inserted automatically at the end of an email with your **contact details** – name, phone number, etc.
- the **address book** allows you to store the **email addresses** of people that you write to

B Email expressions

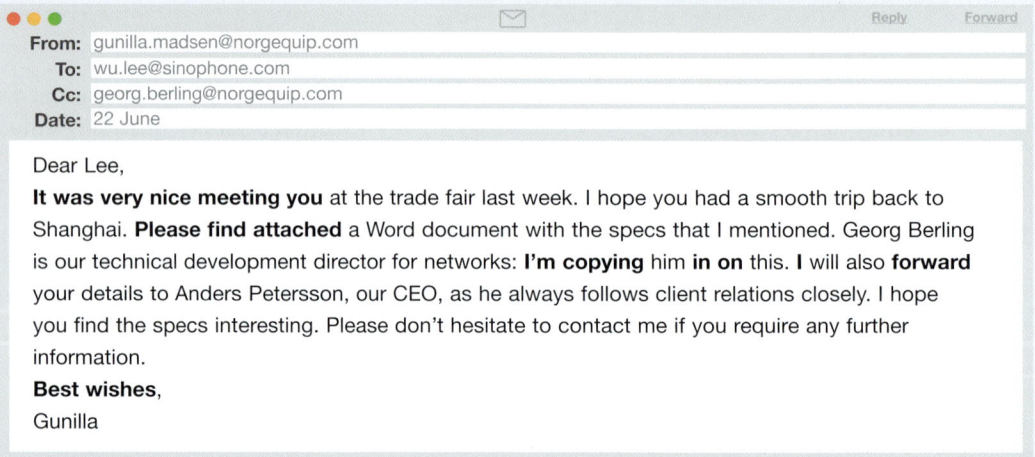

From: gunilla.madsen@norgequip.com
To: wu.lee@sinophone.com
Cc: georg.berling@norgequip.com
Date: 22 June

Dear Lee,
It was very nice meeting you at the trade fair last week. I hope you had a smooth trip back to Shanghai. **Please find attached** a Word document with the specs that I mentioned. Georg Berling is our technical development director for networks: **I'm copying** him **in on** this. **I** will also **forward** your details to Anders Petersson, our CEO, as he always follows client relations closely. I hope you find the specs interesting. Please don't hesitate to contact me if you require any further information.
Best wishes,
Gunilla

C Beginnings and endings

It's important to use the right degree of **formality** – seriousness – and **deference** (see Unit 45).

The following beginnings range from formal to informal: **Dear Sir/Madam** (used when you don't know the person's name), **Dear Ms** Caxton, **Dear** Zoe and **Hi** Zoe.

The following endings range from formal to informal and are used mainly in emails and faxes: **Best regards**, **Regards**, **Best wishes**, **All the best**, **Best**. **Yours faithfully** (BrE only) is used in letters and faxes when you don't know the person's name, **Yours sincerely** (AmE **Sincerely**) is less formal and **Yours** is the least formal ending.

Business Vocabulary in Use Intermediate

Exercises

52.1 Complete these tips on using email with appropriate forms of expressions from A opposite. (Some items are abbreviations and other items are full forms. You can use some items more than once.)

Use the **(1)** .... field to indicate content and purpose. Don't just say, "Hi!" or "From Laura."

Use a signature that includes **(2)** .... To ensure that people know who you are, include a signature that has your contact information, including your mailing address, website, and phone numbers.

Use the copy and **(3)** .... buttons appropriately. Don't use **(4)** .... (abbreviation) to keep others from seeing who you copied; it shows confidence when you directly copy anyone receiving a copy. Do use **(5)** .... (abbreviation), however, when sending to a large distribution list, so recipients won't have to see a huge list of names.

Remember that email isn't private. Email can be **(6)** .... – sent on to someone else – so unintended audiences may see what you've written. You might also send something to the wrong person by mistake, so always keep the content professional to avoid embarrassment. If you are **(7)** .... a message you've received, do not change the wording.

Be economical with group email. Send group email only when it's useful to every recipient. Use the **(8)** ".................................... ...." button only when you need collective input and only if you have something to add.

Summarize long discussions. Scrolling through pages of replies to understand a discussion is annoying. Instead of continuing to **(9)** .... to a series of messages, take a minute to summarize the messages for your reader.

52.2 You are Wu Lee. Reply to the email in B opposite, using the same expressions.

- Open suitably.
- Say it was good to meet Gunilla too.
- You are attaching some information about your company, Sinophone.
- You are informing your colleague Lin Weng, purchasing manager, about the meeting by sending him a copy of the email at the same time.
- You will send Gunilla's details to another colleague in another email, Shu Bao: finance director.
- End suitably.

52.3 Which expressions from C opposite would you use to begin and end each of these emails?

1. You are writing as informally as possible to a friend (Jim) you know very well.
2. You are writing to a company where you would like to work, but you don't know the name of the person who will read your email.
3. You are writing to a woman whose family name you know (Preston) but not her first name; you want to end relatively formally.
4. You are writing to someone you know vaguely (Mike); you want to end with an average level of formality.
5. You are writing to a man (Brian Collins) in your organization who is much more senior than you, and whom you have never met.
6. You are writing to a woman whose name you don't know; end suitably.

```
Over to you
```

- Does email save time – or does it just make more work?
- Should company employees be allowed to send and receive personal emails at work, and surf the internet?

53 CVs, cover letters and emails

A CV tips

A **CV** or **curriculum vitae** is a document about your education, career and objectives. Look at the tips:

a Put your **name** and **contact details** at the top.
b Talk about your **career goal** – professional objective.
c Mention your **skills** (see Unit 4).
d Include your **qualifications** (see Unit 4).
e Write about your **experience** and your **achievements**.
f You can mention relevant **interests**.
g Use **keywords** relevant to the employer, ones that will be picked out by automated systems.
h Avoid **exaggerations** – saying something is better or more important than it really is.
i Be **concise** – not more than two pages, preferably one.

> **Note:** BrE: **CV** or **curriculum vitae**
> AmE: **résumé** or **resume**.
> **Experience** is uncountable in this context: 'I have a lot of experience in this area', not ~~experiences~~.

B Parts of a CV

Layout is the way that information is arranged on the page. Clear layout is very important for CVs.

MARIA SOARES

34 Avenida da Liberdade, 1250 Lisbon, Portugal
email: maria.soares88@gmail.com   mobile: +351 93 472 3792

Career goal: Looking for a **stimulating**[1] career in web design in an **established**[2] design company

Skills:
Visual **creativity**[3]; good **leadership skills**[4]; Understanding of all technical and design issues in website construction and maintenance; **Bilingual**[5] in Portuguese and English

Qualifications:
2016–2017 London Business School – MBA
2011–2012 University of Berlin – Master's degree in Advanced Web Design (course taught in English)
2002–2007 Porto School of Architecture and Design – Architecture degree

Experience:
2012–2016 **Freelance**[6] Web Designer, based in Berlin. Worked with a number of German internationals, contributing design and technical expertise.
2009–2011 Internet Advertising Manager, Publicidades Inovativas, Lisbon. Worked on key client website advertising campaigns.
2007–2009 Architectural Assistant, Projetos do Norte, Porto. Provided support to senior members of the firm, working on commercial building projects.

[1] interesting and exciting
[2] one that has existed for some time
[3] producing new ideas
[4] ability to manage people and lead them in new directions
[5] able to speak two languages
[6] working independently, not as a company employee

C Cover letters and emails

Find out if you should send your application by post or email. If by email, you can copy your **cover letter** into the email, or send it as an attachment. Look at Maria's **cover email**.

To: recruitment@lisbonwebdesign.pt
Subject: Application for **position** of Department Manager

Dear Ms Santos
I am writing with reference to your online advertisement for a department manager. **As you will see** from the **attached CV**, my background is in this area. I have long experience of web design, and I recently completed an MBA in London, where I developed my management and leadership skills.
I would now like to relocate back to Portugal.
I am available for interview on the date that you mention.
I look forward to hearing from you.
Best regards
Maria Soares

> **Note:** **Position** is a formal word for 'job', used especially in the context of job applications.

If writing a letter, start **Dear Sir or Madam**, or **Dear** .... , with the name of the person if you know it, and end **Yours sincerely**. Cover emails and letters should also be concise – less than one page.

Exercises

53.1 A recruiter is making comments about various candidates' CVs. Which point in A opposite does each comment refer to?

1. She's certainly not short and to the point – it's four pages long!
2. He speaks Japanese and Chinese, having lived in each country for 10 years.
3. She hopes to get into senior management one day.
4. He says he has a degree, but we checked with his university – he dropped out and didn't finish the course.
5. She puts her address, mobile number and email address at the top – that's good.
6. He has a degree in marketing and is a member of the Chartered Institute of Marketing – he passed all the exams.
7. She plays hockey, so she must be a good team player.
8. He mentions all the right words – that's why the computer picked out his CV.
9. She talks about her 15-year career with Google and the number of people she managed there.

53.2 Complete this CV with headings from A and B opposite.

Alexandre Duchamp

(1) ....
1999–2002 Mechanical engineering degree, University of Toronto
2002–2003 Master's in electric car engineering, University of Vancouver
(2) ....
To work in the most advanced areas of electric car design and engineering
(3) ....
Good at working independently
Bilingual in French and English
(4) ....
2003–2009 Production engineer at General Motors, Peoria, Illinois
2009–2017 Development engineer, driverless cars, at Tesla Design Center, Hawthorne, California
(5) ....
14350 Manor Drive, Hawthorne, CA 90250
Email: aduchamp1980@hotmail.com   Tel: +1 424 825 3910

53.3 Complete this cover email by choosing the correct expressions from C opposite.

To: jobs@canadelec.com
From: aduchamp1980@hotmail.com
Subject: Application for position of driverless car engineer

Dear Mr Wright
(1) .... from the (2) ...., my background is in electric car engineering, and (3) .... to your online advertisement for driverless car engineers. I have been working in the US for nearly 15 years and (4) .... back to Canada. (5) .... (6) .... for interview on the date that you mention in the advertisement.
Best wishes
Alexandre Duchamp

Over to you

Write your own CV. If you already have one, look at it again and use the ideas and vocabulary in this unit to update it.

54 Interns, trainees and apprentices

A Interns

'Hi, I'm Phoebe. Ten years ago I was doing an economics degree at university and I wanted a career in **financial services** (see Unit 13). I checked online for **paid internships** and I found one at Hearst Banking Group (HBG) which I did while I was still studying. They said we would:

- receive **training** and information on all the careers available in financial services
- gain actual, **hands-on experience** in a real **work environment**
- develop **professional skills** such as leadership and communication
- work with and **learn from** other people with a wide range of knowledge and experience
- **develop** our **network** of contacts
- **build** our **confidence**

'It was all true: I did an internship while I was still a student, and what's more, I got paid! With my experience as an **intern** and just after I **graduated** from university, I was offered a place on HBG's **graduate leadership programme**. And now, 10 years later, I manage some of HBG's most profitable **financial products** (see Unit 35).'

> **Note:** Organizations also talk about offering **work placements** or **job placements**, instead of 'internships'.

B Experience or exploitation?

However, some interns say that the tasks they are given to do are very **menial** – ordinary and boring, like renaming computer files. Another criticism is that there is such a **range of tasks** that interns don't gain particular knowledge of any of them. They may complain that they are **exploited** – some are on very low pay or completely **unpaid**.

> **Note:** The noun related to **exploit** is **exploitation**.

C Trainees and apprentices

Trainees are employees in **entry-level jobs** – the lowest level jobs in an organization. Some companies offer a number of **traineeships** every year. Some governments pay part of the costs of employing trainees and you can apply if you have little or no work experience.

Apprenticeships combine practical training for a job with **part-time study**. **Apprentices** work with experienced employees, gain **job-specific skills**, and study towards a **vocational qualification** at the same time, perhaps one day a week. Apprentices often train to work in manufacturing, construction – building work – or catering – working in restaurants.

> **Note:** Interns may or may not get permanent jobs in the organization, but trainees and apprentices are usually employed long-term.

Business Vocabulary in Use Intermediate

Exercises

54.1 Complete this conversation about an internship in an advertising agency with appropriate forms of words from A and B.

- Where and when did you do your internship?
- It was in an advertising agency, just after I **(1)** _____ university.
- Were you paid?
- They said that we would get €300 a month, but it turned out to be completely **(2)** _____ .
- What sort of tasks did they ask you to do?
- I wanted to gain actual **(3)** _____ - _____ _____ , but they just asked me to do totally **(4)** _____ things like making coffee. And there was such a **(5)** _____ _____ that we didn't get to learn any of them properly.
- Were you able to develop in any way?
- No, they promised we would develop our **(6)** _____ _____ , like meeting skills, but this never happened. They said that we would feel more sure of ourselves, that we would **(7)** _____ _____ _____ , but at the end I felt less sure of myself! And they said we would **(8)** _____ _____ other people, but we never met anyone from whom to learn.
- What about making new contacts?
- As I say, we didn't meet anyone, except other interns, so there was no chance to **(9)** _____ _____ _____ .
- So, it wasn't a positive experience?
- No, the agency just **(10)** _____ us, basically.

54.2 Which words and expressions in C opposite do these examples refer to?

1. Schemes to help new technicians in a television company to gain the required skills, and the people who are helped in this way. (2 words)
2. People getting coffee for technicians working on a film.
3. Going to classes two evenings a week to learn the maths you need in a particular job.
4. Schemes to help manual workers in a metal products firm gain the required skills for operating machines by learning from other employees, and the people who are helped in this way. (2 words)
5. The studies that someone has followed and the skills they have acquired to be a hairdresser, as proved by a certificate.
6. The knowledge and abilities needed in order to be an airline pilot.

```
Over to you
```
Look on the internet for information about internships in an organization that interests you. What kind of experience would you get? Is there anything you don't like about it? Is it paid or unpaid?

Business Vocabulary in Use Intermediate **117**

55 Meetings 1: types of meeting

A Word combinations with 'meeting'

arrange / set up / fix	organize a meeting
bring forward	make a meeting earlier than originally decided
put back / put off / postpone	make a meeting later than originally planned
call off / cancel	decide not to have a meeting
run / chair	be in charge of a meeting
attend	go to a meeting
miss	not go to a meeting

(All combined with "a meeting")

> **Note:** You can say 'bring forward a meeting' or 'bring a meeting forward'. But you can only say 'bring it forward', not 'bring forward it'. The rule is the same for **put back** and **call off**.

B Types of meeting

- **chat** – informal discussion – with colleagues at the coffee machine
- **brainstorming** among colleagues where as many ideas are produced as possible, but are then evaluated later
- **project meeting / team meeting** of employees involved in a particular activity
- **department meeting / departmental meeting**
- **meeting with suppliers** – for example, to negotiate prices for an order
- **meeting with a customer** – for example, to discuss a contract
- **board meeting** – an official, formal meeting of a company's directors
- **AGM: annual general meeting** (BrE) / **annual meeting** (AmE) – where shareholders discuss the company's annual report
- **EGM: extraordinary general meeting** – a shareholders' meeting to discuss an important issue such as a proposed merger

C How was the meeting?

Some colleagues are discussing a meeting they have just come out of.

Anil: I thought it was very **productive**.

Juliet: Well, I thought it was a **waste of time**. I heard nothing I didn't already know.

Barbara: Well, I agree with Anil. I felt we had some very **useful discussions**. We certainly **covered a lot of ground**. We got through an incredible number of things.

Juliet: As usual John was **rambling** and kept **wandering off the point**. He just uses meetings as a chance to **show off**.

Anil: But to be fair, the chair really **kept things moving** – she encouraged people to **stick to the point** by keeping things brief.

Business Vocabulary in Use Intermediate

Exercises

55.1 Replace the underlined expressions with appropriate forms of the verbs in A opposite. In some cases, more than one verb is possible.

Eurotunnel owns and operates the tunnel under the English Channel. A meeting for shareholders had been **(1)** <u>organized</u> for 12 July. The company is experiencing financial problems and some shareholders wanted **(2)** <u>the meeting to take place before then</u>, but in the end the meeting was **(3)** <u>delayed</u>. The Paris commercial law court agreed that the meeting should be **(4)** <u>moved</u> to 27 July to allow time for financial rescue plans to be finalized. Eurotunnel's chairman **(5)** <u>managed</u> the meeting very efficiently, and the new financial plans were agreed. Only very few shareholders **(6)** <u>did not go to</u> it.

55.2 Look at B opposite. At which type of meeting would you be most likely to hear each of these things?

1. I'm pleased to announce another good year for shareholders of this company.
2. I know this sounds crazy, but how about giving away 100,000 free samples?
3. Things in the sales department are getting out of control. We should all start making a real effort.
4. So, you think you can offer 10,000 a month at a unit cost of £4.90?
5. Have you heard? Suzanne is being fired. Her sales figures aren't good enough, apparently.
6. That's a deal, then. Looking forward to working with you. I'm sure you won't be disappointed.
7. Amazingly, we're ahead of schedule on this job.
8. I recommend to shareholders that you accept BP's offer for our company.
9. As you know, BP wants to buy this company. As chief financial offer, what do you think of their offer, Saleem?

55.3 A management consultant is talking about meetings, using expressions from C opposite. Put what she says into the correct order.

a point and rambling. And then there are those who want to show ☐
b moving. If they do this, it's amazing how much ground you can cover. ☐
c Of course, everyone wants meetings to be productive and achieve results. But from personal experience, we know that a lot of them are a waste of ☐
d off – to show how important and clever they are. The chair should keep things ☐
e the point. We've all seen those annoying people who keep wandering off the ☐
f time, and nothing is achieved. In order for discussion to be useful, people should stick to ☐

> **Over to you**
>
> What sort of meetings do you go to in your school or organization? Are they useful?

Business Vocabulary in Use Intermediate 119

56 Meetings 2: the chair

A The role of the chair: before the meeting

A **chairman**, **chairwoman** or **chair** has to be a **good organizer**. What they do before the meeting is as important as the meeting itself. They should ensure that the **agenda** – the list of things to be discussed – is complete by asking those involved what should be on it and then **circulating** – distributing – the agenda to those involved. They should check the **venue**, making sure the room will be free and without interruptions until the end of the meeting.

> **Note:** Don't say **agenda** when you mean **diary**.

B The role of the chair: running the meeting

The **chairperson** should be a **good timekeeper**. They should start the meeting on time. Don't wait for **latecomers**.

> Let's make a start.

They should appoint a **minute-taker**, someone who makes sure that opinions and **action points** – where participants agree to do something, find something out, etc. – are noted.

> Would you mind taking the minutes, Adam?

The chair should make sure that each participant has the chance to **make their point**.

> I think you wanted to say something about this, Brigitte.

Disagreements should be dealt with **tactfully** – without annoying people – making sure that each side feels their point of view has been noted. Avoid **digressions** where people **get off the point**.

> Let's talk about this calmly.

They should make sure each point on the agenda is **allocated** the time it deserves, perhaps indicating this on the agenda. Even if the current item has not been completely covered or **resolved** – decided – make sure that discussion **moves on to the next point**.

> I think we've covered this item.
>
> We can return to this issue at the next meeting.
>
> Let's move on to the next item.

They should ensure that the meeting **finishes on time**, or early.

> OK. Time's up. Thanks for coming.

C Follow-up

After some meetings, it's necessary for the minutes from the previous meeting to be circulated, especially if there are **action points** that particular people are responsible for.

At the next meeting, the chair should ask for the minutes to be read out and make sure that all agree that it is an **accurate record** of what happened, and see if there are any **matters arising** – any points from the last meeting that need to be discussed that are not on the agenda of the current meeting. And they should check what progress has been made on the action points of the previous meeting.

Business Vocabulary in Use Intermediate

Exercises

56.1 This article relates to points in A and B opposite. Read the article and say if the statements below are true or false.

I DON'T KNOW HOW TO CHAIR A MEETING!

I've been asked to chair a meeting about the Christmas office party, but I'm incredibly nervous as I've never chaired one before. Is there a secret for success?

You may never have chaired a meeting, but as you've probably been to lots, you'll have seen it done well and badly. Think about the things that please and annoy you, and build on them. Well-run meetings stick to the point, get things decided and finish on time. Make sure everyone has the agenda well in advance, and that you know enough about the participants and issues to be discussed. Arrange for the room to be cool rather than warm; people will be less likely to go to sleep.

See yourself as a referee whose job it is to ensure fair play through careful watching and listening. It's up to you to encourage the timid, control the talkative, involve the bored, calm down the argumentative and be kind to the minute-taker you have appointed. Getting that individual on your side is essential if you want the record to reflect your desired outcomes. It's normal to suggest what should be left out from the minutes and how any difficult bits should be phrased. Keep things moving by not letting discussions wander off the subject or get over-long. Get decisions made and recorded, even if it's only to postpone matters until the next meeting. If someone is being difficult, defuse things by offering to continue the discussion personally at a more appropriate time.

If the meeting is likely to be more than a couple of hours long, try to include a break at the mid-point; it acts as a marker and stops people getting restless.

Aim to leave everyone feeling they have had a chance to say what they wanted to say, and gain lasting and well-deserved popularity by finishing early.

In planning a successful meeting, you should:

1 think about meetings you have been to in the past.
2 hand out the agenda at the meeting.
3 know something about the participants and the things they will be talking about.
4 treat every participant in the same way.
5 be nice to the person making a record of the meeting.
6 allow people to talk for as long they want.
7 never talk to participants about particular issues after the meeting is over.

56.2 Complete the statements below (1–7) containing expressions from A, B and C opposite with appropriate forms of the verbs that come in front of them.

1 Someone who records what is said _____ the minutes.
2 The chair _____ the person in 1 above as the minute-taker.
3 If you _____ the agenda, you send it out before the meeting.
4 The chair should _____ the right amount of time for each point.
5 When one point has been covered, the meeting should ____ __ to the next point.
6 If you want to save time, _____ digressions.
7 Everyone should _____ that the minutes are an accurate record of what happened at the last meeting.

Over to you

- Are you good at – or would you be good at – chairing meetings? Why? / Why not?
- What do you find annoying in meetings?

57 Meetings 3: points of view

A Opening the meeting

Creative Advertising is a US-owned advertising agency with offices in Soho in London. Its chief executive, Carla Eagleton, is opening a meeting with four of the people who work for the company.

OK, let's get started.

As you know, **I've called this meeting to** discuss the situation in the design department. Until now, the feeling has been that designers are creative types and need the freedom to work as they wish. But things are getting out of control.

You can also say:
- Let's begin, shall we?
- Shall we make a start?
- Let's make a start.
- It's time to get started.
- Let's get down to business.

You can also say:
- I've arranged this meeting to …
- I've organized this meeting to …
- The purpose of this meeting is to …
- The main objective of this meeting is to …

B Asking for and expressing opinions

Would you like to open the discussion, Piers?

I believe the design department needs a certain amount of freedom, but there are limits. They come in at 10.30 when all other employees have already been at work for two hours. This leads to tensions between design people and other employees.

You can also say:
- Would you like to kick off?
- Would you like to get the ball rolling?

What about you, Maria?
- How about you, Maria?
- What do you think, Maria?

In my opinion, they're going much too far. I can't bear to think of the costs involved.
- It looks/seems to me as if …
- It's clear to me that …

You can also say:
- Personally, I think …
- My standpoint is that …

As I see it, I can't run the design department as if it was the accounts department.
- The way I see it …

Of course, we are creative, and need to be given the freedom to work how we like.
- Obviously, …

> **Note**
> The expression **kick off** comes from football. **Get the ball rolling** does not come from any particular sport.
> You use **Of course** and **Obviously** to introduce an idea, but also to show that you think other people will know it or agree with it already. Be careful how you use these expressions, as they can sound rude.

Business Vocabulary in Use Intermediate

Exercises

57.1 Complete the expressions from A and B opposite grouped together below.

1. How .... about you?

2. I've .... this meeting to …

3. Let's .... , ... ?

4. The (main) .... of this meeting is to …

5. It .... to me as if …

57.2 Match the two parts of the expressions from the continuation of the discussion in B opposite.

1. The way
2. Personally,
3. It looks to me
4. It's clear to
5. In my

a I think that the prizes we win help us to attract and keep the best designers.
b as if the design people think of themselves as living on another planet.
c I see it, you should be looking at what we produce, not at the time of day we produce it.
d opinion, we have to think of the needs of each department.
e me that they set a very bad example to the other departments.

Over to you

- How free are people to express their feelings in your organization?
- Are people at all levels encouraged to say what they think?
- Are new employees asked for their opinions?

58 Meetings 4: agreement and disagreement

A Agreeing

Carla's meeting (see previous unit) continues.

The phrases in bold can be used when agreeing with people.

You may be right there. The budget figures are not looking good. But on the other hand we mustn't forget the other benefits for the company.

You're perfectly right. We are the people who are the driving force behind the company.

You can also say:

a **I couldn't agree more.** We got our latest recruits after we won the Advertising Industry Award for best advertisement last year.
b **Precisely.** Creativity comes to some of our people in the middle of the night.
c **Exactly.** It's the creative people who bring in all the money.
d **Absolutely.** It's the output that counts.

You can also say:

e **That's true**, I suppose. But we must think of the company as a whole.
f **I suppose so.** But other employees mustn't be forgotten.

B Disagreeing

That's not really how I see it. Designers and accounts people are all company employees.

I think you're wrong. The design department's costs are justified because of our high-quality work. The costs of the other departments are not justified.

You can also say:

g **I don't really agree.** The prizes that the designers get are important, but people would come to work for us anyway.
h **I can't go along with you there.** I think we need to see people at their desks actually working.
i **I think you're mistaken.** If the designers get to work late, they should be disciplined.
j **I'm afraid I can't agree with you there.** We all depend on each other for the company to make money.
k **I'm sorry, but that's out of the question.** All employees should keep to normal working hours.

You can also say:

l **Of course not.** The latest figures I've seen show that the project is within budget.
m **That's absurd.** You can't expect us to leave at 10 in the evening and be back at 8 in the morning.
n **That's ridiculous.** Each department has very specific needs.

 Note: Be careful with **That's absurd**, **That's ridiculous** and **Of course not**. These expressions are very strong and can be offensive.

Business Vocabulary in Use Intermediate

Exercises

58.1 Put the expressions in A and B opposite into the following groups:

1. mild agreement
2. mild disagreement
3. strong agreement
4. strong disagreement

58.2 The expressions below follow on immediately from those in A opposite. Match the continuations (1–6) with the expressions (a–f).

1. We don't care about the hours that each person in our department works.
2. Besides that, the prizes help us to attract and keep the best designers.
3. Not only do we have these very high costs, but it also sets a very bad example to the other departments and they start going over budget too.
4. We're all in this together.
5. Without us, there would be no profits.
6. You should be looking at what we produce, not at the time of day we produce it.

58.3 Two advertising managers, Georgina and Henry, are exchanging opinions. Use expressions from B opposite (g–n) containing the word in brackets to complete what Henry says. Then match what Georgina says with Henry's replies.

Georgina / Henry

1. The agency should move its offices out of Soho to the suburbs somewhere.
   — .... (absurd). We would lose employees to our competitors if we cut salaries.

2. Times are difficult and everyone should take a 10 per cent pay cut.
   — .... (along). The agency is at its most creative now.

3. The real problem is the number of unproductive people in the agency.
   — .... (ridiculous). We need to stay in the creative heart of London.

4. When they travel on business, everyone should stay at the same low-cost hotels in order to cut costs.
   — .... (afraid). People need to get away from their offices sometimes.

5. One reason for our high costs is employees who go out for coffee in the local bars twice a day.
   — .... (really). Other advertising agencies are doing well, despite the economy.

6. If the agency's less profitable than it was, it's because economic conditions are terrible.
   — .... (course). Everyone in the agency works hard.
   — .... (course). Everyone in the agency works hard.

7. If we could get back to the creativity we had when the agency was founded, all our problems would be solved.
   — .... (question). Some of the accommodation is really bad.

> **Over to you**
>
> - Is it acceptable for people to disagree openly with each other in your company/country?
> - Do you prefer to avoid arguments?

59 Meetings 5: discussion techniques

A Interrupting, referring back, checking understanding, avoiding confrontation

Here are some other expressions used in meetings for different purposes.

To interrupt someone politely:
- If I can just stop you for a moment.
- Can I (just) come in here?
- Sorry to interrupt you, but …

To refer back to what was said earlier:
- To go back to what you were saying earlier …
- As we were saying earlier …
- To go back to what I was just saying …

To check that you understand what someone has said:
- Are you saying that … ?
- Are you suggesting that … ?
- If I understand (you) correctly, …
- If I follow you, …

To avoid direct **confrontation** – disagreement:
- I take your point …
- I understand what you're saying …
- I see/know what you mean, but …
- I hear where you're coming from on this, but …

B Agreement, consensus or compromise?

An **agreement** is when people **agree about** or **on** something.

A **compromise** is an agreement where each side accepts less than it wanted – they each have to **compromise**.

A **consensus** is a situation where most people agree about something.

If people **have a disagreement about** something, they **disagree about** it.

> **Note**
> All the nouns above can be countable and uncountable.
> You can **come to**, **reach** or **find agreement** or **an agreement** (with someone). The same verbs can be used with **compromise** and **consensus**.
> If you disagree (with someone), you have a **disagreement** (with them).

C Concluding

- We've covered a lot of ground.
- It's been a very interesting discussion.
- We're running out of time.
- To go over what's been said …
- To sum up …
- We're going to have to agree to disagree.
- Unless anyone has anything else to add …
- We're going to have to stop there.
- I think that's it.
- Thank you all for coming.

Exercises

59.1 Use complete expressions from A opposite to complete the dialogue, based on the prompts in brackets. The first one has been done for you.

A: We really will have to increase productivity.
B: (coming), but there are limits to how much we can ask of each individual employee. After all, if you look back at the records for …
I hear where you're coming from on this, but …
A: (stop), you have to admit things were different then. That was in the late 1990s.
B: (understand), but that's not so long ago. The pressures were the same.
C: (go back), there are limits as to what we can ask from the creatives. They …
A: (interrupt), but I hate that word 'creative'. A lot of them have created nothing except chaos since they arrived in the company.
C: (suggest) that the creative department has people who shouldn't be there?

59.2 Use the information in B opposite to complete the table below.

Countable noun	Uncountable noun also?	Verb	Expression
agreement			.... / .... / .... (............) agreement
disagreement			.... disagreement
compromise			.... / .... / .... (............) compromise
consensus			.... / .... / .... (............) consensus

59.3 Look at C opposite and put the extracts from this newspaper report into the correct order.

a
out of time and we're going to have to stop there. I'll let you know the committee's decision about the solution to this problem by the end of the month.

b
There were strong differences of opinion at last night's meeting to discuss banning cars from the centre of Cambridge. The chair, Ms Yolanda Johns of the town council's transport committee, organized the meeting well. At the end of the meeting she said, 'We've covered

c
They said it would improve the quality of life. It was not possible to come to

d
a lot of ground and I've listened to both sides of the argument. To sum up the arguments, there were those who thought that banning cars would damage shops and businesses in the town.' Others disagreed.

e
a compromise or consensus. There was total disagreement. After four hours of heated discussion, Ms Johns said, 'It's been a very interesting discussion but we're running

> **Over to you**
>
> In your organization, are decisions based on compromise and consensus – or are they imposed from above? Give an example.

60 Presentations 1: key ideas

A Types of presentation

Here are some examples of business presentations.

a **press conference** – the chief executives of two companies tell journalists why their companies have merged
b **demonstration** – the head of research and development gives a presentation to non-technical colleagues about a new machine that the research and development department has just completed
c **product launch** – a car company announces a new model
d **workshop** – company employees do practical exercises on time management
e **seminar** – a financial adviser gives advice to people about investments

B What makes a good presentation?

A presentation, and the **presenter**, the person giving it, are usually judged by:

1 The way the presentation is **organized**:
- The **ideas** and the **visual aids** (pictures, charts and data designed to help people understand or remember particular information) are **clearly structured** – easy to follow
- how the information is mixed with **interesting examples and stories** – people want to hear how the presenter relates personally to the subject

2 The way the presentation is **delivered**:
- **rapport** with the audience – members feel that the presenter understands them
- **eye contact** – the way the presenter looks at the audience
- **loud enough** voice
- **variety** in your **tone of voice** – it's important not to speak in a monotone and to vary the **speed** that you speak at

3 The way the presenter **feels** about the topic, the audience and himself/herself:
- **confident** and **relaxed look**
- **enthusiastic** about the topic
- **positive attitude**
- **interested in** the audience and getting them **involved** – participating in their minds

C Presentation tools and visual aids

Business Vocabulary in Use Intermediate

Exercises

60.1 Match the presentation types in A opposite with things that people say in them below:

1. Each group has a series of problems faced by a company. I want you to suggest solutions.
2. Now is the right time to get out of company shares and invest in property.
3. The combined resources of our two organizations will allow us to achieve great things.
4. The X300 has the most advanced features of any car in its class.
5. As you can see, this prototype is far in advance of anything we have done before.

60.2 Look at B and C opposite. Then read the article and answer the questions.

Newsonline

Making Sure You Get The Message Across

Your mouth is dry, your voice trembles, your hands shake and you can hear your heart thudding – yes, you are making a presentation. No matter what job we do, most of us will sooner or later have to make one, whether it is delivering a goodbye speech, explaining a project to bosses, or trying to get new business.

Khalid Aziz, of the Aziz Corporation, which teaches senior executives to communicate, says: 'About 60 per cent of the effectiveness of a spoken presentation is nothing to do with the words. It's to do with style, confident body language and the right speed of delivery.' Management consultant Terry Gillen says: 'Your presentation should have a main theme, a single powerful message. It should have a clear structure, with each point leading to the next. Human brains automatically try to organise information received, so if your presentation does not have a structure, your audience will create its own. Attention will wander and listeners may get the wrong idea. And if you structure your presentation, it will be easy for you to remember.' But Mr Gillen warns: 'Reading from a document, whether it's the whole speech or detailed notes, sounds formal and stiff, and switches the audience off.'

Presenters should encourage passive and active audience participation to personalise the message and keep people listening. Mr Gillen says: 'Use phrases such as "What would you think if ..." Encourage them to ask questions or, if you are demonstrating something, get them to join in. They'll do this only if you look friendly and smile. Make eye contact and maybe enter the audience's territory rather than staying stuck behind your desk.' He adds: 'The audience want to enjoy the presentation and are more likely to do so if the presenter also appears to be enjoying it. Nerves and anxiety often show. Audiences notice uncomfortable body language and hesitant speech.' Mr Aziz says: 'Minimise panic by steering clear of coffee for at least two hours before. Practise and rehearse, and visit the venue to remove the fear of the unknown. Beware of complex visual aids which confuse and distract attention from the message, and add extra information with your voice.'

NatWest corporate manager Deborah Buckle, 32, learned to 'Present with Passion' after attending one of Khalid Aziz's courses. Deborah, of Surrey, says: 'Knowing your stuff is not enough. You have to enthuse your audience. I also learned that, unless you're careful, the message received is not always the one given.'

1. Which points in B opposite does Khalid Aziz refer to?
2. Which point in B does Terry Gillen refer to?
3. Is reading from a prepared text a good idea? Why? / Why not?
4. For Terry Gillen, what are four ways of getting audience involvement?
5. For Khalid Aziz, what are two ways of avoiding panic, and one way of using visuals well?
6. What is the most important thing about presentations for Deborah Buckle?
7. She says that 'the message received is not always the one given'. Where is this idea referred to previously in the article?

Over to you

- Do you ever give presentations? What type are they? Who are the audiences?
- In your experience, what makes a good presentation?

Business Vocabulary in Use Intermediate

61 Presentations 2: key steps

A Key steps: introduction

Anne-Marie Duval works for a firm of management consultants. She is responsible for recruiting consultants for the firm. She has been invited as a guest speaker to an international conference in Cannes to talk about the subject of recruitment.

a **My name's** Anne-Marie Duval and I work for Gem Consultants.
b **It's very nice to see so many of you here** in Cannes on such a sunny day!
c **I'm going to talk about** 'Consultancy Skills for the 21st Century'.
d **There are three main areas** I want to look at today.
e **If you have any questions,** I'll be very happy to answer them at the end of the session.

B Key steps: main part

OK. To begin with, let's look at the first type of skills that consultants need: technical skills.
Of course, **related to** technical skills, you need good general knowledge of management subjects.

That's all I have time for on technical skills.
Let's move on to the second area: interpersonal skills.
As you can see on this slide, there are two **key areas in relation to** interpersonal skills.
And **as this transparency shows**, interpersonal skills are complex.

I think **that covers everything on** interpersonal skills.
Time is moving on, so **let's turn to** the third area: people management issues.
This is **the third and most important area** that I want to talk about today.

OK, **that's all I have to say on/about** the key area of people-management issues.

C Key steps: closing

Let me just **sum up. Firstly**, we looked at technical skills, **secondly**, interpersonal skills and **last but not least**, people management issues.
In fact, the secret for success in the future is going to be, **in my view**, these people-management issues. **That brings me to the end** of my presentation. **Are there any questions?**

Business Vocabulary in Use Intermediate

Exercises

61.1 Match the expressions (a–e) in A opposite with what the speaker is doing (1–5).

1 interacts with audience by showing she knows where she is and saying what she thinks of the place
2 identifies herself
3 tells the audience when she will answer questions
4 announces the title of her talk
5 says how it will be structured

61.2 Look at B opposite and correct the mistakes below, from another presentation. There is one mistake in each item.

1 To begin with, let we look at the most basic product in our range.
2 Of course, you will certainly have lots of questions in relation with the product specifications of our basic model.
3 That's all I'm having time for on product specifications.
4 Let's to move on to our mid-range model.
5 As this transparency is showing, there are two key features I want to talk about in relation to our mid-range model.
6 I think that cover everything on our mid-range model.
7 Our top-of-the-range product is the third and more important model I want to talk about.

61.3 Look at C opposite. Is the presenter using the **bold** expressions in the correct place? Why? / Why not?

1 **Are there any questions?** There are three main areas I want to talk about: one – old products, two – new products and three – ideas that are currently under development.
2 Let me just **sum up** as I've covered the three things I wanted to talk about and we're getting near the end of our time.
3 Firstly, we looked at technical skills, secondly, interpersonal skills and **last but not least**, people management issues.
4 **That brings me to the end of my presentation** and fourthly there are the financial aspects and I'm going to spend 20 minutes on them now.
5 In fact, the secret for success in the future is going to be, **in my view**, these people management issues. Of course, other experts in the field have different opinions on this.

Over to you

Think of your last presentation.
- What was it about?
- What went well?
- Did it have a good introduction, a good main part and a good closing?
- What would you change next time?

62 Presentations 3: audience interaction

A Closing and dealing with questions

Anne-Marie is bringing her presentation (see Unit 61) to a close and invites questions from the audience.

> **That brings me to the end** of my presentation. **Are there any questions?**

These are her answers to some of the questions.

a **That's a fair point.** I know that some consultants don't have a very good image. But I think that the results from our organization, Gem Consultants, speak for themselves. I can give you examples of enormously reduced costs or increased profits at companies that have used our services …

b **That's confidential.** I'm afraid I can't tell you.

c **That's not really my field.** But I can put you in touch with someone in my organization who is working on internet applications.

d **T**he questioner would like to know what sort of background the people we recruit usually have. Is that right? Well, we recruit some of our consultants straight out of business school, but mainly …

e **Well, I think that goes beyond the scope of today's presentation.** Today I wanted to concentrate on consultants' skills, not go into particular case studies in consultancy. Well, we've run out of time and I think that's a good place to stop.

f **I'm afraid we've run out of time.** But if you'd like to come and discuss that with me now, I'll try and give you an answer. **I think that's a good place to stop. Thank you for listening.**

B Intercultural aspects

a Avoid **mannerisms** – irritating ways of moving and speaking – such as overusing 'Er …'.
b Be careful with **humour**. For example, don't make jokes about people in the audience.
c **Dress** formally unless you know for sure that the occasion is informal.
d Maintain **eye contact** by looking round the room at each person in the audience for about a second, before moving on to the next person. Don't concentrate on just one or two people.
e **Face the audience** at all times: don't speak to the equipment or the screen.
f **Remain standing**: don't sit. Stay more or less in one place and don't move around too much.
g **Smiling** is fine at appropriate moments, but not too much: it can seem **insincere** – as if you don't mean it.
h Use **gesture** – hand movements – to emphasize key points. Point with your whole hand, rather than just one finger.
i **Respect the audience.** Don't make exaggerated claims – don't say things are better than they really are.

Exercises

62.1 Match these questions (1–6) from the audience with the answers (a–f) that Anne-Marie gives in A opposite.

1. Sorry, but I didn't hear the end of the question – could you repeat what the questioner said?
2. In what ways do you think the internet is going to change the way management consultants work in the future?
3. Some companies refuse to use management consultants. What do you say to people who say that consultants are a waste of time and money?
4. What's the average salary for your consultants?
5. I don't know if you have time to answer this, but can you tell me how I can apply to work for Gem?
6. You say that Gem have enormously increased profits at some companies. Can you give one or two examples of this?

62.2 Look at this presentation that a sales person gave to potential customers. Match his mistakes with the points in B opposite.

Hi, I'm … er … Andy and … er … I'm … er … here to … er … talk about …

What are the main benefits of your products?

How long have you got? Our products are so good I could go on about them all night.

Most people who go to the cinema are between 16 and 30. That's amazing.

There was an Englishman, an Irishman and a Scotsman …

Over to you

- How is body language used in presentations in your country? Which gestures are acceptable and which are not?
- Which of the things mentioned in B opposite do you find the most annoying? Why?

Business Vocabulary in Use Intermediate

63 Negotiations 1: situations and negotiators

A Types of negotiation

If people **negotiate (with each other)**, they talk in order to reach an agreement which is to their **mutual advantage** – good for them both. Examples of these situations in business are:

a **customer–supplier negotiations**
b **wage negotiations**
c **merger or takeover negotiations** (see Unit 34)
d **trade negotiations**
e Negotiations also take place to **settle disputes** – decide arguments.
f **contract disputes**
g **labour disputes**
h **trade disputes**

B Word combinations with 'negotiations'

Intense / Intensive	negotiations	are very difficult and tiring, with a lot being discussed.
Delicate / Tense		are very difficult and could easily fail.
Eleventh-hour / Last-minute		take place very late in relation to the time that an agreement is necessary.
Protracted		take a very long time.

 Note: **Intense** is about twice as frequent as **intensive** in this context.

Someone who takes part in negotiations is a **negotiator**. A **tough negotiator** is someone who is good at getting what they want, but could be difficult to deal with.

C Bargaining

To **bargain** is to discuss and agree the price of something. Someone who does this is a **bargainer**.

Bargaining is used to talk about pay negotiations, especially in phrases like **collective bargaining, pay bargaining, wage bargaining.**

All these refer to discussions between groups of employees and their employers about pay and conditions.

Bargaining is also often used in these combinations.

bargaining	tactic	a particular technique used by a negotiator
	ploy	a technique used by a negotiator that might be considered as unfair
	chip / tool	an issue that a negotiator uses in order to gain an advantage
	point	a particular issue that a negotiator discusses
	power	the degree to which one side is strong enough to obtain what it wants
	process	the way that negotiations develop

Exercises

63.1 Match these headlines (1–7) with the situations (a–g) in A opposite.

1. CAR WORKERS IN TWO-YEAR PAY DEAL TALKS WITH FORD
2. FRANCE BANS US FILMS FOLLOWING TALKS BREAKDOWN
3. WORLD TRADE ORGANIZATION MEMBERS IN WIDE-RANGING DISCUSSIONS
4. PHARMACEUTICALS GIANTS SAY THAT COMBINING WOULD BE 'TO THEIR MUTUAL ADVANTAGE'
5. AIRLINES ATTACK AIRBUS FOR LATE AIRCRAFT DELIVERIES
6. EMPLOYERS REFUSE TO NEGOTIATE WITH STRIKING MINERS
7. EDUCATION MINISTRY AND HP IN 'COMPUTER ON EVERY DESK' TALKS

63.2 Match the two parts of these extracts containing expressions from B opposite.

1. After 48 hours of intensive
2. After tense
3. The agreement on limiting television violence represents the climax of several months of intense
4. Then violence broke out and it took six months of delicate
5. The deal was struck only after eleventh-hour

a. negotiations between the hijackers and air traffic control in Cyprus, the plane was allowed to land at Larnaca airport.
b. negotiations between the US, the European Union and Japan.
c. negotiations in which he slept for only one hour, Mr Prescott said, 'It has been both tough and incredibly complicated.'
d. negotiations to put the process back on track.
e. negotiations between television executives and the National Parent-Teacher Association.

63.3 Complete what an employee representative says with expressions from C opposite.

1. Last night, we were talking with employers until 3 am, but it wasn't really necessary – they were trying to tire us out. It was just a _____ _____.
2. When unemployment is low, we can be more demanding. We have more _____.
3. When neither side is aggressive, things go much better. It improves the whole _____.
4. The most difficult area is negotiating what employees are going to be earning next year, what's called _____ (3 expressions).
5. It's good when you have a piece of information that the other side don't have. It can turn out to be a useful _____ (2 expressions).
6. I usually get what I want. I'm a pretty good _____.

> **Over to you**
>
> • Do you have to negotiate? Do you like it? Why? / Why not?
> • What qualities make a good negotiator?

64 Negotiations 2: preparing

A Preparing to negotiate

When you're going to negotiate, it's important not to rush into things.
a Get as much information as possible about the situation. If you are dealing with people from another culture, find out about its **negotiating styles**[1] and **etiquette**[2], and so on. The more you can find out, the better!
b Work out what your **needs and objectives**[3] are. This gives you your initial **bargaining position**[4].
c Try to estimate the needs and objectives of the other side.
d Prepare a **fallback position**[5].
e Perhaps you are in a position to influence the choice of **venue**[6]. If so, decide whether you prefer:
   – to be **on your own ground**[7]
   – to go and see the other side **on their ground**[8]
   – to meet on **neutral ground**[9], for example in a hotel.
f If you are negotiating as part of a **negotiating team**[10], consult the other members of the team about the points above. Allocate **roles and responsibilities**[11].

[1] the way they negotiate
[2] what they consider to be acceptable and unacceptable behaviour
[3] the things that you want to achieve
[4] conditions that you will accept
[5] conditions that you will accept if the aims you have at the beginning are not met
[6] the place where you are going to meet
[7] in your own offices
[8] in their offices
[9] neither your office nor their office
[10] team that is negotiating
[11] who is going to do what

B Opening the negotiation

Linhas Transatlanticas (LT) is negotiating to buy a number of D740 planes from EPA. Frederica Ramos, LT's chief executive, is talking to Tom Lang, EPA's chief salesman. Here are some of the things she says:

a Mr Lang, **good to see you again**. **How are you? Let me introduce** my colleagues: Sandra Lopes, our head of finance, and this is Fernando dos Santos, head of operations here at LT.
b **Would you like some** coffee or tea, or would you prefer juice? How was the flight?
c **Shall we** go to the conference room and make a start?
d You told me you're flying back on Friday evening, so that gives us three days. I think two days should be enough to cover all the points. On the third day, Friday, **if** we have an agreement, **I'll** ask our lawyers to check it.
e **As you all probably know**, Mr Lang and I met at the Aerospace Trade Fair in Frankfurt last year and we had a very interesting discussion about the possibility of buying a number of D740s from EPA.
f **Well, we've** looked at the potential requirements for the new plane and it looks as if we may need 100 new planes over the next five years.

C Negotiating styles

When you're negotiating with people from other cultures, it's important to think about what they consider as 'normal' behaviour. Think about these areas:

a **body language** – the way you hold your body, the gestures you make, etc.
b **conversational rules** – the acceptability of silence, interrupting others, etc.
c **hierarchy** – awareness of and respect for the relative importance of people on both sides
d **physical contact** – the degree to which it's acceptable to touch someone's shoulder, for example, to make a point
e **relationship building** – how important it is for participants to get to 'know' the other side
f **attitude to time** – do you get down to business immediately, or do you spend some time on 'small talk'?

Exercises

64.1 Tom Lang is EPA's chief salesman. He is hoping to sell a number of 740s to Linhas Transatlanticas (LT) over the next few years. He and his colleagues are meeting LT executives soon, and he is preparing for the negotiations. Match each point in the preparation notes he makes (1–6) with one of the points (a–f) in A opposite.

1 Organize preparatory meeting with our head of manufacturing and head of financing to discuss strategy.
2 Agree to go to LT's offices in Rio de Janeiro.
3 Principal objective: delivery of first 20 planes in 2 years, not earlier; other objectives: get full price on each of €270 million.
4 Rumours that airlines are having problems borrowing money from banks for plane purchases – find out more about this.
5 Will accept price of €260 million per aircraft if order is for 30 or more.
6 Find out more about Brazilian business etiquette!

64.2 Match these points (1–6) with what Frederica Ramos says (a–f) in B opposite.

1 Go to the meeting room and suggest that you get down to business.
2 Have a clear agenda and a timetable.
3 Offer coffee and small talk. Try to create a relaxed atmosphere.
4 Give the background to the negotiations. Just talking about the situation is a good way of reminding people of key facts and issues.
5 Start the actual negotiations, perhaps by finding out more about the priorities of the other side – the things they think are most important – or talking about your own requirements.
6 Greet representatives of the other company, introducing your colleagues. Everybody should be clear about who everyone is.

64.3 Alonso, a representative of Alpha Ltd, is in another country in order to try to get a multimillion-dollar order from Beta Inc, represented by Brian (the most senior), and Belinda and Birgit (who work under Brian). Match each problem with one of the headings in C opposite.

1 Alonso wanted to start the negotiations immediately, but Brian suggested a sightseeing tour of the city where Beta is based, and the next day, a game of golf.
2 At the start of the meeting, Brian asked Alonso about his flight and the hotel.
3 When Alonso made an important point, Brian was silent for two minutes before replying. This made Alonso very nervous.
4 When he was talking, Alonso looked directly at Brian, Belinda and Birgit in turn, giving them equal attention. Brian started to look annoyed.
5 During a coffee break, Alonso put his arm around Brian's shoulders in order to be 'friendly'.
6 When Belinda or Birgit were talking, Brian frequently tapped his fingers on the table.

> **Over to you**
>
> - What are the normal 'rules' in your country for a buyer–customer negotiation?
> - Give one or two tips to a business person visiting your country in order to negotiate.

Business Vocabulary in Use Intermediate

65 Negotiations 3: win-win

A Probing

The idea with **win-win** is that in negotiations there shouldn't be winners and losers. The negotiators try to reach a **win-win solution** – an agreement of equal benefit to them both.

One way of starting out is **probing** – asking the right questions and listening carefully to the answers – to find out more about the objectives of the other side, in order to build on the information you collected before the negotiation.

a **What is the situation on** production at your plant at the moment?

b **What sort of** quantities **are you looking for?**

c **What are we looking at in the way of** a discount?

d **What did you have in mind regarding** specifications?

e **What were you thinking of in terms of** delivery dates?

f **How important to you** is the currency for payment?

B Positive positions

Through a series of **proposals** or **offers** and **counter-proposals** or **counter-offers** from the other side, the two sides work towards an agreement that will benefit them both.

1 **If** you offer more attractive financing, **we will be able to** increase our order.
2 **As long as** the planes are delivered on time, **we could consider** ordering more in the future.
3 **On condition that** you deliver 20 planes by May, **we will start** negotiating a second order then.
4 **Supposing that** you provide good technical support, **we may be prepared** to pay a higher price.
5 **Provided** you understand our immediate needs, **we might agree** to later delivery of some of the planes.

> **Note:** Notice that you use the **-ing** form after **consider**. You can also use the **-ing** form (as well as the infinitive) after **start**.
> You can say **provided (that)** and **providing (that)**: **that** is optional with both.

C Negative positions

These can be expressed with 'if' or 'unless'.

1 **If you don't / Unless you** reduce the price, we will go elsewhere.
2 **If you fail to / Unless you** deliver on time, we will go to a commercial court for compensation.
3 **If you can't / Unless you** sort out the technical problems, we will cancel our order.
4 **If you refuse to / Unless you** take account of the issues we've mentioned, we won't continue these negotiations.

D Concessions and trade-offs

When you offer to change your position to one that is less favourable to yourself, you **concede** something or **make a concession**. A series of concessions in exchange for concessions from the other side is a series of **trade-offs**.

Even in a friendly negotiation, there may be **horse-trading**, with each side making a series of concessions. (This expression is often used to show disapproval.)

Exercises

65.1 Match the replies (1–6) with the probing questions (a–f) in A opposite.

1. In the long term, perhaps 100 units per year over five years.
2. We can offer 10 per cent if the quantities are right.
3. We'd like to see a 10 per cent improvement in performance
4. We'd prefer US dollars.
5. We'll need the first 30 planes in 18 months.
6. We're operating at full capacity.

65.2 The EPA–LT negotiations in 64.1 and 64.2 have reached a stage where each side is making proposals and counter-proposals. Use expressions and structures from the item with the same number in B opposite to complete the phrases below, using the correct form of the words in brackets. The first one has been done for you.

1. offer more flexible payment conditions / be able / (pay) / higher price
   If you offer more flexible payment conditions, we will be able to pay a higher price.
2. guarantee increased fuel economy / could consider / (pay) €25.5 million per unit
3. you sign the agreement today / will / start / (deliver) the planes / July (2 expressions)
4. send us your personnel for training / may / prepared (add) special features / to the planes that you order
5. accept our conditions / might agree / (work) / you / future (2 expressions)

65.3 Change these expressions from C opposite and others so that they begin with 'Unless'. The first one has been done for you.

1. If you don't reduce the price, we will contact Boeing to see what they have to offer.
   Unless you reduce the price, we will contact Boeing to see what they have to offer.
2. If you fail to consider our particular requirements, we will end these discussions.
3. If you can't deal with our order as a priority, we will cancel it.
4. If you are unable to offer more environmentally friendly versions, we will go to see your competitor.
5. If you don't stop using unfair techniques, we will break off negotiations.

65.4 Use appropriate forms of expressions from D opposite to complete these extracts. Use each expression once only.

1. Management has made _____ in return for the withdrawal of the shareholders' proposal to fire the entire board of directors.
2. Diplomats and oil executives believe a compromise could be reached through intensive horse _____ .
3. The contract negotiating strategy will be based on the _____ between time, cost and quality, and attitude to risk.
4. Parkside had been passing on price increases to customers, but in May was forced to _____ a 10 per cent cut to its largest customer.

> **Over to you**
> - Is every negotiation potentially a win-win one?
> - Have you ever needed to make concessions? When, and how?

Business Vocabulary in Use Intermediate

66 Negotiations 4: reaching agreement

A Deadlock and mediators

BASEBALL STRIKE

Every year in the US there are negotiations between the baseball players' union and the baseball team owners about pay and conditions for the coming season. One year, after months of negotiations, there was **deadlock**[1] and the negotiations **broke down**[2]. Some commentators said there was **stalemate**[3]; others, an **impasse**[4]. There were **irreconcilable differences**[5] between the two sides and it was impossible to reach an agreement. The baseball players went on strike. The two sides agreed to bring in a **mediator**[6] and the process of **mediation**[7] began. The person they chose was a retired politician. His role was not to **impose**[8] an agreement. He recommended a **cooling-off period**[9]. The players ended their strike, for the time being at least. Another month passed, and still there was no progress. The two sides said they would accept an agreement imposed by an **arbitrator**[10]. A judge, who also loved baseball, was chosen. She looked at the claims of each side and imposed a **settlement**[11] or a **resolution**[11] to the dispute, fixing the salaries and the working conditions of the players for the coming season. The public was glad that **arbitration**[12] had settled the dispute. Baseball matches continued and life returned to normal.

[1] the situation was completely stuck
[2] failed because there was a problem
[3] a situation in which neither group of people can win
[4] a situation where no progress could be made
[5] it was impossible to find agreement between the two sides
[6] someone from outside to help restart the negotiations and bring the two sides closer together
[7] helping the two sides to agree
[8] force
[9] a period where each side would take no action against the other for a certain period of time
[10] a person who has been chosen to make a decision
[11] an arrangement to end the disagreement
[12] the process of solving a disagreement between two groups of people

B Agreements and contracts

An agreement of any kind is a **deal**. When you reach an agreement, you can talk about **closing a deal** or **clinching a deal**.

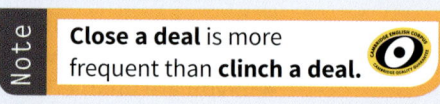

Note: **Close a deal** is more frequent than **clinch a deal**.

A **bargain** is also an agreement reached through negotiation. People who get what they want in a negotiation and make few concessions are said to **drive a hard bargain**.

An agreement may be in the form of a **contract**.

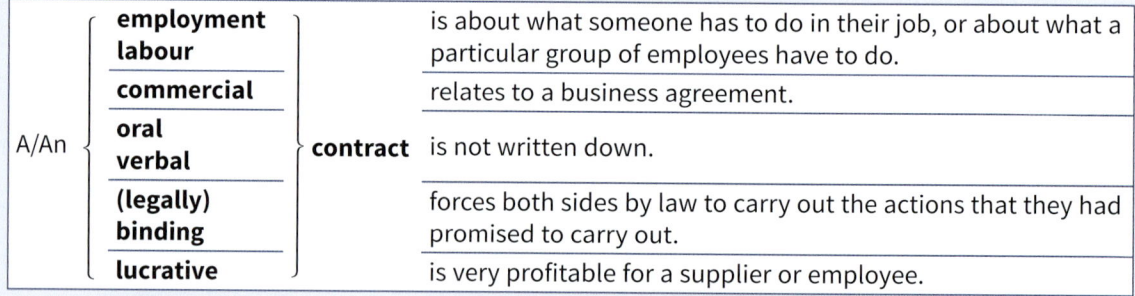

A/An		contract	
	employment / labour		is about what someone has to do in their job, or about what a particular group of employees have to do.
	commercial		relates to a business agreement.
	oral / verbal		is not written down.
	(legally) binding		forces both sides by law to carry out the actions that they had promised to carry out.
	lucrative		is very profitable for a supplier or employee.

C Checking the deal

It's important to check the points of an agreement to avoid misunderstandings. You could say:

- **Let me just go/run over** – repeat and summarize – the main points.
- **On A**, we agreed that …
- **As far as B is concerned,** – In relation to B, – we agreed …
- **We still have the question of C to settle** – decide and agree on.
- And there's still the **outstanding** – remaining undecided – **issue** of D.
- We'll send you a **written proposal**.
- We'll **draw up** – write – **a contract** based on those points.
- **I think that covers everything.**

Exercises

66.1 Look at the words from A opposite and say if these statements are true or false.

1. Someone who helps two sides to reach an agreement is an arbitrator.
2. If two sides in a dispute use arbitration, no outsiders are involved.
3. It's not usual for mediators to impose agreements.
4. If you're in an impasse, you think that progress is possible.
5. If negotiations break down, they stop, at least for a time.
6. Irreconcilable differences are not important.
7. If the two sides agree on a cooling-off period of one week, negotiations continue the next day.

66.2 Complete these extracts using words that can come in front of 'contract' from B opposite.

1. Buyer and seller enter into a legally .... contract once an offer has been accepted.

2. DAF is bidding for a .... contract to supply trucks to the British army.

3. If two people agree on something and sign a sheet of paper, is that a .... contract?

4. Peters claimed that Schaffer was an employee in real estate ventures of Peters's company, but Schaffer asserted that an unwritten, ... contract made them partners.

5. She had an .... contract due to expire later in the year and wanted to take time off work.

66.3 The EPA–LT negotiations are ending. Arrange the phrases that Frederica Ramos uses to close the negotiations into the correct order. The first one is a.

a I'll just run over the main points. On the issue of the numbers of planes we wish to order,
b I think that covers everything. That's it for today.
c If we agree to the proposal, you'll draw up a contract based on those points.
d payment to settle, and there is also still the outstanding issue of documentation.
e we agreed that you would install the most economical Rolls-Royce engines now available.
f we agreed that you would supply us with 120 planes over four years. As far as fuel economy is concerned,
g We still have the question of the currency for
h You agreed to send us a written proposal on these last two issues.

> **Over to you**
>
> - When would you drive a hard bargain?
> - If there were irreconcilable differences in negotiations that you were involved in, what would you do to help resolve them?

Answer key

1.1
1. I work *on*
2. In fact, I *run*
3. I *manage*
4. One of my *main responsibilities*
5. I'm also *in charge of*
6. I deal *with*
7. I'm *responsible for*
8. I work closely *with*

1.2
1. to 2. to 3. at 4. off
5. in 6. out

1.3
2. full-time work
3. part-time work
4. a temporary job
5. permanent work
6. a permanent job

Over to you (sample answers)
If you work:
- I'm a pilot for a regional airline. I'm in charge of flying small planes (30 passengers) on short flights. My main responsibility is for the safety of the passengers, of course. My other responsibilities include leaving and arriving on time, and not using too much fuel.
- I usually leave home at 4.30 in the morning. The first flight is at 6 and I usually arrive at the airport at 5. I don't take a lot of time off work – I like flying too much!

If you don't work:
- I'd like to do something that involves working with other people.
- I'd like to work in a job with a regular routine, where I can leave home at 8 and know that I'll get back at 6. A nice comfortable office job would be nice!
- Some people prefer to work part-time because they have children to look after, or because they have other things that interest them. Some people like temporary jobs because they don't want to work for the same organization all the time. Other people like them because they want to take regular breaks so that they can travel, for example.

2.1
1. b 2. d 3. a 4. f 5. c 6. e

2.2
1. c working, boring, involves
2. e being / to be
3. a travelling, demanding, dealing
4. d tiring
5. b stimulating, repetitive

Over to you (sample answers)
If you work:
- Yes, I have a nine-to-five job in a bank. I don't have to clock on and clock off. We have a swipe card we use when we enter the building. There is no flexitime system – we have to be there before the bank opens until after it closes. There are people who do shiftwork – taking calls from customers in our call centres.
- I deal with bank customers, so it would be difficult to do my job working from home!
- I like my colleagues, but I don't like some of our customers, who can be very rude!

If you don't work:
- I'd like to have regular hours. I wouldn't like any kind of shiftwork – it would be too stressful for me.
- I wouldn't like to work from home: I need to be with other people.
- I'd like a job that involves teamwork, working with figures, solving problems, working outdoors and helping other people.

3.1
Across
5. recruited
6. headhunt
8. appoint

Down
1. accepts
2. turns down
3. offers
4. hired
7. apply

3.2
1. recruit, headhunt, appoint, offer, hire
2. accept, turn down, apply

3.3
1. turned down
2. an interview
3. his referees
4. offered him
5. accepted
6. applications
7. CVs
8. applicants
9. their qualifications
10. shortlisted six people
11. psychometric tests

Over to you (sample answers)
If you work:
I work as a laboratory technician, and the recruitment process was quite long. I replied to

142 Business Vocabulary in Use Intermediate

an advertisement on a jobs website – I sent them my CV with references and a covering letter. I was interviewed twice, first by the head of the laboratory and then by some of the people who worked with her. They checked my references, offered me the job, and I accepted it.

If you're a student:

> Dear Sir/Madam
>
> I saw the advertisement for gardeners on the Bristol City Council jobs website, and I would like to apply. I'm currently finishing a degree in garden design at University College Falmouth, and I would like to start a career in this area. I attach a CV, and I can provide references from my lecturers at University College.
>
> I can travel at any time to Bristol for an interview.
>
> Looking forward to hearing from you,
>
> Yours sincerely,

4.1
1 from, with, in
2 in, as
3 as
4 on, in

4.2
1 skilled
2 highly skilled
3 semi-skilled
4 unskilled
5 unskilled
6 highly skilled
7 semi-skilled
8 skilled

4.3
1 computer-literate, proactive, self-starter, team-player
2 numerate
3 motivated, driven
4 self-starter, methodical, systematic, organized
5 talented, motivated

Over to you (sample answer)
The job of sports shop manager requires someone who is good at sport, preferably good at three sports or more, so that they can advise customers on the right equipment to buy. Someone in this position has to be a self-starter, methodical and organized. You have to be computer-literate so that you can control stock and order new stock on time, and be good with people, as you will manage a staff of up to 15 people.

5.1
1 salary
2 overtime, commission
3 bonus
4 perks
5 company car
6 pension
7 benefits package

5.2
1 compensation payment, severance payment
2 compensation package, severance package
3 performance-related bonus
4 fat cats

Over to you (sample answers)
I'm a senior manager in a construction company. My basic salary is the most important thing. The benefits in order of importance are:
1 The performance-related bonuses that we get when we finish projects on time.
2 The share options that I get, based on the profits made by the company.
3 I hope to retire when I'm 55 or 60, and my pension is very important – so this is next.
4 And of course, the company car is a nice perk to have – I have a Jaguar.
5 The health plan that the company contributes to is another nice perk.

6.1
Across
2 white
5 staff
6 manual
7 strike
9 employee
10 outs
12 personnel
13 labour
15 collar

Down
1 payroll
2 workforce
3 unions
4 blue
5 shopfloor
8 stoppage
11 slow
14 go

6.2
1 office
2 head office
3 headquarters
4 open-plan
5 administrative staff
6 support
7 human resources department
8 HRD

Over to you (sample answers)
- Henkel has its head office in Dusseldorf, Germany. It has about 55,000 employees worldwide. It is a very large company with three main activities, and people work on different sites depending on the activity they work in. Some employees, for example administrative and support staff, work in open-plan offices.

Business Vocabulary in Use Intermediate

- Personally, I would prefer to have my own office, rather than work in an open-plan office.

7.1

Noun	Verb
retirement	retire
demotion	demote
lay-off	layoff
dismissal	dismiss
termination	terminate

Noun	Adjective
seniority	senior
freelance(r)	freelance
redundancy	redundant
insecurity	insecure
flexibility	flexible

7.2 1 b 2 d 3 e 4 c 5 a

7.3
1 reviews
2 off
3 contracts
4 freelancers
5 laying
6 flatter
7 leaner
8 redundant
9 outplacement

Over to you (sample answers)
- Performance reviews are designed to help employees understand their weak and strong points, and to help them change the way that they work in order to improve their performance.
- An organization often restructures in order to become more efficient and profitable. Perhaps the structure that existed before is no longer suitable for new activities or objectives.
- The main advantage of outsourcing is that it allows an organization to concentrate on what it does best, rather than having to manage a range of activities that it does not do so well.
- People are dismissed for all sorts of reasons – perhaps because they have behaved in an unacceptable way, or because their performance is not as good as it should be and they have not reached their objectives.

8.1
1 bullying
2 sexual harassment, harassed
3 glass ceiling, sex discrimination
4 racial discrimination, racist, discriminated
5 Affirmative action, affirmative action

8.2 1 b 2 a 3 f 4 e 5 d
6 c 7 g

Over to you (sample answer)
There are many health and safety hazards in the chemical industry. There are hazardous substances everywhere, and in some areas of the industry there is a risk of explosions. Activities have to be managed very carefully to avoid industrial accidents.

9.1
1 marketing director
2 research director
3 finance director
4 human resources director
5 customer services manager
6 sales manager

9.2
1 President and CEO – Maria Montebello
2 Non-executive director – George Gomi
3 Non-executive director – Julia Jones
4 CFO – Stan Smith
5 VP Marketing – Clarissa Chang
6 VP Research – Richard Roberts
7 VP Personnel – Deirdre Dawes

Over to you (sample answers)
Management Organigram

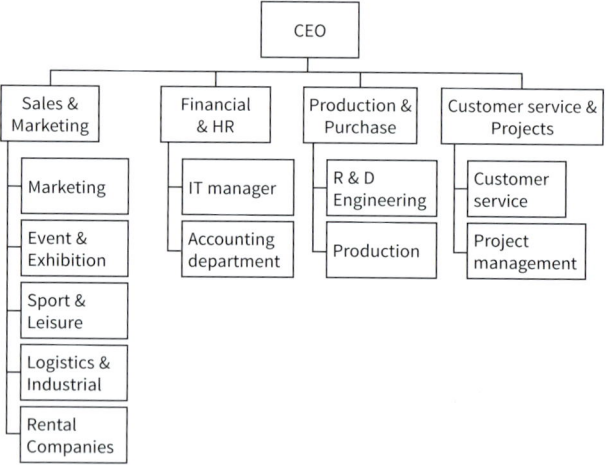

If you don't work:
I think I would be a very good lawyer. Even when I was at school, I was good at solving disagreements between people. I like speaking in public, and defending people Wwho have been badly affected by the actions of others. I'd like to work in a law firm, working with other lawyers.

10.1
1. entrepreneurs
2. entrepreneurial
3. founded
4. start-up
5. grow
6. leadership
7. empire

10.2
Güler Sabancı: banking entrepreneur
Cath Kidston: retail entrepreneur
Jack Ma: e-commerce mogul
Elon Musk: electric car entrepreneur
Zhang Xin: property tycoon
Mark Zuckerberg: social media website founder

Over to you (sample answers)
- In the UK, one famous entrepreneur is Richard Branson. He has founded all sorts of businesses. They form the Virgin group of companies. The group contains everything from a transatlantic airline to cable television services. Some of the companies are more successful than others. He likes to get into businesses that previously he knew nothing about. Branson is famous for his casual clothes, his long hair and his beard.
- Entrepreneurs are born, in my opinion. They seem to have unusual curiosity and enthusiasm. They are not easily discouraged when they don't succeed the first time. They are often good at knocking on doors and finding the right people to help them develop their ideas.

11.1   1 d   2 c   3 a   4 f   5 b   6 e

11.2
1. state-owned companies, government-owned companies, nationalized companies
2. commercial airline
3. bureaucracy
4. commercial land
5. commercial television
6. enterprise
7. commercial artist
8. commercial disaster

11.3
1. free enterprise
2. private enterprise
3. enterprise economy
4. enterprise culture
5. enterprise zone

Over to you (sample answers)
- In France, the public sector is very big. Public sector workers have good conditions: a short working week, and earlier retirement than in the private sector. But they are paid less than they would be in the private sector. However, public sector workers' conditions are slowly changing and becoming more like those in the private sector.
- Among the industries mentioned, electricity supply and rail transport are in the public sector. Telephone services have been privatized in the last few years.

12.1
1. partnership
2. plc
3. corporation
4. freelancer / sole trader / sole owner
5. limited company

12.2
1. demutualization
2. building society
3. members
4. demutualized
5. demutualize
6. mutual

12.3   1 b   2 c   3 e   4 a   5 d

Over to you (sample answer)
In my country, a lot of charities work on social problems such as poverty or homelessness. Others work abroad to help people in poverty there, or to help them after natural disasters such as hurricanes. There are also charities which work on medical problems such as cancer.

13.1
1. computer software
2. computer hardware
3. pharmaceuticals
4. aerospace
5. cars
6. media
7. financial services
8. retail

13.2
1. property
2. tourism
3. financial services
4. defence
5. pharmaceuticals

13.3
Across
1. aerospace
3. steel
4. service
6. manufacturing
8. media
9. industrial
11. emerging
12. growth
13. pharmaceuticals

Down
1. automobile
2. defence
5. catering
7. health
10. light

Business Vocabulary in Use Intermediate   **145**

Over to you (sample answers)
- A wide range of goods is manufactured in my country, Turkey: everything from pharmaceuticals to trucks. There are a lot of plants in cities around Istanbul, and also in places such as Izmir and Bursa.
- The economy is quite diversified.

14.1
2 observations
3 surveys
4 moderator
5 low response rates
6 field trials

14.2
a Market research
b beta version
c product launch
d researchers
e focus groups
f safe
g industrial scale
h designers
i testing/trialling
j CAD/CAM

14.3
1 market
2 groups
3 consumer
4 surveys
5 launch
6 design
7 recall

Over to you (sample answers)
- Before it can release a new drug, a pharmaceutical company needs to do a lot of trials to make sure the drug is effective and safe. It then needs to get agreement from the authorities before the drug can be sold.
- I once took part in a survey where I had to taste a new brand of cola. The cola company who had organized the survey wanted to make sure that the taste of the new cola was more acceptable than the existing brands among young cola drinkers.
- If a company finds a problem in a product after the launch, they may have to recall the product in order to fix it. If this involves recalling tens of thousands of cars, for example, it can be very expensive, and some owners may not be aware of the recall.

15.1
1 innovation
2 state-of-the-art
3 development
4 cutting edge
5 technologies
6 developed
7 technology
8 develop
9 release

15.2
1 j 2 i 3 d 4 e 5 a
6 b 7 h 8 g 9 c 10 f

Over to you (sample answers)
- Word processors like Amstrad and Wang became obsolete when personal computers appeared, and word processing – as well as many other things – could be done on a PC.
- Companies try to prevent illegal downloading by using technical devices such as copy protection, and by taking legal action against people who download material in large quantities, perhaps in order to sell it. Downloading is so common that companies will find it very difficult to stop it completely.

16.1
1 manufacture / manufacturing / production, make(s) / manufacture(s) / produce(s), maker / manufacturer / producer
2 provider, services
3 producer, production
4 provider
5 producer, produced
6 provision

16.2
1 c 2 b 3 d 4 g 5 a
6 f 7 e 8 h

16.3
1 a 2 d 3 c 4 b

Over to you (sample answer)
It depends. Tailor-made – hand-made – clothes may fit better than mass-produced clothes, but entirely hand-made cars, put together without the help of computers and advanced machines, may not be such a good idea!

17.1
1 capital
2 knowledge
3 stocks / inventories
4 raw materials
5 components
6 parts
7 labour
8 work-in-progress
9 stocks / inventories
10 finished goods

17.2
1 c 2 a 3 d 4 e 5 f 6 b

17.3
1 just-in-time
2 warehouses
3 finance
4 store
5 efficient
6 lean manufacturing/production

Over to you (sample answers)
- The advantage of outsourcing is that your company can concentrate on what it does best. But critics say that if you know enough about an activity to outsource it and to stay in control of it, then you might be able to do it just as well yourself.
- The advantage of asking for components 'just-in-time' is that the customer does not have to stock them and finance them before they are used. The disadvantage is that if they don't arrive on time, production has to stop.

18.1
1 Wikinomics
2 benchmarking
3 the long tail
4 mass customization

18.2 1 e 2 a 3 d 4 b 5 f 6 c

18.3
1 model
2 benchmarking
3 industrial secrets
4 long tail
5 catalogue

Over to you (sample answer)
My organization is trying to improve efficiency by improving the flow of information between departments. It's difficult when people in one department don't know what those in another department are doing.

19.1 1 b 2 c 3 f 4 e 5 d 6 a

19.2
1 buyer, consumer, customer, purchaser
2 customer base
3 client
4 client base, clientele
5 seller
6 seller, vendor
7 buyer, purchaser
8 street vendor
9 buyer, purchaser, buying manager, purchasing manager
10 user, end-user

19.3
1 market-place
2 market reforms
3 Market prices
4 market forces / market pressures
5 market forces / market pressures
6 market economy

Over to you (sample answers)
- In the UK, Marks and Spencer has a very large customer base, especially among the middle class.
- The purchasing manager in a large office is responsible for buying furniture, computer equipment and supplies, stationery, etc.

20.1
1 penetrate
2 cornered
3 entering
4 monopolized
5 penetrate

20.2
1 are the market leader
2 have a 55 per cent market share
3 Market growth is
4 market segments
5 market segmentation

20.3
1 500
2 yes
3 A
4 A and B
5 B, C, D and E
6 no

Over to you (sample answer)
In the UK mobile phone market, there are five competitors. Competition is very strong. The two market leaders are EE, with 32.9 per cent of the market, and O2, with 20.9 per cent. The other key players are Vodafone with 18.2 per cent and 3 Mobile with 10 per cent. The fifth, much smaller, competitor is Tesco Mobile, with 8.5 per cent.

21.1
2 features
3 benefits
4 the product
5 the promotion
6 the place
7 the price
8 marketing mix
9 the packaging
10 marketers, marketeers

21.2 1 f 2 d 3 a 4 e 5 g 6 b 7 c

Over to you (sample answer)
Disney theme parks are famous for being market-oriented. They have the knowledge and understanding of customer needs that allow them to keep visitors happy: everything from supplying special raincoats when it rains, managing the queues for the different attractions, to serving the right food in the restaurants.

22.1
1 placement
2 mix
3 lines
4 lifecycle
5 positioning
6 portfolio

Business Vocabulary in Use Intermediate

22.2
1 consumer durables
2 raw materials
3 consumer durables
4 fast-moving consumer goods
5 fast-moving consumer goods

22.3 1 c   2 a   3 g   4 h
5 b   6 d   7 e   8 f

Over to you (sample answers)
- James Bond films provide possibilities for product placement for everything from cars to clothes to plasma TVs.
- The most famous brands of chocolate in the UK: Nestlé, Cadbury; soft drinks: Coca-Cola, Pepsi-Cola; breakfast cereal: Kellogg's; fast food: McDonald's, Kentucky Fried Chicken

23.1
1 true   4 true
2 false   5 false
3 false   6 true

23.2
1 hike
2 boom
3 cuts
4 controls

23.3
1 It had an upmarket image.
2 No, this added to its appeal.
3 No, it also bought competitors, and launched products in addition to coffee.
4 It has improved a lot.
5 No, it's squeezed from below by fast food chains and from above by more sophisticated coffee shop chains.

Over to you (sample answers)
- In France, most people buy their cars through dealers. Other sources such as the internet are not much used.
- The lowest costs for home furniture are found at large specialized furniture shops on the edge of towns. As in many places, IKEA is increasing its number of shops.
- There are some supermarkets in town centres, but they do not usually have low prices. People go to out-of-town supermarkets like Casino and Intermarché, but there are even cheaper chains such as Lidl.
- The immediate advantage might be increased sales, but the long-term disadvantage might be damage to the company's brand image.

24.1
1 distribution channel   4 resellers
2 wholesalers   5 customer
3 retailers   6 retailers / resellers

24.2
1 shopping mall   4 discounter
2 shopping centre   5 department store
3 convenience store   6 hypermarket

24.3
1 junk mail   4 cold calling
2 call centre   5 direct marketing
3 mailshot   6 telemarketing

Over to you (sample answers)
- City centre shops can be good: there are some good department stores where I live. But it can be difficult to park. With out-of-town shops, parking is free, but you have to drive there, and they can be a bit 'soul-less' – without character.
- In the UK, wine companies often advertise by direct mail.
- As a consumer, telemarketing can be very annoying. The phone rings at inconvenient times, like mealtimes. I don't think I've ever bought anything following a telemarketing call.

25.1 Across   Down
4 promotions   1 hoarding
6 displays   2 loyalty
7 samples   3 commercials
10 prizes   5 territory
11 agency   7 sign
14 force   9 manager
15 gifts   12 medium
16 advertisers   13 area
17 women

25.2 1 d   2 e   3 a   4 c   5 b

Over to you (sample answers)
- Manchester United are currently sponsored by Adidas, a German sportswear manufacturer, in a ten-year £750 million agreement.
- Many supermarket chains offer loyalty cards. Some coffee-shop chains do too: if you buy nine coffees, you get a tenth one free.

26.1 1 B2C   3 B2B   5 B2C
2 B2G   4 B2G

148 Business Vocabulary in Use Intermediate

26.2
1. fashion products
2. no
3. no
4. She can get information about buying things that she previously knew nothing about.
5. Because the general economic situation is so bad.
6. a) yes, b) yes

26.3
1. travel
2. banking
3. fundraising
4. brokerage
5. gambling

Over to you (sample answers)
Some of the potential problems of shopping online:
- the goods you see on the website may not be the ones that are actually available
- the goods you want to order are out of stock
- the goods you order might not arrive or might not arrive on time, or at all
- fraud: your credit card details may be taken to make unauthorised purchases

27.1
1. e   2. f   3. d   4. a   5. b
6. a   7. c

27.2
1. costings
2. expenses
3. the sales
4. sales
5. variable, fixed, fixed
6. overheads

27.3
1. indirect cost
2. fixed cost
3. COGS
4. overhead cost
5. variable cost
6. direct cost

27.4
1. €14
2. €10
3. 25 per cent
4. 20 per cent

Over to you (sample answer)
McDonald's Big Mac has the highest sales of all its products. The company's main costs are its restaurants, staff and raw materials (food supplies).

28.1
1. armchairs, sofas, dining tables
2. armchairs
3. chairs
4. coffee tables
5. armchairs

28.2
1. overspending
2. under budget
3. budget for
4. spend / expenditure
5. budget

28.3
1. emerging markets
2. more users ready to buy second phones with more features
3. no
4. 60 per cent
5. economies of scale

Over to you (sample answers)
- The money spinners are electronic gadgets of all kinds: mobile phones, iPods, games consoles …
- The biggest advertisers are food and drink companies: there are a lot of advertisements for snacks and soft drinks, and the supermarkets also have expensive campaigns.
- Economies of scale allow companies to reduce costs: with some products, the more that is produced and sold, the cheaper each product is.

29.1   1 b   2 f   3 d   4 c   5 e   6 a

29.2
1. Cashflow
2. upfront
3. trade credit
4. discount
5. credit policy, payment terms

29.3
1. key accounts
2. debtors
3. creditors
4. bad debts
5. write them off

Over to you (sample answers)
- The standard delivery time for ordering books online is 3–4 days, by ordinary post. But on some sites you can order books to be delivered overnight.
- Car dealers offer discounts all the time. People say that you should never pay the official price for a car, but should always negotiate. There are times of year when car dealers can offer particularly low prices in order to keep selling.

30.1
1. fixed assets
2. current assets
3. fixed asset
4. not an asset
5. current asset
6. not an asset
7. intangible asset
8. not an asset

30.2
2. amortization, book value
3. current liabilities

Business Vocabulary in Use Intermediate

　　　　4　depreciated / amortized
　　　　5　wrote down
　　　　6　long-term liabilities

30.3　1　false　　3　false　　5　false
　　　　2　true　　 4　true

Over to you (sample answer)
The Clifton Building Company's main assets are its vans and other equipment. (Another asset is the knowledge and skill of its builders, but these are not shown on its balance sheet.) Its main liabilities are the money it owes to suppliers, and to the tax authorities.

31.1　Across　　　　　　　　Down
　　　　1　profit and loss　　2　account
　　　　6　standards　　　　　3　statement
　　　　7　exceptional　　　　4　results
　　　　8　report　　　　　　　5　pretax
　　　　11　bottom line　　　　9　rule
　　　　　　　　　　　　　　　10　loss

31.2　1　false　　　4　true
　　　　2　false　　　5　true
　　　　3　false　　　6　true

Over to you (sample answers)
- Airlines and other transport companies are likely to bleed red ink if the price of oil rises.
- Creative accounting that is not illegal should be identified by auditors, who should tell the company's accountants to present the information in a more acceptable way. Creative accounting that is illegal could be punished by a fine or even by time in prison.

32.1　1　b　　2　a　　3　d　　4　e　　5　c

32.2　1　loan capital / borrowing
　　　　2　collateral / security
　　　　3　leverage / gearing
　　　　4　highly geared, highly leveraged
　　　　5　overleveraged

Over to you (sample answers)
- I've thought of opening a restaurant. Family and friends could supply the capital, and I might also go to a bank for a loan.
- Existing companies normally get capital on the stockmarket: the stockmarkets are dynamic, but they are not always ready to support a good business idea. The cost of issuing shares can be high, and it's not possible to control the 'owners' of the company when shares change hands. Companies can also borrrow money from banks, but there have been periods recently when banks are unwilling to lend.

33.1　1　b　　2　a　　3　f　　4　e　　5　d　　6　c

33.2　1　collapse, burden　　4　bailout, crisis
　　　　2　repayment　　　　　5　turning, ailing
　　　　3　Recovery

33.3　1　administration　　　5　wind up
　　　　2　protection　　　　　6　ceases trading
　　　　3　creditors　　　　　　7　liquidation
　　　　4　goes into
　　　　　　receivership

Over to you (sample answers)
- If a company defaults on its debt repayments, it may try to restructure its debts, or it may go bankrupt.
- General Motors may go bankrupt.
- The US government has bailed out ailing car manufacturers, but many economists say that this is not a good way of using money. Supporters of bailouts say that in difficult economic times it's better that people are not laid off but that they continue working, rather than being unemployed and receiving money from the government.

34.1　1　b　　2　c　　3　e　　4　a　　5　d

34.2　1　bid　　　　　　4　predators
　　　　2　restructure　　 5　merger
　　　　3　hostile bid　　　6　joint venture

34.3　1　diversified into　　5　refocusing
　　　　2　subsidiaries　　　6　disposals
　　　　3　parent　　　　　　7　non-core assets
　　　　　　company　　　　8　divestments
　　　　4　demerging　　　　9　core

Over to you (sample answers)
- Companies form joint ventures to combine their different skills so that they can make a product or provide a service that neither of them could do by itself.
- In the UK, Lloyds TSB has merged with HBOS. The UK government encouraged them to merge as the banking crisis meant that they might not have been able to survive on their own.

- The biggest company in the Czech Republic is Škoda Auto and its core activity is making cars.

35.1
1 false
2 false
3 true
4 true
5 false
6 true

35.2 1 c 2 a 3 b 4 d 5 f 6 e

35.3
1 a, b
2 b, c
3 mortgages, travel and health insurance
4 increased: loan payment protection insurance, current accounts;
decreased: travel and health insurance

Over to you (sample answers)
- The main advantage of online banking is convenience: not having to drive to the bank, etc. The main disadvantage is the potential for fraud.
- BNP Paribas is the biggest bank in France. It's an international bank.

36.1
1 brokers
2 traders
3 speculators
4 Wall Street
5 financial institutions
6 centres
7 City
8 Square Mile

36.2
1 gone public
2 raise, flotations
3 oversubscribed
4 raising capital
5 stockmarkets
6 listed *or* floated

36.3
1 securities house
2 futures contract
3 commodities
4 currencies
5 commercial paper
6 bonds
7 securities
8 commodities exchange
9 options contract

Over to you (sample answers)
- Zurich is Switzerland's main financial centre.
- In the US, many commodities are traded, including, for example, farm products on the Chicago Board of Trade.

37.1
1 Hong Kong
2 Nikkei
3 Dow Jones
4 Nasdaq
5 London
6 CAC 40
7 Frankfurt

37.2
1 blue chips
2 trading
3 high turnover
4 bullish
5 bull market
6 bearish
7 barrier

37.3 1 c 2 d 3 b 4 a

Over to you (sample answers)
- It would be good to buy shares in Google, as the company will probably continue to grow and grow.
- Panic selling might start on the stock market if investors think that the economy is going to slow down very fast, and many companies' sales are going to fall quickly.
- In a bull market share prices are rising, and people expect them to continue to rise. In a bear market share prices are falling, and people expect them to continue to fall.

38.1
2 economics
3 economic
4 uneconomic
5 economical
6 uneconomical
7 economics
8 finances
9 financial

38.2
1 growth rate
2 out of work
3 labour shortages
4 trade balance
5 exports
6 trade gap
7 trade deficit
8 widen

38.3

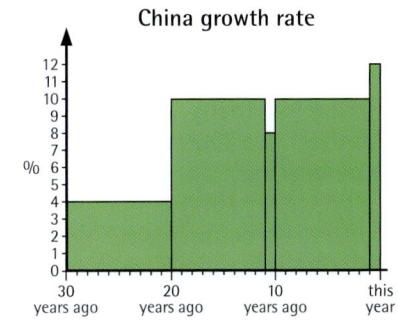

China growth rate

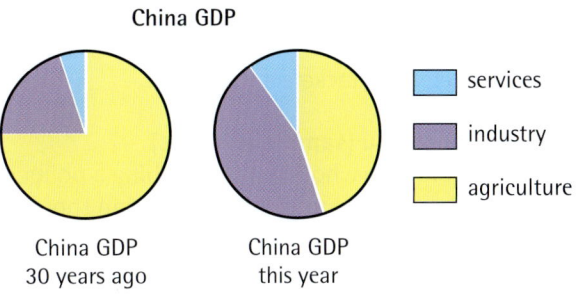

China GDP 30 years ago

China GDP this year

services
industry
agriculture

Business Vocabulary in Use Intermediate 151

Over to you (sample answers)
- If a country has a trade surplus, it exports more than it imports. If it has a trade deficit, it imports more than it exports.
- Inflation here in Italy is about 2 per cent per year, and falling.
- The three countries with the highest GDP are the US ($18.558 trillion in 2016), China ($11.383 trillion), Japan ($4.412 trillion).

39.1 1 false 2 true 3 true 4 false 5 true 6 true 7 false

39.2
Across
1 depression
5 peaks
9 levels off
11 bottoms out

Down
2 recession
3 slump
4 negative
6 stagflation
7 stagnation
8 steady
10 boom

Over to you (sample answers)
- Here in Italy, banks have cut interest rates this year.
- Stagnation is when the economy grows slowly, or not at all. Stagflation is when prices are rising during a period of stagnation.

40.1
1 price fixing
2 bribery
3 sleaze
4 insider dealing / insider trading; Chinese walls
5 bribe / kickback / sweetener / backhander; bribery / corruption / sleaze
6 identity theft

40.2
embezzlement, embezzler, embezzles, embezzlement, embezzled
faking, faker, fakes, a fake, fake
forgery, forger, forges, a forgery, forged
money laundering, money launderer, launders, –, –
racketeering, racketeer, –, a racket, –

Over to you (sample answers)
- Someone who is guilty of bribing a politician should go to prison. The politician should lose his job, and should also go to prison.
- On the internet, one common kind of wrongdoing is hacking into computers, gaining access to confidential information. Another is writing programs that contain viruses and infecting other computers with them.

41.1
Across
4 affirmative
7 sweatshop labour
9 discrimination
12 code of ethics
13 exploit
14 action
15 stake
16 issues

Down
1 responsible
2 carbon emissions
3 offset
5 ethical
6 green
8 environmental
10 minority
11 moral

Over to you (sample answers)
- One UK company that has a reputation for social responsibility is the Cooperative Bank. For example, it does not invest in companies that have unethical activities.
- In my country, there are a number of companies with affirmative action programs. They are keen to employ people from ethnic minorities. Women are fairly represented at all levels of management, and half their board members are women.

42.1
1 timescale / timeframe
2 schedule
3 longer than planned
4 overlapped
5 make up
6 behind
7 stage / phase / step / task
8 delays
9 downtime

42.2
2 You should avoid interruptions.
3 You should avoid distractions.
4 You shouldn't aim for perfectionism when it isn't necessary.
5 You should plan your day in advance.
6 You should go on a time management course.

Over to you (sample answers)
- If a company is behind schedule on a project, it can employ more people on the project. But this may not always be a good idea, as the new people have to be told what to do. For example, software-writing projects that are behind schedule are often still not completed on time even if new programmers are found.

- My best personal tip on time management is to concentrate on one task at a time and to finish it before starting another one.

43.1 1 d   2 a   3 b   4 e   5 c

43.2
1 rat race, treadmill
2 overwhelmed, stressed out
3 downshift, rebalance
4 quality of life
5 stress-induced
6 quality time
7 stress, pressure
8 demands
9 overwork
10 burned out

Over to you (sample answers)
- I sometimes get stressed at work. I play basketball and go swimming to reduce this.
- Symptoms of stress include headaches, a tendency to get angry for no reason, feelings of helplessness, etc.
- Some people who downshift complain of boredom and of feeling that they are not part of the modern world.

44.1
1 drive, dynamism, energy
2 vision
3 subordinates
4 leadership skills
5 command and control

44.2
Across
1 decision
5 authoritarian
8 distant
9 approach
11 consult
12 top
13 delegate
14 decentralized

Down
2 empower
3 bureaucratic
4 initiative
6 consensual
7 making
10 imposed

Over to you (sample answers)
- I think the CEO of my last company was really charismatic – everybody admired him.
- During a process of consultation, the decision maker talks to everyone who will be affected by the decision so that they can influence it.
- Here in Denmark, the management style is quite democratic. There are typically not that many management layers, and everyone is involved in the decision-making process. And once the decision has been taken, people tend to accept it, even if they disagreed with it before.

45.1
1 macho culture
2 long-hours culture
3 learning culture
4 company / corporate culture
5 business culture
6 sales culture

45.2
1 a ABC
   b SBC
2 a SBC
   b ABC
3 a ABC
   b SBC

Over to you (sample answer)
Here in Greece, students show quite a lot of deference to teachers, and employees are quite deferential towards managers. The attitude is that teachers are the ones with the knowledge, and should teach it. Managers are the ones who know what to do, and employees should obey them.

46.1
1 collectivist, individualist
2 connections
3 trust
4 loyalty
5 individualism, collectivism
6 independent entities

46.2 1 c   2 e   3 b   4 a   5 d

46.3
1 h   2 e   3 g   4 f
5 d   6 a   7 c   8 b

Over to you (sample answers)

Working hours
In the US, people start work at 8 or 8.30 and officially finish at 5, though many managers start later and stay at work much longer.

Holidays
There are not a lot of public holidays during the year. Many employees only have two weeks' holiday a year. Trade fairs and conferences (what Americans call 'conventions') are very important, as they allow people to get away from their desks without using holiday time.

Meals and entertaining
The lunch break is usually quite short, but some business is done over restaurant lunches. The working breakfast is an important occasion for discussions. There are lots of snacks between meals, and coffee.

Punctuality
Punctuality is extremely important. Don't be late for meetings!

Boundaries
It's OK to phone people at home about work, but not late in the evening.

47.1
1 VoIP
2 videoconferencing
3 mobile phone
4 cordless phone
5 public telephone / payphone
6 voicemail / text message
7 webcam and microphone

47.2
1 It would be good to see Anna soon. I'll phone ~~to~~ her and see when she's free.
2 3
3 Why don't you ring ~~to~~ Pizza Palace and order some takeaway pizza?
4 3
5 Call me up next time you're in New York.
6 3
7 I'll give her a bell and we'll go out for a meal.
8 When you get some news, give me a call.

47.3
a press 4   c press 6   e press 5
b press 3   d press 2

Over to you (some ideas)
- **Advantages of using call centres:**
1 You can talk to a human being who can offer advice, etc.
2 You don't need computer knowledge.
3 You can be more sure that the transaction has been successful and has gone through.
   Advantages of using the internet:
1 You can see all the information available and have time to look at different options and to think about it.
2 You don't have to worry about the mood of the person you're dealing with at the call centre!
- The last time I phoned an organization was when I called Xara last week. The person who answered the phone was very pleasant and put me through to the department I wanted. They dealt with my enquiry very efficiently – it was about a late delivery. The person I spoke to gave me their extension number and said that I could phone again the next day if the goods still hadn't arrived then.

48.1
1 you put me through
2 One moment
3 putting you through
4 the line's busy
5 want to hold
6 call back later
7 hold, please
8 busy
9 again later
10 the number of
11 direct line

48.2 (sample answers)
1 You're through to Steve Fox's voicemail. I'm on holiday till Monday the 12th and I won't be picking up messages. I will respond when I get back. If your enquiry is urgent, please contact my colleague Rob Timmins on extension 8359. If you'd like to leave a message, please leave it after the tone.
2 You're through to the voicemail of Sue Leighton. I'm away on a business trip till Thursday. I will pick up any messages, so please leave a message after the tone and I'll get back to you as soon as possible.
3 Hello. You're through to Rod Baxter's voicemail. I'm on a training course until the 20th of January. I won't be picking up my voicemail. You can leave a message and I will respond when I get back. If you have any urgent queries, please call my PA, Jill Salford. Her direct line is 8466.
4 You're through to Tina Preston's voicemail. I'll be in meetings all day today, Friday. If you'd like to leave a message, I'll get back to you on Monday morning. If there are any urgent matters, please call my colleague Keith Samson on extension 8521.

48.3
1 is   3 to   5 on   7 on
2 from   4 at   6 on

Over to you (sample answers)
- I think it's difficult on the phone in English when people talk too fast and I have to ask them politely to slow down. It's difficult to remember 'specific' telephone expressions. It's also hard to end calls without seeming rude.
- You're through to Maria Karlovski's voicemail. I'm on holiday until Tuesday the 20th and I won't be picking up messages. I will respond when I get back. If your enquiry is urgent, please contact my colleague Pavel Schmidt on extension 242. If you'd like to leave a message, please speak after the tone.
- I prefer voicemail because it's easier to use – you don't need to go to a computer. But putting your message across clearly and politely can be difficult. At least with modern systems you can go back and 'improve' it. However, email gives you time to think about what you want to say!

49.1 1
A: <u>I'd like</u> to speak to Ms Sangster, please.
B: <u>I'm afraid she's not available.</u>
A: <u>It's</u> Sven Nyman <u>here</u>.
B: <u>May I ask what it's about?</u>
A: <u>I'm calling about</u> her order.
B: I'll <u>ask</u> her to call you when she's free.

2
A: Hello. Is Jack Bronson <u>available</u>?
B: <u>No, I'm afraid he's not available. May I ask who's calling? Which company are you calling from?</u>
A: <u>This is Rosario Gonzalez calling from Excelsior Media Services. Could I leave a message for him? I'm calling to confirm that I've received his cheque.</u>
B: <u>I'll give him your message.</u>

49.2 2 V for Victor, A for Alpha, L for Lima, L for Lima, A for Alpha, D for Delta, O for Oscar, L for Lima, I for India, D for Delta.
3 W for Whisky, E for Echo, B for Bravo, E for Echo, R for Romeo.
4 h t t p colon slash slash www dot, britishcouncil all as one word dot org slash courses.
5 P for Papa, E for Echo, T for Tango, E for Echo, R for Romeo, new word, H for Hotel, O for Oscar, U for Uniform, S for Sierra, E for Echo.
6 M for Mike, A for Alpha, C for Charlie, P for Papa, H for Hotel, E for Echo, R for Romeo, S for Sierra, O for Oscar, N for November.
7 john hyphen smith at cambridge dot ac dot UK.

49.3 1 g   2 d   3 b   4 f
5 c   6 e   7 a   8 h

Over to you (sample answers)
- Cambridge: C for Charlie, A for Apple, M for Mike, B for Bravo, R for Romeo, I for India, D for Delta, G for Golf, E for Echo.
- My email address is rosariogonzalez@hotmail.com: rosariogonzalez – all one word – at hotmail dot com. My company's website is http://peo.cambridge.org: h t t p colon slash slash p e o dot cambridge dot org.

50.1 1 f   2 b   3 j   4 a   5 h   6 d
7 k   8 e   9 i   10 c   11 g

50.2 1 natural
2 illogical: A gives a definite time when they will next meet (tomorrow), but B says just that they will talk 'soon'.
3 natural
4 illogical: A gives a definite time (this afternoon) when they will actually meet but B says just that they will be 'back in touch soon'.
5 natural

50.3 1 e   2 c   3 b   4 a   5 d

Over to you (sample answers)
- I prefer to use email because it gives people time to think about their response before replying to me.
OR I prefer to use the phone because that way you get immediate answers to questions, queries, etc.
- It can be difficult to end calls without seeming rude. The best way to do this is to confirm the things that have been decided during the call and say when the next contact will be: an email for example, or another phone call.

51.1 1 George should have taken the card with both hands.
2 He shouldn't have written on it.
3 He did not read it carefully.

4 He should have treated it with more care and respect, and put it somewhere such as his briefcase.
5 He should have ensured that he had enough business cards of his own.

51.2

via Lamborghini, 21
20154 Milano, Italy
Tel +39 81 532 7000
Email: frossi@modac21.it[7]

Francesca[1] **Rossi**[3] **PhD**[5]**, IPM**[6]
Textiles Purchasing Manager[4]

51.3
1 email address
2 attachment
3 get back to me
4 to give me a call
5 by courier

Over to you (sample answer)

Dear Leila,

It was very nice meeting you at the IT conference in San Antonio. Hope you got back to Beirut OK. Please find attached, as promised, some information about my institution, Heriot-Watt University, and its Department of Information Technology. We offer PhD courses, with a large number of overseas students. The university is just outside Edinburgh, and an ideal place to study – I hope the attached information is useful. Please don't hesitate to get in touch if you require any further information.

Best regards,

Daniella

52.1
1 subject
2 contact details / contact information
3 blind copy
4 bcc
5 bcc
6 forwarded
7 forwarding
8 reply to all
9 reply

52.2 (sample answer)

From: wu.lee@sinophone.com
To: gunilla.madsen@norgequip.com
cc: lin.weng@sinophone.com
22 June 2016
Dear Gunilla,
It was very nice meeting you too at the trade fair last week. I hope you had a smooth trip back to Oslo. Please find attached a document with information about Sinophone. Lin Weng is our purchasing manager: I'm copying him in on this. I will also forward your details to Shu Bao, our finance director. Please don't hesitate to contact me if you require any further information.
Best regards
Wu Lee

52.3
1 Hi Jim; Best
2 Dear Sir/Madam; Best regards
3 Dear Ms Preston; Regards
4 Dear Mike; All the best
5 Dear Mr Collins; Best regards
6 Dear Madam; Best regards

Over to you (sample answers)
- In my view, email doesn't save time. It creates more work, because people send messages that they wouldn't bother sending if they had to write a letter or phone.
- Company employees shouldn't be allowed to send and receive personal emails at work, or surf the internet, because it wastes the company's time and costs the company money.

53.1
| 1 i | 2 c | 3 b | 4 h | 5 a |
| 6 d | 7 f | 8 g | 9 e | |

53.2
1 Qualifications
2 Career goal
3 Skills
4 Experience
5 Contact details

53.3
1 As you will see
2 attached CV
3 I am writing with reference
4 I would now like to relocate
5 I look forward to hearing from you
6 I am available

Over to you (sample answer)

DAVID MARCOS

Contact details
7050 Fairmount Drive, San Jose, CA 95148
email: dmarcos1980@hotmail.com   mobile: +408 972 3792

Career goal
Looking for a more senior management role in a telecommunications company

Skills
Good management skills
Team leader
Combined technical and business knowledge of mobile phone networks

Qualifications
1999–2002 University of the East, Manila – Electrical engineering degree
2002–2003 University of Sydney, Australia – Master's degree in Electronics
2010–2011 Wharton Business School, United States – MBA (Masters in Business Administration)

Experience
2003–2006 Electrical engineer, Samsung, Seoul, S. Korea. Worked on development of mobile network technology
2007–2010 Team Leader, ZTE Corp. Managed a team of 20 mobile network specialists
2011–Present Department Manager, Cisco Systems, San Jose, California. Managing a group of 50 engineers working with business clients on next-generation mobile technology. Involved in both technical and financial issues.

54.1
1 graduated from
2 unpaid
3 hands-on experience
4 menial
5 range of tasks
6 professional skills
7 build our confidence
8 learn from
9 develop our network
10 exploited

54.2
1 traineeships, trainees
2 entry-level jobs
3 part-time study
4 apprenticeships, apprentices
5 vocational qualification
6 job-specific skills

Over to you (sample answer)
I have just graduated with a law degree and I found a law firm that specializes in commercial law. The internship that they offer sound very interesting. They allow interns to work with more senior lawyers on the writing of contracts. It all sounds good – no menial tasks. What's more, the internship is paid – about €500 a month.

55.1
1 arranged / set up / fixed
2 to bring forward the meeting / the meeting to be brought forward
3 put back / put off / postponed
4 put back / put off / postponed
5 chaired / ran
6 did not attend / missed

55.2
1 AGM
2 brainstorming
3 department/departmental meeting
4 meeting with suppliers
5 chat
6 meeting with a customer
7 project meeting
8 EGM or AGM
9 board meeting

55.3   1 c   2 f   3 e   4 a   5 d   6 b

Over to you (sample answer)
In my organization, I go to monthly sales meetings with the other sales people, to discuss our results for the month. These are quite useful, as I can see how much I'm selling in relation to my colleagues.

56.1
1 true   5 true
2 false   6 false
3 true   7 false
4 false

Business Vocabulary in Use Intermediate

56.2
1 takes
2 appoints
3 circulate
4 allocate
5 move on
6 avoid
7 agree

Over to you (sample answers)
- I think I'm quite good at chairing meetings because people feel that I give everyone an equal opportunity to speak and the decisions we take are based on a full discussion of the facts.
- What I find annoying in meetings is people who don't stick to the point and people who talk too much – they're often the same people!

57.1

1 | How / What | about you? |

2 | I've | called / organized / arranged | this meeting to … |

3 | Let's | begin, shall we? / get down to business. / get started. / make a start. |

4 | The (main) | objective / purpose | of this meeting is to … |

5 | It | looks / seems | to me as if … |

57.2 1 c 2 a 3 b 4 e 5 d

Over to you (sample answers)
- In my organization, people are free to express their feelings.
- People at every level are encouraged to express their feelings and opinions – the management is very interested in what they have to say.
- Even the opinions of new employees are highly valued.

58.1 1 e–f 2 g–j 3 a–d 4 k–n

58.2 1 d 2 a 3 f 4 e 5 c 6 b

58.3
1 That's ridiculous. We need to stay in the creative heart of London.
2 That's absurd. We would lose employees to our competitors if we cut salaries.
3 Of course not. Everyone in the company works hard.
4 I'm sorry, but that's out of the question. Some of the accommodation is really bad.
5 I'm afraid I can't agree with you there. People need to get away from their offices sometimes.
6 I don't really agree. Other advertising agencies are doing well, despite the economy.
7 I can't go along with you there. The agency is at its most creative right now.

Over to you (sample answers)
- People are encouraged to disagree – as long as they are polite to each other. Our boss thinks that disagreements can lead to interesting new ideas, and she thinks that forcing people to keep quiet makes potential problems worse.
- No, I'm happy to have arguments if they resolve problems.

59.1
A: If I can just stop you for a moment, you …
B: I understand what you're saying, but …
C: To go back to what I was just saying, there are …
A: Sorry to interrupt you, but …
C: Are you suggesting that …

59.2
agreement: yes, agree, come to / reach / find (an) agreement
disagreement: yes, disagree, have a disagreement
compromise: yes, compromise, come to / reach / find (a) compromise
consensus: yes, –, come to / reach / find (a) consensus

59.3 1 b 2 d 3 c 4 e 5 a

Over to you (sample answers)
In my organization, decisions are imposed from above. For example, recently we were told that the company was going to move its offices from the city centre to the suburbs, about 20 kilometres away. The announcement was made without any discussion or consultation with employees.

60.1 1 d 2 e 3 a 4 c 5 b

60.2
1 confident and relaxed look, speed that you speak at, visual aids
2 clear structure
3 No. It can sound formal and stiff.
4 Use phrases such as 'What would you think if …'. Encourage the audience to ask questions or get them to join in by looking friendly and smiling. Make eye contact and don't stay behind your desk. Show that you're enjoying giving your presentation.
5 Visit the venue beforehand. Avoid coffee before you speak. Keep visual aids simple.
6 Enthusing your audience.
7 '… if your presentation does not have a structure, your audience will create its own.' (para 2)

Over to you (sample answers)
- I'm in research and development, and I give a lot of demonstrations of the products we are developing. These can be to the company's employees or to customers.
- A good presenter is someone who knows their audience and is able to adjust what they say to the audience. Also, enthusiasm is good, but it is not enough. The presenter must know what they are talking about.

61.1 1 b 2 a 3 e 4 c 5 d

61.2
1 To begin with, *let's* look at the most basic product in our range.
2 Of course, you will certainly have lots of questions in relation *to* the product specifications of our basic model.
3 That's all *I have* time for on product specifications.
4 *Let's move on* to our mid-range model.
5 As this transparency *shows*, there are two key features I want to talk about in relation to our mid-range model.
6 I think that *covers* everything on our mid-range model.
7 Our top-of-the-range product is the third and *most* important model I want to talk about.

61.3
1 No. The presenter asks if the audience has any questions, which usually happens at the end of a presentation, and then goes on to discuss the topic of the presentation.
2 Yes. The presenter says he/she is going to sum up and gives his/her reasons.
3 No. The presenter says the presentation is finished and then says he/she will talk about something else.
4 Yes. The presenter gives his/her own opinions and says that there will naturally be other opinions.

Over to you (sample answers)
- My last presentation was about a new product my company was about to launch.
- I had prepared clearly structured ideas and visuals and I was also very confident and relaxed.
- My presentation had a very strong introduction that led to a good main part in a clear way, but the closing was slightly sudden and I'm not sure the audience understood my message.
- Next time, I would make sure my closing sums up the main idea of my presentation, so that people go away with a single, clear message in their minds.

62.1 1 d 2 c 3 a 4 b 5 f 6 e

62.2 1 c 2 a 3 f 4 i 5 e 6 b

Over to you (sample answers)
- My last presentation was about a new product my company was about to launch.
- I had prepared clearly structured ideas and visuals and I was also very confident and relaxed.
- My presentation had a very strong introduction that led to a good main part in a clear way, but the closing was slightly sudden and I'm not sure the audience understood my message.
- Next time, I would make sure my closing sums up the main idea of my presentation, so that people go away with a single, clear message in their minds.

63.1 1 b 2 h 3 d 4 c 5 f 6 g 7 a

63.2 1 c 2 a 3 e 4 d 5 b

63.3
1 bargaining ploy
2 bargaining power
3 bargaining process
4 collective bargaining / pay bargaining / wage bargaining

Business Vocabulary in Use Intermediate

5 bargaining chip / bargaining tool
6 bargainer

Over to you (sample answers)
- I sometimes have to negotiate with suppliers of equipment. I quite like this – it's interesting to see how we reach agreement on prices, quantities, etc. and to see how each side's requirements are met.
- A good negotiator is someone who can keep an objective view of the overall situation, while being sensitive to and aware of the priorities and goals of each side.

64.1 1 f   2 e   3 b   4 c   5 d   6 a

64.2 1 c   2 d   3 b   4 e   5 f   6 a

64.3 1 e   2 f   3 b   4 c   5 d   6 a

Over to you (sample answers)
- A business person visiting India should not be surprised if there is a lot of small talk before the beginning of the actual negotiation. People want to get to know the contacts that they are dealing with.
- Don't be surprised if questions can be quite personal – about your family, children, and so on.

65.1 1 b   2 c   3 d   4 f   5 e   6 a

65.2
1 If you offer more flexible payment conditions, we will be able to pay a higher price.
2 As long as you guarantee increased fuel economy, we could consider paying €25.5 million per unit.
3 On condition that you sign the agreement today, we will start delivering / to deliver the planes in July.
4 Supposing that you send us your personnel for training, we may be prepared to add special features to the planes that you order.
5 Provided (that) / Providing (that) you accept our conditions, we might agree to work with you in the future.

65.3
2 Unless you consider our particular requirements, we will end these discussions.
3 Unless you can deal with our order as a priority, we will cancel it.
4 Unless you are able to offer more environmentally friendly versions, we will go to see your competitor.
5 Unless you stop using unfair techniques, we will break off negotiations.

65.4 1 concessions   3 trade-off
         2 trading   4 concede

Over to you (sample answers)
- There are some negotiations where the two sides are unequal and win-win is difficult. For example, the owner of a house or flat who wants to rent it out in a recession may have to accept a much lower rent than the one they originally wanted.
- I needed to make concessions when I went to my boss to ask for a rise. I had to accept much less than I originally asked for!

66.1 1 true   5 true
         2 false   6 false
         3 true   7 false
         4 false

66.2 1 binding
         2 commercial
         3 binding / legally binding
         4 oral / verbal
         5 employment

66.3 1 a   2 f   3 e   4 g
         5 d   6 h   7 c   8 b

Over to you (sample answers)
- I would try to drive a hard bargain with a car salesman who has a lot of unsold cars in stock.
- I would try to resolve seemingly irreconcilable differences by allowing a cooling-off period, where the two sides would have time to think about their position and any concessions they might be willing to make.

Index

The numbers in the Index are **Unit** numbers, not page numbers.

abandon a market /əˈbændən ə ˌmɑːkɪt/ 20
absurd /əbˈsɜːd/ 58
academic qualifications /ækəˌdemɪk kwɒlɪfɪˈkeɪʃənz/ 51
accept /əkˈsept/ 3
accessible /əkˈsesəbl/ 44, 45
account /əˈkaʊnt/ 29, 31, 35
account balance /əˈkaʊnt ˌbælənts/ 35
accountancy (BrE) /əˈkaʊntəntsi/ 31
accountancy firm /əˈkaʊntəntsi ˌfɜːm/ 31
accountant /əˈkaʊntənt/ 31
accounting /əˈkaʊntɪŋ/ 31
accounting rules /əˈkaʊntɪŋ ruːlz/ 31
accounting standards /əˈkaʊntɪŋ ˌstændədz/ 31
accounts payable (AmE) /əˌkaʊnts ˈpeɪəbl/ 29
accounts receivable (AmE) /əˌkaʊnts rɪˈsiːvəbl/ 29
accurate record /ˌækjʊrət ˈrekɔːd/ 56
achievement /əˈtʃiːvmənt/ 53
acquire /əˈkwaɪə/ 34
acquire experience /əˌkwaɪər ɪkˈspɪərɪənts/ 4
acquisition /ˌækwɪˈzɪʃən/ 34
action point /ˈækʃən ˌpɔɪnt/ 56
address book /əˈdres bʊk/ 52
admin /ˈædmɪn/ 6
administration /ædˌmɪnɪˈstreɪʃən/ 6
administrative staff /ædˈmɪnɪstrətɪv ˌstɑːf/ 6
administrator /ədˈmɪnɪstreɪtə/ 33
advance /ədˈvɑːnts/ 39
advertise /ˈædvətaɪz/ 25
advertiser /ˈædvətaɪzə/ 25
advertising agency /ˈædvətaɪzɪŋ ˌeɪdʒəntsi/ 25
advertising campaign /ˈædvətaɪzɪŋ kæmˌpeɪn/ 25
aerospace /ˈeərəʊspeɪs/ 13
affirmative action (AmE) /əˌfɜːmətɪv ˈækʃən/ 8, 41
affirmative action program (AmE) /əˌfɜːmətɪv ˈækʃən ˌprəʊɡræm/ 41
agenda /əˈdʒendə/ 56

AGM (annual general meeting) (BrE) /ˌeɪdʒiːˈem/ 55
agree /əˈɡriː/ 58
agree about /əˈɡriː əˌbaʊt/ 59
agree on /əˈɡriː ɒn/ 59
agreement /əˈɡriːmənt/ 59
ahead of schedule /əhed əv ˈʃedjuːl/ 42
ailing /ˈeɪlɪŋ/ 33
All the best /ɔːl ðə ˈbest/ 52
alliance /əˈlaɪəns/ 34
allocate /ˈæləkeɪt/ 56
amortization /əˌmɔːtɪˈzeɪʃən/ 30
amortize /əˈmɔːtaɪz/ 30
annual /ˈænjuəl/ 31
annual general meeting (AGM) (BrE) /ˈænjuəl ˈdʒenərəl ˈmiːtɪŋ/ 55
annual meeting (AmE) /ˈænjuəl ˈmiːtɪŋ/ 55
annual report /ˌænjuəl rɪˈpɔːt/ 31
applicant /ˈæplɪkənt/ 3
application form /ˌæplɪˈkeɪʃən fɔːm/ 3
apply for /əˈplaɪ fɔː/ 3
apply for a personal loan /əˌplaɪ fər ə pɜːsənəl ˈləʊn/ 35
appoint /əˈpɔɪnt/ 3
apprentice /əˈprentɪs/ 54
apprenticeship /əˈprentɪsʃɪp/ 54
approachable /əˈprəʊtʃəbl/ 44, 45
arbitration /ˌɑːbɪˈtreɪʃən/ 66
arbitrator /ˈɑːbɪtreɪtə/ 66
area code /ˈeərɪə ˌkəʊd/ 47
arrange a meeting /əˈreɪndʒ ə miːtɪŋ/ 55
as long as /əz lɒŋ əz/ 65
as you will see /əz juː wɪl siː?/ 53
assembly line /əˈsembli laɪn/ 16
asset /ˈæset/ 12, 30
attach /əˈtætʃ/ 51, 52
attached /əˈtætʃt/ 52
attached CV /əˈtætʃt ˌsiːˈviː/ 53
attachment /əˈtætʃmənt/ 51, 52
attend a meeting /əˈtend ə miːtɪŋ/ 55
attitude to time /ˌætɪtjuːd tʊ: ˈtaɪm/ 64
auction site /ˈɔːkʃən saɪt/ 26
audit /ˈɔːdɪt/ 31
auditor /ˈɔːdɪtə/ 31
authoritarian /ˌɔːθɒrɪˈteərɪən/ 44
automobile (AmE) /ˈɔːtəməbiːl/ 13

available /əˈveɪləbl/ 49
axe (verb) /æks/ 39

background /ˈbækɡraʊnd/ 3
backhander (BrE) /ˌbækˈhændə/ 40
bad debt /bæd ˈdet/ 29
bad working environment /bæd ˈwɜːkɪŋ ɪnˌvaɪrənmənt/ 8
bail out /beɪl ˈaʊt/ 33
balance of payments /ˌbælənts əv ˈpeɪmənts/ 38
balance sheet /ˈbælənts ʃiːt/ 30
ban (verb) /bæn/ 40
bank /bæŋk/ 35
bank holiday /ˌbæŋk ˈhɒlɪdeɪ/ 46
bar (verb) /bɑː/ 40
bargain (noun) /ˈbɑːɡɪn/ 66
bargain (verb) /ˈbɑːɡɪn/ 63
bargainer /ˈbɑːɡɪnə/ 63
bargaining chip /ˈbɑːɡɪnɪŋ ˌtʃɪp/ 63
bargaining ploy /ˈbɑːɡɪnɪŋ plɔɪ/ 63
bargaining point /ˈbɑːɡɪnɪŋ pɔɪnt/ 63
bargaining position /ˈbɑːɡɪnɪŋ pəˌzɪʃən/ 64
bargaining power /ˈbɑːɡɪnɪŋ paʊə/ 63
bargaining process /ˈbɑːɡɪnɪŋ ˌprəʊses/ 63
bargaining tactic /ˈbɑːɡɪnɪŋ ˌtæktɪk/ 63
bargaining tool /ˈbɑːɡɪnɪŋ tuːl/ 63
barrier /ˈbærɪə/ 37
basic /ˈbeɪsɪk/ 23
basic salary /ˌbeɪsɪk ˈsæləri/ 5
bcc /ˌbiːsiːˈsiː/ 52
be in touch /ˌbiː ɪn ˈtʌtʃ/ 51
bear market /ˈbeə ˌmɑːkɪt/ 37
bearish /ˈbeərɪʃ/ 37
become stressed out /bɪkʌm ˌstrest ˈaʊt/ 43
behind schedule /bɪˌhaɪnd ˈʃedjuːl/ 42
belief /bɪˈliːf/ 45
benchmarking /ˈbentʃˌmɑːkɪŋ/ 18
benefit /ˈbenɪfɪt/ 21
benefits package /ˈbenəfɪts ˌpækɪdʒ/ 5
Best /best/ 52
best practice /ˌbest ˈpræktɪs/ 18
Best regards /best rɪˈɡɑːdz/ 52
Best wishes /best ˈwɪʃɪz/ 52

Business Vocabulary in Use Intermediate **161**

beta version /ˈbiːtə ˌvɜːʒən/ 14
bid /bɪd/ 26
big business /bɪg ˈbɪznɪs/ 11
bilingual /baɪˈlɪŋgwəl/ 53
billing /ˈbɪlɪŋ/ 29
binding /ˈbaɪndɪŋ/ 66
bleed red ink /bliːd ˌred ˈɪŋk/ 31
blog /blɒg/ 26
blue chip /ˈbluː tʃɪp/ 37
board /bɔːd/ 9
board meeting /ˈbɔːd miːtɪŋ/ 55
boardroom /ˈbɔːdrʊm/ 9
boardroom row /ˌbɔːdruːm ˈraʊ/ 5
body language /ˈbɒdi ˌlæŋgwɪdʒ/ 64
bond /bɒnd/ 32, 36
bonus /ˈbəʊnəs/ 5
bonus payment /ˈbəʊnəs ˌpeɪmənt/ 42
book value /ˈbʊk ˌvæljuː/ 30
booking (BrE) /ˈbʊkɪŋ/ 47
bookings line (BrE) /ˈbʊkɪŋz laɪn/ 47
book-keeper /ˈbʊkiːpə/ 31
boom /buːm/ 39
boom and bust /ˌbuːm ən ˈbʌst/ 39
boring /ˈbɔːrɪŋ/ 2
born leader /bɔːn ˈliːdə/ 44
borrower /ˈbɒrəʊə/ 32
borrowing /ˈbɒrəʊɪŋ/ 32
boss /bɒs/ 9
bottom line /ˌbɒtəm ˈlaɪn/ 31
bottom out /ˌbɒtəm ˈaʊt/ 39
bottom-end /ˌbɒtəmˈend/ 23
boundaries between work and private life /baʊndriz bɪtwiːn ˌwɜːk ən ˈpraɪvɪt laɪf/ 46
bourse /bɔːs/ 36
brainstorming /ˈbreɪnˌstɔːmɪŋ/ 55
branch /brɑːntʃ/ 35
brand /brænd/ 22, 30
brand awareness /brænd əˈweənəs/ 22
brand identity /brænd aɪˈdentɪti/ 22
brand image /brænd ˈɪmɪdʒ/ 22
brand manager /ˈbrænd ˌmænɪdʒə/ 22
brand name /ˈbrænd neɪm/ 15, 22
brand recognition /brænd rekəgˈnɪʃən/ 22
branded /ˈbrændɪd/ 22
branding /ˈbrændɪŋ/ 22
breach /briːtʃ/ 41
break down /ˌbreɪk ˈdaʊn/ 66
break even /ˌbreɪk ˈiːvən/ 28
breakdown /ˈbreɪk daʊn/ 43

breakthrough /ˈbreɪkθruː/ 15
bribe (noun) /braɪb/ 40
bribery /ˈbraɪbəri/ 40
bring forward a meeting /ˌbrɪŋ ˈfɔːwəd ə miːtɪŋ/ 55
broker /ˈbrəʊkə/ 36
budget for /ˈbʌdʒɪt fɔː/ 28
bug /bʌg/ 14
build confidence /bɪld ˈkɒnfɪdəns/ 54
build up /bɪld ˈʌp/ 33
building society /ˈbɪldɪŋ səˌsaɪəti/ 12, 35
bull market /ˈbʊl ˌmɑːkɪt/ 37
bullish /ˈbʊlɪʃ/ 37
bullish sentiment /ˈbʊlɪʃ ˌsentɪmənt/ 37
bully /ˈbʊli/ 8
bullying /ˈbʊliɪŋ/ 8
bureaucracy /bjʊəˈrɒkrəsi/ 11
bureaucratic /ˌbjʊərəˈkrætɪk/ 11, 44
burn out /ˈbɜːn aʊt/ 43
business /ˈbɪznɪs/ 11
business card /ˈbɪznɪs ˌkɑːd/ 51
business contact /ˈbɪznɪs ˌkɒntækt/ 51
business culture /ˈbɪznɪs ˌkʌltʃə/ 45
business empire /ˈbɪznɪs ˌempaɪə/ 10
business leader /ˈbɪznɪs liːdə/ 10
business year /ˌbɪznɪs ˈjɪə/ 31
businessman /ˈbɪznɪsmən/ 10
businessperson /ˈbɪznɪspɜːsən/ 10
business-to-business (B2B) /ˌbɪznɪstəˈbɪznɪs/ 26
business-to-consumer (B2C) /ˌbɪznɪstəkənˈsjuːmə/ 26
business-to-government (B2G) /ˌbɪznɪstəˈgʌvənmənt/ 26
businesswoman /ˈbɪznɪsˌwʊmən/ 10
busy /ˈbɪzi/ 48
buyer /ˈbaɪə/ 18, 19
buying manager /ˈbaɪɪŋ ˌmænɪdʒə/ 19

CAD/CAM /kædkæm/ 14, 16
calendar (AmE) /ˈkælɪndə/ 42
call (verb) /kɔːl/ 47
call back /kɔːl ˈbæk/ 48
call centre (BrE) /kɔːl ˈsentə/ 13, 24, 35, 47
call off a meeting /kɔːl ˈɒf ə miːtɪŋ/ 55

call up /kɔːl ˈʌp/ 14, 47
cancel a meeting /ˈkæntsəl ə miːtɪŋ/ 55
candidate /ˈkændɪdət/ 3
capacity /kəˈpæsɪti/ 16
capital /ˈkæpɪtəl/ 17, 32
capital market /ˌkæpɪtəl ˈmɑːkɪt/ 36
captains of industry /ˌkæptɪnz əv ˈɪndʌstri/ 10
car (BrE) /kɑː/ 13
carbon emissions /ˌkɑːbən əˈmɪʃənz/ 41
carbon footprint /ˌkɑːbən ˈfʊtprɪnt/ 41
carbon offset /ˌkɑːbən ˈɒfset/ 41
carbon-neutral /ˌkɑːbə nˈnjuːtrəl/ 41
career goal /kəˈrɪə gəʊl/ 53
career ladder /kəˈrɪə ˌlædə/ 7
career path /kəˈrɪə pɑːθ/ 7
cash cow /ˈkæʃ kaʊ/ 28
cash mountain /ˈkæʃ maʊntɪn/ 33
cash pile /ˈkæʃ paɪl/ 33
cashflow /ˈkæʃfləʊ/ 29
catalogue /ˈkætəlɒg/ 18
catering /ˈkeɪtərɪŋ/ 13
cc /siːˈsiː/ 52
cease trading /ˌsiːs ˈtreɪdɪŋ/ 33
cellphone (AmE) /ˈselfəʊn/ 47
CEO (chief executive officer) /ˌsiːiːˈəʊ/ 9
CFO (chief financial officer) /ˌsiːefˈəʊ/ 9
chain store /ˈtʃeɪn stɔː/ 24
chair (noun) /tʃeə/ 56
chair a meeting /ˈtʃeər ə miːtɪŋ/ 55
chairman /ˈtʃeəmən/ 9, 56
chairperson /ˈtʃeəpɜːsən/ 56
chairwoman /ˈtʃeəˌwʊmən/ 9, 56
challenging /ˈtʃælɪndʒɪŋ/ 43
change hands /ˌtʃeɪndʒ ˈhændz/ 37
charge (noun) /tʃɑːdʒ/ 30, 35
charge (verb) /tʃɑːdʒ/ 23
charisma /kəˈrɪzmə/ 44
charismatic /ˌkærɪzˈmætɪk/ 44
charity /ˈtʃærɪti/ 12
chase an invoice /ˌtʃeɪs ən ˈɪnvɔɪs/ 29
chat (noun) /tʃæt/ 55
cheap /tʃiːp/ 23
chief executive officer (CEO) /tʃiːf ɪgˌzekjʊtɪv ˈɒfɪsə/ 9
chief financial officer (CFO) /tʃiːf faɪˈnænʃəl ˌɒfɪsə/ 9

162   Business Vocabulary in Use Intermediate

chief operating officer /tʃiːf
 'ɒpəreɪtɪŋ ˌɒfɪsə/ 9
child labour /tʃaɪld 'leɪbə/ 41
Chinese walls /ˌtʃaɪniːz 'wɔːlz/ 40
churn out /'tʃɜːn aʊt/ 16
circulate /'sɜːkjʊleɪt/ 56
the City /ðə 'sɪti/ 36
clearly /'klɪəli/ 60
client /'klaɪənt/ 19
client base /'klaɪənt beɪs/ 19
clientele /ˌkliːɒn'tel/ 19
climate change /'klaɪmət
 tʃeɪndʒ/ 41
clinch a deal /ˌklɪntʃ ə 'diːl/ 66
clinical trial /'klɪnɪkəl traɪəl/ 14
clock in /klɒk 'ɪn/ 2
clock off /klɒk 'ɒf/ 2
clock on /klɒk 'ɒn/ 2
clock out /klɒk 'aʊt/ 2
close (noun) /kləʊz/ 37
close a deal /kləʊz ə 'diːl/ 66
close down /kləʊz 'daʊn/ 37
close up /kləʊz 'ʌp/ 37
co-creation /ˌkəʊkriː'eɪʃən/ 18
code of conduct /ˌkəʊd əv
 'kɒndʌkt/ 41
code of ethics /ˌkəʊd əv 'eθɪks/ 41
cold call /ˌkəʊld 'kɔːl/ 24
collaboration /kəˌlæbə'reɪʃən/ 18
collaborative site /kəˌlæbərətɪv
 'saɪt/ 26
collapse (noun) /kə'læps/ 37
collapse (verb) /kə'læps/ 33
collateral /kə'lætərəl/ 32
collective bargaining /kəˌlektɪv
 'bɑːgɪnɪŋ/ 63
collectivism /kə'lektɪvɪzəm/ 46
collectivist /kə'lektɪvɪst/ 46
come to (an) agreement /ˌkʌm tuː
 (ən) ə'griːmənt/ 59
command and control /kəˌmɑːnd
 ən kən'trəʊl/ 44
commerce /'kɒmɜːs/ 11
commercial (adj) /kə'mɜːʃəl/ 11
commercial paper /kəˌmɜːʃəl
 'peɪpə/ 36
commission /kə'mɪʃən/ 5, 26
commodities exchange
 /kəˌmɒdətiz ɪksˌtʃeɪndʒ/ 36
commodity /kə'mɒdəti/ 36
commute /kə'mjuːt/ 2
commuter /kə'mjuːtə/ 2
company /'kʌmpəni/ 11
company car /ˌkʌmpəni 'kɑː/ 5

company culture /ˌkʌmpəni
 'kʌltʃə/ 45
company doctor /ˌkʌmpəni
 'dɒktə/ 33
company hierarchy /ˌkʌmpəni
 'haɪərɑːki/ 7
company pension scheme
 /ˌkʌmpəni 'penʃən skiːm/ 35
compensation /ˌkɒmpen'seɪʃən/ 5
compensation package
 /ˌkɒmpen'seɪʃən ˌpækɪdʒ/ 5
compensation payment
 /ˌkɒmpen'seɪʃən ˌpeɪmənt/ 5
compete /kəm'piːt/ 20
competition /ˌkɒmpə'tɪʃən/ 20, 25
competitor /kəm'petɪtə/ 20
completion /kəm'pliːʃən/ 42
component /kəm'pəʊnənt/ 17
compromise /'kɒmprəmaɪz/ 59
computer hardware /kəmˌpjuːtə
 'hɑːdweə/ 13
computer software /kəmˌpjuːtə
 'sɒftweə/ 13
computer-aided design and
 manufacturing /kəmˌpjuːtəreɪdɪd
 dɪ'zaɪn ən mænjə'fæktʃərɪŋ/ 16
computer-assisted design
 and manufacturing
 /kəmˌpjuːtərəsɪstɪd dɪ'zaɪn
 ən mænjə'fæktʃərɪŋ/ 16
computer-literate
 /kəmˌpjuːtə'lɪtərət/ 4
concede /kən'siːd/ 65
concern /kən'sɜːn/ 11
concise /kən'saɪs/ 53
confident look /ˌkɒnfɪdənt 'lʊk/ 60
confidential /ˌkɒnfɪ'denʃəl/ 62
conglomerate /kən'glɒmərət/ 34
connection /kə'nekʃən/ 46
consensual /ˌkən'sensʊəl/ 44
consensus /kən'sentsəs/ 44, 59
consolidation /kənˌsɒlɪ'deɪʃən/ 34
construction /kən'strʌkʃən/ 13
consultation /ˌkɒnsʌl'teɪʃən/ 44
consumer /kən'sjuːmə/ 19
consumer durables /kənˌsjuːmə
 'djʊərəblz/ 22
consumer goods /kənˌsjuːmə
 'gʊdz/ 22
contact details /'kɒntækt
 ˌdiːteɪlz/ 51, 52, 53
contact information /'kɒntækt
 ɪnfəˌmeɪʃən/ 52
contract (noun) /'kɒntrækt/ 63, 66

contract dispute /'kɒntrækt
 dɪˌspjuːt/ 63
contractor /kən'træktə/ 7
contribution /ˌkɒntrɪ'bjuːʃən/ 35
convenience store /kən'viːniənts
 stɔː/ 24
conversational rules
 /kɒnvəˌseɪʃənəl 'ruːlz/ 64
cooling-off period /ˌkuːlɪŋ'ɒf
 ˌpɪəriəd/ 66
copy in on /ˈkɒpi ɪn ˌɒn/ 52
copyright /'kɒpiraɪt/ 15
copyright infringement /ˌkɒpiraɪt
 ɪn'frɪndʒmənt/ 15
cordless /'kɔːdləs/ 47
cordless phone /'kɔːdləs fəʊn/ 47
core activities /ˌkɔːr æk'tɪvɪtiz/ 34
corner a market /ˌkɔːnə ə 'mɑːkɪt/ 20
corporate /'kɔːpərət/ 11, 41
corporate culture /ˌkɔːpərət
 'kʌltʃə/ 11, 45
corporate social responsibility
 (CSR) /ˌkɔːpərət ˌsəʊʃəl
 rɪspɒnsɪ'bɪlɪti/ 41
corporation /ˌkɔːpər'eɪʃən/ 11, 12
corrupt (adj) /kə'rʌpt/ 40
corruption /kə'rʌpʃən/ 40
cost /kɒst/ 42
cost of goods sold /ˌkɒst əv gʊdz
 'səʊld/ 27
cost-effective /ˌkɒstɪ'fektɪv/ 16
costing /'kɒstɪŋ/ 27
costings /'kɒstɪŋz/ 27
costs /kɒsts/ 27
counterfeit /'kaʊntəfɪt/ 40
counterfeit notes /ˌkaʊntəfɪt
 'nəʊts/ 40
counterfeiting /'kaʊntəfɪtɪŋ/ 40
counter-offer /'kaʊntərˌɒfə/ 65
counter-proposal
 /'kaʊntəprə'pəʊzəl/ 65
country code /'kʌntri ˌkəʊd/ 47
courier /'kʊriə/ 51
course /kɔːs/ 4
cover /'kʌvə/ 61
cover a lot of ground /ˌkʌvər ə lɒt
 əv 'graʊnd/ 55
cover an item /ˌkʌvər ən 'aɪtəm/ 56
cover email /'kʌvə 'iːmeɪl/ 53
cover letter (AmE) /ˌkʌvə 'letə/ 3, 53
covering letter (BrE) /ˌkʌvərɪŋ
 'letə/ 3
craft industry /'krɑːft ˌɪndəstri/ 16
crash (noun) /kræʃ/ 37

Business Vocabulary in Use Intermediate **163**

creative accounting /kriːˌeɪtɪv əˈkaʊntɪŋ/ 31
creativity /ˌkriːɪˈtɪvɪti/ 53
credit card /ˈkredɪt kɑːd/ 35
credit card company /ˈkredɪt kɑːd ˌkʌmpəni/ 35
credit crunch /ˈkredɪt krʌntʃ/ 35
credit policy /ˈkredɪt ˌpɒlɪsi/ 29
creditor (BrE) /ˈkredɪtə/ 29, 33
cross-promotion /ˌkrɒsprəˈməʊʃən/ 25
CSR (corporate social responsibility) /ˌsiːesˈɑː/ 41
cultural difference /ˌkʌltʃərəl ˈdɪfərənts/ 45
cultural dimension /ˌkʌltʃərəl daɪˈmenʃən/ 45
culture /ˈkʌltʃə/ 45
currency /ˈkʌrənsi/ 36
current account (BrE) /ˈkʌrənt əˌkaʊnt/ 35
current assets /kʌrənt ˈæsets/ 30
current liabilities /kʌrənt laɪəˈbɪlɪtiz/ 30
curriculum vitae (CV) (BrE) /kəˌrɪkjʊləm ˈviːtaɪ/ 3, 53
custom-built /ˌkʌstəmˈbɪlt/ 18
customer /ˈkʌstəmə/ 19, 24
customer base /ˈkʌstəmə beɪs/ 19
customer needs /ˌkʌstəmə ˈniːdz/ 21
customer–supplier negotiations /ˈkʌstəmə səˈplaɪə nəˌɡəʊʃiˈeɪʃənz/ 63
cut (verb) /kʌt/ 39
cut out the middleman /kʌt aʊt ðə ˈmɪdlmæn/ 24
cutting edge /ˌkʌtɪŋ ˈedʒ/ 15
CV (curriculum vitae) (BrE) /ˌsiːˈviː/ 3, 53

dangerous machinery /ˌdeɪndʒərəs məˈʃiːnəri/ 8
date of birth (DoB) /ˌdeɪt əv ˈbɜːθ/ 54
day shift /ˈdeɪ ʃɪft/ 2
deadlock /ˈdedlɒk/ 66
deal (noun) /diːl/ 66
deal with /ˈdiːl wɪð/ 1
dealer /ˈdiːlə/ 24, 36
Dear /dɪər/ 53
Dear Sir or Madam /dɪər sɜːr ər ˈmædəm/ 53

debenture /dɪˈbentʃə/ 32
debt /det/ 32
debt burden /ˈdet ˌbɜːdən/ 33
debt crisis /ˈdet ˌkraɪsɪs/ 33
debt default /ˈdet dɪˌfɔːlt/ 33
debt repayment /ˌdet rɪˈpeɪmənt/ 33
debt rescheduling /ˌdet rɪˈʃedjʊlɪŋ/ 33
debt restructuring /ˌdet rɪˈstrʌktʃərɪŋ/ 33
debt servicing /ˈdet ˌsɜːvɪsɪŋ/ 33
debtor (BrE) /ˈdetə/ 29
decentralized /diːˈsentrəlaɪzd/ 44
decision making /dɪˈsɪʒən ˌmeɪkɪŋ/ 44, 45
decline (noun) /dɪˈklaɪn/ 37
defence (BrE) /dɪˈfens/ 13
deference /ˈdefərənts/ 45, 52
degree /dɪˈɡriː/ 4
delay /dɪˈleɪ/ 42
delayer /diːˈleɪə/ 7
delayering /diːˈleɪərɪŋ/ 45
delegate (verb) /ˈdelɪɡeɪt/ 44
delegation /ˌdelɪˈɡeɪʃən/ 44
delete /dɪˈliːt/ 48, 52
delicate negotiations /ˈdelɪkət nəˌɡəʊʃiˈeɪʃənz/ 63
deliver /dɪˈlɪvə/ 60
demand (noun) /dɪˈmɑːnd/ 37, 39, 43
demanding /dɪˈmɑːndɪŋ/ 2
demerge /dɪˈmɜːdʒ/ 34
demonstration /ˌdemənˈstreɪʃən/ 60
demote /dɪˈməʊt/ 7
demutualization /diːˌmjuːtʃʊəlaɪzeɪʃən/ 12
demutualize /diːˈmjuːtʃʊəlaɪz/ 12, 35
department meeting /dɪˌpɑːtmənt ˈmiːtɪŋ/ 55
department store /dɪˈpɑːtmənt stɔː/ 24
departmental meeting /diːpɑːtˌmentəl ˈmiːtɪŋ/ 55
deposit account /dɪˈpɒzɪt əˌkaʊnt/ 35
depreciate /dɪˈpriːʃieɪt/ 30
depreciation /dɪˌpriːʃiˈeɪʃən/ 30
depression /dɪˈpreʃən/ 39
derivative /dɪˈrɪvɪtɪv/ 36
design /dɪˈzaɪn/ 15, 21
design defect /dɪˈzaɪn ˌdiːfekt/ 14
design fault /dɪˈzaɪn ˌfɔːlt/ 14

designer /dɪˈzaɪnə/ 14, 15
develop /dɪˈveləp/ 15
develop a network /dɪˈveləp ə ˈnetwɜːk/ 54
developer /dɪˈveləpə/ 14, 15
development /dɪˈveləpmənt/ 15
diary (BrE) /ˈdaɪəri/ 42
dignity at work policy /ˌdɪɡnɪti ət ˈwɜːk ˌpɒləsi/ 8
digression /daɪˈɡreʃən/ 56
direct costs /ˌdaɪrekt ˈkɒsts/ 27
direct line /daɪrekt ˈlaɪn/ 48
direct mail /daɪrekt ˈmeɪl/ 24
direct marketing /daɪrekt ˈmɑːkɪtɪŋ/ 24
direct production costs /daɪrekt prəˈdʌkʃən ˌkɒsts/ 27
disagree /ˌdɪsəˈɡriː/ 59
discount (noun) /ˈdɪskaʊnt/ 23, 25, 29
discounter /ˈdɪskaʊntə/ 24
discounting /ˈdɪskaʊntɪŋ/ 23
discriminate against /dɪˈskrɪmɪneɪt əˌɡenst/ 8
discrimination /dɪˌskrɪmɪˈneɪʃən/ 41
diseconomies of scale /dɪsɪˌkɒnəmɪz əv ˈskeɪl/ 28
dismiss /dɪˈsmɪs/ 7
dispatch (verb) /dɪˈspætʃ/ 29
disposal /dɪˈspəʊzəl/ 34
distance /ˈdɪstənts/ 46
distant /ˈdɪstənt/ 44, 45
distraction /dɪˈstrækʃən/ 42
distribute /dɪˈstrɪbjuːt/ 21, 33
distributor /dɪˈstrɪbjʊtə/ 24
dive (verb) /daɪv/ 39
diversified /daɪˈvɜːsɪfaɪd/ 13
diversify into /daɪˈvɜːsɪfaɪ ɪntuː/ 34
divest /daɪˈvest/ 34
divestment /daɪˈvestmənt/ 34
dividend /ˈdɪvɪdend/ 32
DoB (date of birth) /ˌdiːəʊˈbiː/ 54
dominate a market /ˈdɒmɪneɪt ə ˌmɑːkɪt/ 20
donate /dəʊˈneɪt/ 12
donation /dəʊˈneɪʃən/ 12
don't hesitate /dəʊnt ˈhezɪteɪt/ 51
dot-com bust /ˈdɒtkɒm bʌst/ 26
downmarket (BrE) /daʊnˈmɑːkɪt/ 23
downscale (AmE) /ˈdaʊnskeɪl/ 23
downshifter /ˈdaʊnʃɪftə/ 43
downshifting /ˈdaʊnʃɪftɪŋ/ 43
downsize /ˈdaʊnsaɪz/ 7

downsizing /ˈdaʊnsaɪzɪŋ/ 7
downtime /ˈdaʊntaɪm/ 42
dress (verb) /dres/ 62
drive (noun) /draɪv/ 44
drive a company out of a market /ˈdraɪv ə ˌkʌmpəni aʊt əv ə ˌmɑːkɪt/ 20
dull /dʌl/ 2
dynamism /ˈdaɪnəmɪzəm/ 44

early retirement /ˌɜːli rɪˈtaɪəmənt/ 7
earn /ɜːn/ 5
earnings /ˈɜːnɪŋz/ 31, 33
ease /iːz/ 39
e-commerce /ˌiːˈkɒmɜːs/ 11, 26
economic /iːkəˈnɒmɪk/ 38
economic indicators /iːkəˌnɒmɪk ˈɪndɪkeɪtəz/ 38
economic output /iːkəˌnɒmɪk ˈaʊtpʊt/ 38
economic problems /iːkəˌnɒmɪk ˈprɒbləmz/ 38
economical /ˌiːkəˈnɒmɪkəl/ 38
economics /ˌiːkəˈnɒmɪks/ 38
economies of scale /ɪˌkɒnəmɪz əv ˈskeɪl/ 18, 28
economy /ɪˈkɒnəmi/ 13, 38
educational qualification /ˌedʒuˈkeɪʃənəl ˌkwɒlɪfɪˈkeɪʃən/ 53
effective /ɪˈfektɪv/ 14
efficiency /ɪˈfɪʃəntsi/ 7
efficient /ɪˈfɪʃənt/ 17
EGM (extraordinary general meeting) /ˌiːdʒiːˈem/ 55
electronics /ɪˌlekˈtrɒnɪks/ 13
eleventh-hour negotiations /ɪˈlevənθˌaʊə nəˌɡəʊʃiˈeɪʃənz/ 63
email /ˈiːmeɪl/ 51
email address /ˈiːmeɪl əˌdres/ 51, 52
embezzle /ɪmˈbezl/ 40
embezzlement /ɪmˈbezlmənt/ 40
emerging industry /ɪˌmɜːdʒɪŋ ˈɪndəstri/ 13
employ /ɪmˈplɔɪ/ 3
employee /ɪmˈplɔɪiː/ 6
employment agency /ɪmˈplɔɪmənt ˌeɪdʒəntsi/ 3
empowerment /ɪmˈpaʊəmənt/ 44
end-user /endˈjuːzə/ 19
energy /ˈenədʒi/ 44
enter a market /ˈentər ə ˌmɑːkɪt/ 20
enterprise /ˈentəpraɪz/ 11

enterprise culture /ˌentəpraɪz ˈkʌltʃə/ 11
enterprise economy /ˌentəpraɪz ɪˈkɒnəmi/ 11
enterprise zone /ˈentəpraɪz zəʊn/ 11
enthusiastic /ɪnˌθjuːziˈæstɪk/ 60
entrepreneur /ˌɒntrəprəˈnɜː/ 10
entrepreneurial /ˌɒntrəprəˈnɜːriəl/ 10
entry-level /ˈentriˌlevəl/ 23, 54
environmental issues /ɪnˌvaɪərənˈmentəl ˌɪʃuːz/ 41
e-procurement /ˌiːprəˈkjʊəmənt/ 26
equal opportunities (BrE) /ˌiːkwəl ˌɒpəˈtjuːnɪtiz/ 8
equity /ˈekwɪti/ 32
establish /ɪˈstæblɪʃ/ 10, 53
establishment /ɪˈstæblɪʃmənt/ 10
ethical /ˈeθɪkəl/ 41
ethical investing /ˌeθɪkəl ɪnˈvestɪŋ/ 41
ethnic minority /ˌeθnɪk maɪˈnɒrɪti/ 41
etiquette /ˈetɪket/ 51, 64
event /ɪˈvent/ 42
exaggeration /ɪɡˌzædʒəˈreɪʃən/ 53
examples and stories /ɪɡˈzɑːmpəlz ən ˈstɔːriz/ 60
exceptional loss /ɪkˌsepʃənəl ˈlɒs/ 31
exceptional profit /ɪkˌsepʃənəl ˈprɒfɪt/ 31
exciting /ɪkˈsaɪtɪŋ/ 2
exclusive /ɪkˈskluːsɪv/ 23
exec /ɪɡˈzek/ 9
executive /ɪɡˈzekjʊtɪv/ 9
expenditure /ɪkˈspendɪtʃə/ 28
expenses /ɪkˈspentsɪz/ 27
expensive /ɪkˈspentsɪv/ 23
experience (noun) /ɪkˈspɪəriənts/ 3, 53
experience curve /ɪkˈspɪəriənts kɜːv/ 28
exploit /ɪkˈsplɔɪt/ 41, 54
exploitation /ˌeksplɔɪˈteɪʃən/ 54
export (noun) /ˈekspɔːt/ 38
extension /ɪkˈstentʃən/ 47, 48
extraordinary general meeting (EGM) (BrE) /ˈɪkstrɔːdənəri ˈdʒenərəl ˈmiːtɪŋ/ 55
eye contact /ˈaɪ ˌkɒntækt/ 46

face the audience /ˌfeɪs ði ˈɔːdiənts/ 62

fair point /feə ˈpɔɪnt/ 62
fake (adj) /feɪk/ 15
fake (noun) /feɪk/ 40
fake (verb) /feɪk/ 40
fall (noun) /fɔːl/ 37
fallback position /ˈfɔːlbæk pəˌzɪʃən/ 64
familiar /fəˈmɪliə/ 45
family name /ˈfæməli ˌneɪm/ 51
fascinating /ˈfæsɪneɪtɪŋ/ 2
fast-moving consumer goods (FMCG) /fɑːstmuːvɪŋ kənˌsjuːmə ˈɡʊdz/ 22
fat cat /ˈfæt kæt/ 5
feature (noun) /ˈfiːtʃə/ 21
feel /fiːl/ 60
fend off /fend ˈɒf/ 34
field /fiːld/ 62
field trial /ˈfiːld ˌtraɪəl/ 14
fierce competition /ˈfɪəs kɒmpəˌtɪʃən/ 20
file for bankruptcy protection /ˌfaɪl fə ˈbæŋkrʌptsi prəˌtekʃən/ 33
finance (noun) /ˈfaɪnænts/ 38
finance (verb) /ˈfaɪnænts/ 17
finances /ˈfaɪnæntsɪz/ 38
financial /faɪˈnæntʃəl/ 38
financial centre (BrE) /faɪˌnænʃəl ˈsentə/ 36
financial crime /faɪˌnænʃəl ˈkraɪm/ 40
financial institution /faɪˌnænʃəl ˌɪnstɪˈtjuːʃən/ 35, 36
financial market /faɪˌnænʃəl ˈmɑːkɪt/ 36
financial problems /faɪˌnænʃəl ˈprɒbləmz/ 38
financial product /faɪˌnænʃəl ˈprɒdʌkt/ 35, 36, 54
financial reporting /faɪˌnænʃəl rɪˈpɔːtɪŋ/ 31
financial results /faɪˌnænʃəl rɪˈzʌlts/ 31
financial services /faɪˌnænʃəl ˈsɜːvɪsɪz/ 13, 54
financial year /faɪˌnænʃəl ˈjɪə/ 30, 31
find (an) agreement /ˌfaɪnd (ən) əˈɡriːmənt/ 59
fine (verb) /faɪn/ 40
finish on time /ˌfɪnɪʃ ɒn ˈtaɪm/ 56
finished goods /fɪnɪʃd ˈɡʊdz/ 17, 22
fire (verb) /faɪə/ 7
fire hazards /ˈfaɪə ˌhæzədz/ 8

Business Vocabulary in Use Intermediate

firm /fɜːm/ 11
first aid /ˌfɜːst ˈeɪd/ 8
first name /ˈfɜːst neɪm/ 51
first thing /ˌfɜːst ˈθɪŋ/ 48
first-half results /ˌfɜːsthɑːf rɪˈzʌlts/ 31
fiscal year /ˈfɪskəl ˌjɪə/ 31
fix a meeting /ˈfɪks ə miːtɪŋ/ 55
fixed assets /ˌfɪkst ˈæsets/ 30
fixed costs /ˌfɪkst kɒsts/ 27
flatter /ˈflætə/ 7
flexibility /ˌfleksɪˈbɪlɪti/ 7
flexitime (BrE) /ˈfleksitaɪm/ 2
flextime (AmE) /ˈflekstaɪm/ 2
flipchart /ˈflɪptʃɑːt/ 60
float /fləʊt/ 36
flotation /fləʊˈteɪʃən/ 36
FMCG (fast-moving consumer goods) /ˌefˈemˌsiːˈʤiː/ 22
focus group /ˈfəʊkəs gruːp/ 14
follow the etiquette /ˌfɒləʊ ði ˈetɪket/ 51
food processing /fuːd ˈprəʊsesɪŋ/ 13
foreign exchange /ˌfɒrɪn ɪksˈtʃeɪndʒ/ 36
forex /ˈfɒreks/ 36
forge /fɔːdʒ/ 40
forgery /ˈfɔːdʒəri/ 40
form of address /fɔːm əv əˈdres/ 45
formality /fɔːˈmæləti/ 52
forward /ˈfɔːwəd/ 52
found /faʊnd/ 10
founder /ˈfaʊndə/ 10
4G /fɔː dʒiː/ 47
the four Ps /ðə fɔː ˈpiːz/ 21
franchise /ˈfræntʃaɪz/ 24
franchisee /ˌfræntʃaɪˈziː/ 24
franchisor /ˈfræntʃaɪzə/ 24
fraud /frɔːd/ 40
fraud squad /ˈfrɔːd skwɒd/ 40
free enterprise /friː ˈentəpraɪz/ 11
free gift /friː ˈgɪft/ 25
the free market /ðə ˌfriː ˈmɑːkɪt/ 19
free sample /friː ˈsɑːmpəl/ 25
freelance (adj) /ˈfriːlɑːnts/ 12, 53
freelance (noun) /ˈfriːlɑːnts/ 7
freelancer /ˈfriːlɑːntsə/ 7
freephone number /ˈfriːfəʊn ˌnʌmbə/ 47
friendly bid /ˌfrendli ˈbɪd/ 34
fringe benefits /ˌfrɪndʒ ˈbenəfɪts/ 5
full-time job /ˌfʊltaɪm ˈdʒɒb/ 1
fundraising /ˈfʌndˌreɪzɪŋ/ 12
future-proof /ˈfjuːtʃəpruːf/ 15

futures contract /ˈfjuːtʃəz ˌkɒntrækt/ 36
fwd /ˈfɔːwəd/ 52

gain /geɪn/ 37
Gantt chart /ˈgænt tʃɑːt/ 42
GDP (gross domestic product) /ˌdʒiːdiːˈpiː/ 38
GDP per capita /dʒiːdiːˌpiː pɜː ˈkæpɪtə/ 38
gearing (BrE) /ˈgɪərɪŋ/ 32
generic product /dʒəˌnerɪk ˈprɒdʌkt/ 22
generics /dʒəˈnerɪks/ 22
gesture /ˈdʒestʃə/ 46, 62
get back in touch /get ˌbæk ɪn ˈtʌtʃ/ 50
get back to someone /get ˈbæk tə ˌsʌmwʌn/ 48, 51
get down to business /get ˌdaʊn tə ˈbɪznɪs/ 57
get off the point /ˌget ɒf ðə ˈpɔɪnt/ 56
get out of a market /get ˈaʊt əv ə ˌmɑːkɪt/ 20
get the ball rolling /get ðə ˌbɔːl ˈrəʊlɪŋ/ 57
give someone a bell (BrE) /ˌgɪv sʌmwʌn ə ˈbel/ 47
give someone a buzz (BrE) /ˌgɪv sʌmwʌn ə ˈbʌz/ 47
give someone a call (BrE) /ˌgɪv sʌmwʌn ə ˈkɔːl/ 47
give someone a ring (BrE) /ˌgɪv sʌmwʌn ə ˈrɪŋ/ 7
give someone the sack (BrE) /ˌgɪv sʌmwʌn ðə ˈsæk/ 47
glass ceiling /glɑːs ˈsiːlɪŋ/ 8
global warming /ˌgləʊbəl ˈwɔːmɪŋ/ 41
glut /glʌt/ 16
GNP (gross national product) /ˌdʒiːenˈpiː/ 38
go along with /gəʊ əˈlɒŋ wɪð/ 58
go bankrupt /gəʊ ˈbæŋkrʌpt/ 12, 33
go bust /gəʊ ˈbʌst/ 33
go into administration /gəʊ ɪntuː ədˈmɪnɪstreɪʃən/ 33
go into liquidation /ˌgəʊ ɪntə lɪkwɪˈdeɪʃən/ 33
go into receivership /ˌgəʊ ɪntə rɪˈsiːvəʃɪp/ 33

go into the red /ˌgəʊ ɪntə ðə ˈred/ 35
go out of business /ˌgəʊ aʊt əv ˈbɪznɪs/ 33
go overdrawn /ˌgəʊ ə ʊvəˈdrɔːn/ 35
go public /gəʊ ˈpʌblɪk/ 36
going concern /ˌgəʊɪŋ kənˈsɜːn/ 30
good organizer /ˌgʊd ˈɔːgənaɪzə/ 56
good timekeeper /ˌgʊd ˈtaɪmkiːpə/ 56
good with /ˈgʊd wɪð/ 4
goodbye /gʊdˈbaɪ/ 46
goods /gʊdz/ 16, 17, 22
goodwill /gʊdˈwɪl/ 30
go-slow /ˌgəʊˈsləʊ/ 6
government-owned company /ˌgʌvənməntˌəʊnd ˈkʌmpəni/ 11
graduate (noun) /ˈgrædʒuwət/ 4, 54
graduate (verb) /ˈgrædʒueɪt/ 54
graduate leadership programme /ˈgrædʒuət ˈliːdəʃɪp ˈprəʊgræm/ 54
graduate from /ˈgrædʒuweɪt frəm/ 4
green issues /ˈgriːn ɪʃuːz/ 41
greeting /ˈgriːtɪŋ/ 46, 48
gross domestic product (GDP) /grəʊs dəˌmestɪk ˈprɒdʌkt/ 38
gross margin /ˌgrəʊs ˈmɑːdʒɪn/ 27
gross national product (GNP) /grəʊs ˌnæʃnəl ˈprɒdʌkt/ 38
gross profit /grəʊs ˈprɒfɪt/ 31
group discussion /ˌgruːp dɪsˈkʌʃən/ 3
grow /grəʊ/ 10, 38
growth /grəʊθ/ 38
growth industry /ˈgrəʊθ ɪndəstri/ 13
growth rate /ˈgrəʊθ reɪt/ 38

halve /hɑːv/ 18
hand in your notice /ˌhænd ɪn jə ˈnəʊtɪs/ 7
handle (verb) /ˈhændl/ 17
handout /ˈhændaʊt/ 60
hand-made /ˈhændmeɪd/ 16
hands-on experience /ˌhændˈzɒn ɪkˈspɪəriəns/ 54
hang up /hæŋ ˈʌp/ 48
harass /ˈhærəs/ 8
hard /hɑːd/ 2
harmony /ˈhɑːməni/ 46
have a disagreement about /hæv ə dɪsəˈgriːmənt əbaʊt/ 59

hazardous substances /ˌhæzədəs ˈsʌbstəntsɪz/ 8
head (noun) /hed/ 9
head (up) /hed (ʌp)/ 9
head office /ˌhed ˈɒfɪs/ 6
headhunt /ˈhedhʌnt/ 3
headhunter /ˈhedˌhʌntə/ 3
headhunting /ˈhedˌhʌntɪŋ/ 3
headquarters (HQ) /hedˈkwɔːtəz/ 6
health and safety inspector /ˌhelθ ən ˈseɪfti ɪnˌspektə/ 8
health and safety issue /ˌhelθ ən ˈseɪfti ˌɪʃuː/ 8
health plan /ˈhelθ plæn/ 5
healthcare /ˈhelθkeə/ 13
heating and air-conditioning /ˈhiːtɪŋ ən ˌeəkənˈdɪʃənɪŋ/ 8
heavy industry /ˌhevi ˈɪndəstri/ 13
helpline /ˈhelplaɪn/ 47
hierarchical /ˌhaɪəˈrɑːkɪkəl/ 45
hierarchy /ˈhaɪərɑːki/ 51, 64
high finance /haɪ ˈfaɪnænts/ 38
high power–distance culture /haɪ paʊəˈdɪstənts ˌkʌltʃə/ 45
high turnover /haɪ ˈtɜːnəʊvə/ 37
high-end /haɪˈend/ 23
highest bidder /haɪɪst bɪdə/ 26
highly geared /ˌhaɪli ˈɡɪəd/ 32
highly leveraged /ˌhaɪli liːvərɪdʒd/ 32
highly skilled /ˌhaɪli ˈskɪld/ 4
high-priced /haɪˈpraɪst/ 23
hire (verb) /haɪə/ 3
hi-tech /ˌhaɪˈtek/ 15
hold (verb) /həʊld/ 48
hold shares /həʊld ˈʃeəz/ 32
holding /ˈhəʊldɪŋ/ 41
holding in a company /ˈhəʊldɪŋ ɪn ə ˌkʌmpəni/ 34
holiday (BrE) /ˈhɒlɪdeɪ/ 46
horse-trading /ˈhɔːstreɪdɪŋ/ 65
host /həʊst/ 26
hostile bid /ˌhɒstaɪl ˈbɪd/ 34
hotline /ˈhɒtlaɪn/ 47
household goods /ˌhaʊshəʊld ˈɡʊdz/ 13
HQ (headquarters) /ˌeɪtʃˈkjuː/ 6
HR (human resources) /ˌeɪtʃˈɑː/ 6
HRD (human resources department) /ˌeɪtʃɑːˈdiː/ 6
HRM (human resource management) /ˌeɪtʃɑːˈem/ 6

human resource management (HRM) /ˌhjuːmən rɪˈzɔːs ˌmænɪdʒmənt/ 6
human resources (HR) /ˌhjuːmən rɪˈzɔːsɪz/ 6
human resources department (HRD) /ˌhjuːmən rɪˈzɔːsɪz dɪˌpɑːtmənt/ 6
human rights /ˌhjuːmən ˈraɪts/ 41
humour (noun) (BrE) /ˈhjuːmə/ 46
hypermarket /ˈhaɪpəˌmɑːkɪt/ 24

I am available /aɪ əm əˈveɪləbəl/ 53
I am writing with reference /aɪ əm ˈraɪtɪŋ wɪð ˈrefərəns/ 53
I look forward to hearing from you /aɪ lʊk ˈfɔːwəd tʊ ˈhɪərɪŋ frəm juː/ 53
I would now like to relocate /aɪ wəd naʊ laɪk tʊ ˌriːləʊˈkeɪt/ 53
idea /aɪˈdɪə/ 60
identity theft /aɪˈdentɪti θeft/ 40
illegal downloading /ɪˌliːɡəl ˈdaʊnləʊdɪŋ/ 15
impasse /ˈɪmpæs/ 66
import (noun) /ˈɪmpɔːt/ 38
impose /ɪmˈpəʊz/ 44, 66
in charge of /ɪn ˈtʃɑːdʒ əv/ 1
in stock /ɪn ˈstɒk/ 17
in the black /ˌɪn ðə ˈblæk/ 31, 35
in the red /ˌɪn ðə ˈred/ 31
inbox /ˈɪnbɒks/ 52
Inc (incorporated) /ɪŋk/ 12
income statement (AmE) /ˈɪŋkʌm ˌsteɪtmənt/ 31
incorporated (Inc) /ɪnˈkɔːpəreɪtɪd/ 12
indebtedness /ɪnˈdetɪdnəs/ 32
independent entity /ˌɪndɪˈpendənt ˈentɪti/ 46
index /ˈɪndeks/ 37
indirect costs /ˌɪndaɪrekt kɒsts/ 27
individual savings account (ISA) (BrE) /ɪndɪˌvɪdjuːəl ˈseɪvɪŋz əkaʊnt/ 35
individualism /ˌɪndɪˈvɪdjuəlɪzəm/ 46
individualist /ˌɪndɪˈvɪdjuəlɪst/ 46
industrial /ɪnˈdʌstriəl/ 13
industrial accident /ɪnˌdʌstriəl ˈæksɪdənt/ 8
industrial action /ɪnˌdʌstriəl ˈækʃən/ 6
industrial buyer /ɪnˌdʌstriəl ˈbaɪə/ 19

industrial goods /ɪnˌdʌstriəl ˈɡʊdz/ 22
industrial robot /ɪnˌdʌstriəl ˈrəʊbɒt/ 16
industrial scale /ɪnˌdʌstriəl ˈskeɪl/ 14
industrial secret /ɪnˌdʌstriəl ˈsiːkrət/ 18
industrialize /ɪnˈdʌstriəlaɪz/ 13
industry /ˈɪndəstri/ 13
inflation /ɪnˈfleɪʃən/ 38
inflation rate /ɪnˈfleɪʃən reɪt/ 38
inflationary /ɪnˈfleɪʃənəri/ 38
information line /ɪnfəˈmeɪʃən ˌlaɪn/ 47
in-house /ˌɪnˈhaʊs/ 7, 17
in-house training /ɪnˌhaʊs ˈtreɪnɪŋ/ 4
initial public offering /ɪˌnɪʃəl ˌpʌblɪk ˈɒfərɪŋ/ 36
initiative /ɪˈnɪʃətɪv/ 44
innovate /ˈɪnəʊveɪt/ 15
innovation /ˌɪnəʊˈveɪʃən/ 15
innovative /ˈɪnɒvətɪv/ 15
innovator /ˈɪnəʊveɪtə/ 15
in-person survey /ɪnˌpɜːsən ˈsɜːveɪ/ 14
input (noun) /ˈɪnpʊt/ 17
insider dealing /ɪnˌsaɪdə ˈdiːlɪŋ/ 40
insider trading /ɪnˌsaɪdə ˈtreɪdɪŋ/ 40
insolvent /ɪnˈsɒlvənt/ 33
insurance policy /ɪnˈʃɔːrənts ˌpɒlɪsi/ 35
intangible assets /ɪnˌtændʒɪbl ˈæsets/ 30
intellectual property /ɪntəlektjuəl ˈprɒpəti/ 15
intense competition /ɪnˈtens kɒmpəˌtɪʃən/ 20
intense negotiations /ɪnˌtens nəˌɡəʊʃiˈeɪʃənz/ 63
intensive negotiations /ɪnˌtensɪv nəˌɡəʊʃiˈeɪʃənz/ 63
interest /ˈɪntrəst/ 32, 35, 53
interest in a company /ˈɪntrəst ɪn ə ˌkʌmpəni/ 34
interest rate /ˈɪntrəst reɪt/ 35
interested in /ˈɪntrəstɪd ˌɪn/ 60
interesting /ˈɪntrəstɪŋ/ 60
intern /ɪnˈtɜːn/ 54
internet banking /ˌɪntənet ˈbæŋkɪŋ/ 35
internet seller /ˈɪntənet ˌselə/ 26
internet selling /ˈɪntənet ˌselɪŋ/ 26

interrupt /ˌɪntəˈrʌpt/ 59
interruption /ˌɪntəˈrʌpʃən/ 42
interview (noun) /ˈɪntəvjuː/ 3
invent /ɪnˈvent/ 15
invention /ɪnˈventʃən/ 15
inventor /ɪnˈventə/ 15
investment /ɪnˈvestmənt/ 32
investment company
 /ɪnˈvestmənt ˌkʌmpəni/ 35
investor /ɪnˈvestə/ 32, 36
invoice (noun) /ˈɪnvɔɪs/ 29
invoicing /ˈɪnvɔɪsɪŋ/ 29
involved /ɪnˈvɒlvd/ 60
ISA (individual savings account)
 (BrE) /ˈaɪsə/ 35
issue (verb) /ˈɪʃuː/ 32, 36

job insecurity /ˌdʒɒb ɪnsɪˈkjʊərɪti/ 7
job offer /ˈdʒɒb ˌɒfə/ 3
job placement /dʒɒbˈpleɪsmənt/ 54
job-specific skills /dʒɒb spəˈsɪfɪk
 skɪlz/ 54
job title /ˈdʒɒb ˌtaɪtl/ 51
(the) jobless /ðə ˈdʒɒbləs/ 38
jobs website /ˌdʒɒbz ˈwebsaɪt/ 3
join /dʒɔɪn/ 3
joint account /ˌdʒɔɪnt əˈkaʊnt/ 35
joint venture /ˌdʒɔɪnt ˈventʃə/ 34
jump (verb) /dʒʌmp/ 39
junk mail /ˈdʒʌŋk meɪl/ 24
just-in-time /ˌdʒʌstɪnˈtaɪm/ 17

keep things moving /ˌkiːp θɪŋz
 ˈmuːvɪŋ/ 55
key account /kiː əˈkaʊnt/ 29
key area /ˌkiː ˈeəriə/ 61
key player /kiː ˈpleɪə/ 20
keyword /ˈkiːwɜːd/ 53
kick off /kɪk ˈɒf/ 57
kickback /ˈkɪkbæk/ 40
knowledge /ˈnɒlɪdʒ/ 17

labor union (AmE) /ˈleɪbə ˌjuːniən/ 6
laboratory /ləˈbɒrətri/ 14, 15
labour (BrE) /ˈleɪbə/ 6, 17
labour costs /ˈleɪbə kɒsts/ 6
labour dispute /ˈleɪbə dɪsˌpjuːt/ 6, 63
labour leader /ˈleɪbə liːdə/ 6
labour relations /ˌleɪbə rɪˈleɪʃənz/ 6
labour shortage /ˈleɪbə ˌʃɔːtɪdʒ/ 6, 38
labour unrest /ˌleɪbər ʌnˈrest/ 6
labour-intensive
 /ˌleɪbərɪnˈtensɪv/ 16
landline /ˈlændlaɪn/ 47

laptop /ˈlæptɒp/ 60
last but not least /ˌlɑːst bʌt nɒt
 ˈliːst/ 61
last name /ˈlɑːst neɪm/ 51
last-minute negotiations
 /ˌlɑːstˈmɪnɪt nəˌgəʊʃiˈeɪʃənz/ 63
latecomer /ˈleɪtˌkʌmə/ 56
lay off /leɪ ˈɒf/ 7
layout /ˈleɪaʊt/ 53
lead time /ˈliːd taɪm/ 42
leadership /ˈliːdəʃɪp/ 44
leadership skills /ˈliːdəʃɪp
 skɪlz/ 10, 44, 53
leading edge /ˌliːdɪŋ ˈedʒ/ 15
lean manufacturing /liːn
 mænjʊˈfæktʃərɪŋ/ 17
lean production /liːn
 prəˈdʌkʃən/ 17
leaner /ˈliːnə/ 7
leap (verb) /liːp/ 39
learn from /lɜːn frəm/ 54
learning culture /ˈlɜːnɪŋ ˌkʌltʃə/ 45
learning curve /ˈlɜːnɪŋ kɜːv/ 18, 28
leave a market /ˈliːv ə ˌmɑːkɪt/ 20
leave a message /ˌliːv ə ˈmesɪdʒ/ 49
leave a voice message /liːv ə ˈvɔɪs
 ˌmesɪdʒ/ 47
(legally-)binding
 /(ˌliːgəli)ˈbaɪndɪŋ/ 66
leisure /ˈleʒə/ 13
lender /ˈlendə/ 32
lending /ˈlendɪŋ/ 32
level /ˈlevəl/ 37
level off /ˌlevəl ˈɒf/ 39
level out /ˌlevəl ˈaʊt/ 39
leverage /ˈliːvərɪdʒ/ 32
liabilities /ˌlaɪəˈbɪlɪtiz/ 30
life insurance /ˈlaɪf ɪnˌʃɔːrəns/ 35
life insurance company /laɪf
 ɪnˈʃɔːrəns ˌkʌmpəni/ 12
lifestyle /ˈlaɪfstaɪl/ 43
light industry /laɪt ˈɪndəstri/ 13
limited company (Ltd) /ˌlɪmɪtɪd
 ˈkʌmpəni/ 12
limited liability /ˌlɪmɪtɪd
 laɪəˈbɪlɪti/ 12
limited liability partnership (LLP)
 /ˌlɪmɪtɪd laɪəbɪlɪti ˈpɑːtnəʃɪp/ 12
line /laɪn/ 47
list /lɪst/ 36
list price /ˈlɪst praɪs/ 23
LLP (limited liability partnership)
 /ˌelelˈpiː/ 12
loan capital /ˈləʊn ˌkæpɪtəl/ 32

the long tail /ðə ˌlɒŋ ˈteɪl/ 18
long-hours culture /lɒŋˈaʊəz
 ˌkʌltʃə/ 45
long-term liabilities /ˌlɒŋtɜːm
 ˌlaɪəˈbɪlɪtiz/ 30
loss-leader /ˈlɒsliːdə/ 23, 28
loss-making /ˈlɒsˌmeɪkɪŋ/ 28
loud enough /ˌlaʊd ɪˈnʌf/ 60
low (noun) /ləʊ/ 37
low power–distance culture /ləʊ
 paʊəˈdɪstənts ˌkʌltʃə/ 45
low pricing /ləʊ ˈpraɪsɪŋ/ 23
low response rate /ləʊ rɪˈspɒns
 reɪt/ 14
low-end /ˈləʊend/ 23
low-key /ˌləʊˈkiː/ 20
low-priced /ləʊˈpraɪst/ 23
low-tech /ˌləʊˈtek/ 15
loyalty /ˈlɔɪəlti/ 46
loyalty card /ˈlɔɪəlti kɑːd/ 25
Ltd (limited company) /ˈlɪmɪtɪd/ 12
lunch break /ˈlʌntʃ breɪk/ 46

macho culture /ˈmætʃəʊ ˌkʌltʃə/ 45
magnate /ˈmægnət/ 10
mail survey /ˈmeɪl sɜːveɪ/ 14
mailing /ˈmeɪlɪŋ/ 24
mailshot /ˈmeɪlʃɒt/ 24
majority holding /məˌdʒɒrɪti
 ˈhəʊldɪŋ/ 34
majority interest /məˌdʒɒrɪti
 ˈɪntrəst/ 34
majority stake /məˌdʒɒrɪti ˈsteɪk/ 34
make (noun) /meɪk/ 22
make (verb) /meɪk/ 16
make a concession /ˌmeɪk ə
 kənˈseʃən/ 65
make a loss /meɪk ə ˈlɒs/ 28, 31
make a profit /meɪk ə ˈprɒfɪt/ 28, 31
make acquisitions /meɪk
 ækwɪˈzɪʃənz/ 33
make an application /ˌmeɪk ən
 æplɪˈkeɪʃən/ 3
make redundant /ˌmeɪk
 rɪˈdʌndənt/ 7
make up time /ˌmeɪk ʌp ˈtaɪm/ 42
make your point /ˌmeɪk jɔː
 ˈpɔɪnt/ 56
maker /ˈmeɪkə/ 16
mall /mɔːl/ 24
manage /ˈmænɪdʒ/ 1
management /ˈmænɪdʒmənt/ 6
management development
 /ˌmænɪdʒmənt dɪˈveləpmənt/ 4

management layer /ˌmænɪdʒmənt 'leɪə/ 45
management style /'mænɪdʒmənt ˌstaɪl/ 44
mannerism /'mænərɪzəm/ 62
manufacture /ˌmænjʊ'fæktʃə/ 16
manufacturer /ˌmænjʊ'fæktʃərə/ 16
manufacturing /ˌmænjʊ'fæktʃərɪŋ/ 16
manufacturing factory /ˌmænjʊfæktʃərɪŋ 'fæktəri/ 16
manufacturing industry /mænjʊ'fæktʃərɪŋ ˌɪndəstri/ 13
manufacturing operation /mænjʊ'fæktʃərɪŋ ɒpəˌreɪʃən/ 17
manufacturing plant /ˌmænjʊ'fæktʃərɪŋ plɑːnt/ 16
manufacturing sector /mænjʊ'fæktʃərɪŋ ˌsektə/ 13
manufacturing works /ˌmænjʊ'fæktʃərɪŋ wɜːks/ 16
marker /'mɑːkə/ 60
market /'mɑːkɪt/ 19, 20, 21
market abuse /ˌmɑːkɪt ə'bjuːs/ 40
market capitalization /ˌmɑːkɪt kæpɪtəlaɪ'zeɪʃən/ 37
market economy /ˌmɑːkɪt ɪ'kɒnəmi/ 19
market forces /ˌmɑːkɪt 'fɔːsɪz/ 19
market growth /ˌmɑːkɪt 'grəʊθ/ 20
market leader /ˌmɑːkɪt 'liːdə/ 20
market orientation /ˌmɑːkɪt ɔːrɪen'teɪʃən/ 21
market pressures /ˌmɑːkɪt 'preʃəz/ 19
market price /ˌmɑːkɪt 'praɪs/ 19
market reforms /ˌmɑːkɪt rɪ'fɔːmz/ 19
market research /ˌmɑːkɪt rɪ'sɜːtʃ/ 14
market rigging /ˌmɑːkɪt rɪgɪŋ/ 40
market segment /ˌmɑːkɪt 'segmənt/ 20
market segmentation /ˌmɑːkɪt segmən'teɪʃən/ 20
market share /ˌmɑːkɪt 'ʃeə/ 20
market-driven /'mɑːkɪtˌdrɪvən/ 21
marketeer /ˌmɑːkɪ'tɪə/ 21
marketer /'mɑːkɪtə/ 21
marketing /'mɑːkɪtɪŋ/ 21
marketing concept /'mɑːkɪtɪŋ ˌkɒnsept/ 21
marketing department /'mɑːkɪtɪŋ dɪˌpɑːtmənt/ 21

marketing mix /'mɑːkɪtɪŋ ˌmɪks/ 21
marketing plan /'mɑːkɪtɪŋ ˌplæn/ 21
market-led /ˌmɑːkɪt'led/ 21
market-oriented /ˌmɑːkɪt'ɔːrɪəntɪd/ 21
market-place /'mɑːkɪtpleɪs/ 19
mark-up /'mɑːkʌp/ 27
mass collaboration /ˌmæs kəˌlæbə'reɪʃən/ 18
mass customization /ˌmæs ˌkʌstəmaɪ'zeɪʃən/ 18
mass market /mæs 'mɑːkɪt/ 23
mass production /ˌmæs prə'dʌkʃən/ 18
matters arising /ˌmætəz ə'raɪzɪŋ/ 56
MBA (Master of Business Administration) /ˌembiː'eɪ/ 4
meals and entertaining /ˌmiːlz 'ənd entə'teɪnɪŋ/ 46
media /'miːdiə/ 13
mediator /'miːdieɪtə/ 66
mediation /ˌmiːdieɪʃən/ 66
medium (noun) /'miːdiəm/ 25
meeting with a customer /ˌmiːtɪŋ wɪð ə 'kʌstəmə/ 55
meeting with suppliers /ˌmiːtɪŋ wɪð sə'plaɪəz/ 55
member /'membə/ 12
membership of professional organizations /'membəʃɪp əv prə'feʃənəl ɔːgənaɪ'zeɪʃənz/ 51
menial /'miːniəl/ 54
merge /mɜːdʒ/ 34
merger /'mɜːdʒə/ 34
merger negotiations /ˌmɜːdʒə nəˌgəʊʃi'eɪʃənz/ 63
methodical /mə'θɒdɪkəl/ 4
microphone /'maɪkrəfəʊn/ 47
middle initial /ˌmɪdl ɪ'nɪʃəl/ 51
middleman /'mɪdlmæn/ 24
mid-priced /ˌmɪd'praɪst/ 23
mid-range /ˌmɪd'reɪndʒ/ 23
minimum wage /ˌmɪnɪməm 'weɪdʒ/ 5
minority holding /maɪˌnɒrɪti 'həʊldɪŋ/ 34
minority interest /maɪˌnɒrɪti 'ɪntrəst/ 34
minority stake /maɪˌnɒrɪti 'steɪk/ 34
minute-taker /'mɪnɪtˌteɪkə/ 56
miss a meeting /ˌmɪs ə 'miːtɪŋ/ 55

mistaken /mɪ'steɪkən/ 58
mobile Internet /ˌməʊbaɪl 'ɪntənet/ 47
mobile phone (BrE) /ˌməʊbaɪl 'fəʊn/ 47
model (noun) /'mɒdəl/ 18, 22, 23
moderator /'mɒdəreɪtə/ 14
mogul /'məʊgəl/ 10
money laundering /'mʌni ˌlɔːndərɪŋ/ 40
money spinner /'mʌni ˌspɪnə/ 28
monopolize a market /mə'nɒpəlaɪz ə ˌmɑːkɪt/ 20
moral issues /'mɒrəl ɪʃuːz/ 41
mortgage /'mɔːgɪdʒ/ 35
motivated /'məʊtɪveɪtɪd/ 4
move downmarket /muːv daʊn'mɑːkɪt/ 23
move on /muːv 'ɒn/ 61
move on to the next point /muːv ɒn tə ðə ˌnekst 'pɔɪnt/ 56
move upmarket /muːv ʌp'mɑːkɪt/ 23
multinational (noun) /ˌmʌlti'næʃənəl/ 11
mutual (noun) /'mjuːtʃuəl/ 12
mutual advantage /ˌmjuːtʃuəl əd'vɑːntɪdʒ/ 63

narrow (verb) /'nærəʊ/ 38
nationalized /'næʃənəlaɪzd/ 11
nationalized company /ˌnæʃənəlaɪzd 'kʌmpəni/ 11
needs /niːdz/ 18
needs and objectives /ˌniːdz ənd əb'ʤektɪvz/ 64
negative equity /ˌnegətɪv 'ekwɪti/ 35
negative growth /ˌnegətɪv 'grəʊθ/ 39
negotiate /nəˌgəʊʃi'eɪt/ 63
negotiating style /nə'gəʊʃieɪtɪŋ ˌstaɪl/ 64
negotiating team /nə'gəʊʃieɪtɪŋ ˌtiːm/ 64
negotiations /nəˌgəʊʃi'eɪʃənz/ 63
negotiator /nəˌgəʊʃi'eɪtə/ 63
net margin /ˌnet 'mɑːdʒɪn/ 27
net profit /net 'prɒfɪt/ 31
neutral ground /ˌnjuːtrəl 'graʊnd/ 64
niche /niːʃ/ 23
night shift /'naɪt ʃɪft/ 2
nine-to-five /naɪntə'faɪv/ 2

Business Vocabulary in Use Intermediate   169

non-core assets /ˌnɒnkɔː ˈæsets/ 34
non-executive director /nɒnɪɡˌzekjʊtɪv daɪˈrektə/ 9
non-profit organization (BrE) /nɒnˈprɒfɪt ɔːɡənaɪˌzeɪʃən/ 12
note /nəʊt/ 42
not-for-profit organization (AmE) /nɒtfəˈprɒfɪt ɔːɡənaɪˌzeɪʃən/ 12
number /ˈnʌmbə/ 47
numerate /ˈnjuːmərət/ 4

objective /əbˈdʒektɪv/ 57
observation /ˌɒbzəˈveɪʃən/ 14
obsolete /ˌɒbsəˈliːt/ 15
obviously /ˈɒbviəsli/ 57
of course /əv ˈkɔːs/ 57
offer (noun) /ˈɒfə/ 65
offer (verb) /ˈɒfə/ 3, 7
office /ˈɒfɪs/ 6
office worker /ˈɒfɪs wɜːkə/ 2
0800 number /əʊeɪt ˈhʌndrəd ˌnʌmbə/ 47
on condition that /ɒn kənˈdɪʃən ðət/ 65
on schedule /ɒn ˈʃedjuːl/ 42
on your own ground /ɒn jɔː əʊn ˈɡraʊnd/ 64
1-800 number /wʌn eɪt ˈhʌndrəd ˌnʌmbə/ 47
online banking /ɒnlaɪn ˈbæŋkɪŋ/ 26
online brokerage /ˌɒnlaɪn ˈbrəʊkərɪdʒ/ 26
online dating /ˌɒnlaɪn ˈdeɪtɪŋ/ 26
online fundraising /ˌɒnlaɪn ˈfʌndreɪzɪŋ/ 26
online gambling /ˌɒnlaɪn ˈɡæmblɪŋ/ 26
online gaming /ˌɒnlaɪn ˈɡeɪmɪŋ/ 26
online selling /ˈɒnlaɪn selɪŋ/ 26
online survey /ˌɒnlaɪn ˈsɜːveɪ/ 14
online travel /ˌɒnlaɪn ˈtrævəl/ 26
open /ˈəʊpən/ 37
open the discussion /ˌəʊpən ðə dɪˈskʌʃən/ 57
open-plan office /ˌəʊpənˈplæn ˌɒfɪs/ 6
operating expenses /ˌɒpəreɪtɪŋ ɪkˈspentsɪz/ 27
options contract /ˈɒpʃənz ˌkɒntrækt/ 36
order (verb) /ˈɔːdə/ 29
organize /ˈɔːɡənaɪz/ 60
organized /ˈɔːɡənaɪzd/ 4
out of work /aʊt əv ˈwɜːk/ 1, 38

outplacement /ˈaʊtpleɪsmənt/ 7
output /ˈaʊtpʊt/ 16
outside supplier /ˌaʊtsaɪd səˈplaɪə/ 17
outsource /ˈaʊtsɔːs/ 7
outsourcing /ˈaʊtˌsɔːsɪŋ/ 17
over budget /ˌəʊvə ˈbʌdʒɪt/ 28
overdraft /ˈəʊvədrɑːft/ 35
overdraft facility /ˈəʊvədrɑːft fəˌsɪlɪti/ 35
overhead costs /ˈəʊvəhed ˌkɒsts/ 27
overheads /ˈəʊvəhedz/ 27
overlap (verb) /ˌəʊvəˈlæp/ 42
overleveraged /ˌəʊvəˈliːvərɪdʒd/ 32
overproduction /ˌəʊvəprəˈdʌkʃən/ 16
overspend /ˌəʊvəˈspend/ 28
oversubscribed /ˌəʊvəsəbˈskraɪbd/ 36
overtime /ˈəʊvətaɪm/ 2, 5
overtime ban /ˈəʊvətaɪm bæn/ 6
overwhelmed /ˌəʊvəˈwelmd/ 43
overwork /ˌəʊvəˈwɜːk/ 43
own-brand product (BrE) /ˌəʊnˌbrænd ˈprɒdʌkt/ 22
own-label product (AmE) /ˌəʊnˌleɪbəl ˈprɒdʌkt/ 22

packaging /ˈpækɪdʒɪŋ/ 21
paid internship /peɪd ˈɪntɜːnʃɪp/ 54
panic selling /ˈpænɪk ˌselɪŋ/ 37
paper qualifications /ˈpeɪpə ˌkwɒlɪfɪˈkeɪʃənz/ 4
parent company /ˈpeərənt ˌkʌmpəni/ 34
part /pɑːt/ 17
part-time study /ˌpɑːtˈtaɪm ˈstʌdi/ 54
partner /ˈpɑːtnə/ 12, 17
partnership /ˈpɑːtnəʃɪp/ 12, 17
passive smoking /ˌpæsɪv ˈsməʊkɪŋ/ 8
patent /ˈpeɪtənt/ 15
pay and conditions /peɪ ən kənˈdɪʃənz/ 5
pay bargaining /peɪ ˈbɑːɡɪnɪŋ/ 63
pay off /peɪ ˈɒf/ 35
pay out /peɪ ˈaʊt/ 35
payables (AmE) /ˈpeɪəblz/ 29
payment terms /ˈpeɪmənt tɜːmz/ 29
payphone /ˈpeɪfəʊn/ 47
payroll /ˈpeɪrəʊl/ 6
peak /piːk/ 39

peer collaboration /pɪə kəˌlæbəˈreɪʃən/ 18
penalty /ˈpenəlti/ 42
penetrate a market /ˈpenɪtreɪt ə ˌmɑːkɪt/ 20
pension /ˈpenʃən/ 5
pension fund /ˈpenʃən fʌnd/ 35
perfectionism /pəˈfekʃənɪzəm/ 42
performance /pəˈfɔːməns/ 5, 18
performance review /pəˈfɔːməns rɪˌvjuː/ 7
performance-related bonus /pəˌfɔːməns rɪleɪtɪd ˈbəʊnəs/ 5
perk /pɜːk/ 5
permanent job /ˌpɜːmənənt ˈdʒɒb/ 1
personal assets /ˌpɜːsənəl ˈæsets/ 12
personal interview /ˌpɜːsənəl ˈɪntəvjuː/ 14
personal organizer /ˌpɜːsənəl ˈɔːɡənaɪzə/ 42
personnel /ˌpɜːsənˈel/ 6
personnel department /pɜːsənˈel dɪˌpɑːtmənt/ 6
pharmaceutical /fɑːməˈsjuːtɪkəl/ 13
phase /feɪz/ 42
phone /fəʊn/ 46, 47
phone number /ˈfəʊn ˌnʌmbə/ 51
phonecard /ˈfəʊnkɑːd/ 47
physical contact /ˌfɪzɪkl ˈkɒntækt/ 46, 64
pick up /pɪk ˈʌp/ 48
piracy /ˈpaɪrəsi/ 15
place /pleɪs/ 21
place an order /ˌpleɪs ən ˈɔːdə/ 29
plan /plæn/ 21
plastic /ˈplæstɪk/ 35
PLC (public limited company) /ˌpiːelˈsiː/ 12
plummet /ˈplʌmɪt/ 39
point (noun) /pɔɪnt/ 37
poison pill /ˈpɔɪzən ˌpɪl/ 34
pool /puːl/ 14
position (noun) /pəˈzɪʃən/ 3, 53
positive attitude /ˌpɒzətɪv ˈætɪtjuːd/ 60
positive discrimination /ˌpɒzətɪv dɪskrɪmɪˈneɪʃən/ 8
post (noun) /pəʊst/ 3
postal address /ˈpəʊstəl əˌdres/ 51
postpone a meeting /pəʊstˈpəʊn ə ˈmiːtɪŋ/ 55

Business Vocabulary in Use Intermediate

power–distance /ˌpaʊəˈdɪstənts/ 45
predator /ˈpredətə/ 34
premium (adj) /ˈpriːmiəm/ 23
present (noun) /ˈprezənt/ 46
presenteeism /ˌprezənˈtiːɪzm/ 46
presenter /prɪˈzentə/ 60
president (AmE) /ˈprezɪdənt/ 9
press conference /ˈpres
 ˌkɒnfərənts/ 60
pressure /ˈpreʃə/ 43
pre-tax loss /ˌpriːtæks ˈlɒs/ 31
pre-tax profit /ˌpriːtæks ˈprɒfɪt/ 31
prey /preɪ/ 34
price /praɪs/ 21
price boom /ˈpraɪs buːm/ 23
price controls /ˈpraɪs
 kənˌtrəʊlz/ 23
price cut /ˈpraɪs kʌt/ 23
price fixing /ˈpraɪs fɪksɪŋ/ 40
price hike /ˈpraɪs haɪk/ 23
price tag /ˈpraɪs tæg/ 23
price war /ˈpraɪs wɔː/ 23
principal /ˈprɪnsəpəl/ 32
prioritize /praɪˈɒrɪtaɪz/ 42
priority /praɪˈɒrɪti/ 42
prison /ˈprɪzən/ 40
private enterprise /ˌpraɪvət
 ˈentəpraɪz/ 11
private pension /ˌpraɪvət
 ˈpenʃən/ 35
privatization
 /ˌpraɪvətaɪˈzeɪʃən/ 11
privatize /ˈpraɪvətaɪz/ 11
prize /praɪz/ 25
proactive /ˌprəʊˈæktɪv/ 4
probe (verb) /prəʊb/ 65
produce /ˈprɒdjuːs/ 16
producer /prəˈdjuːsə/ 16
product /ˈprɒdʌkt/ 16
product catalogue (BrE) /ˈprɒdʌkt
 ˌkætəlɒg/ 22
product category /ˌprɒdʌkt
 ˈkætəgəri/ 22
product endorsement /ˈprɒdʌkt
 ɪnˌdɔːsmənt/ 25
product launch /ˈprɒdʌkt
 ˌlɔːntʃ/ 14, 60
product lifecycle /ˌprɒdʌkt
 ˈlaɪfsaɪkəl/ 22
product line /ˌprɒdʌkt ˈlaɪn/ 22
product mix /ˌprɒdʌkt ˈmɪks/ 22
product placement /ˌprɒdʌkt
 ˈpleɪsmənt/ 22, 25

product portfolio /ˌprɒdʌkt
 ˌpɔːtˈfəʊliəʊ/ 22
product positioning /ˌprɒdʌkt
 pəˈzɪʃənɪŋ/ 22
product range /ˌprɒdʌkt ˈreɪndʒ/ 22
production /prəˈdʌkʃən/ 16
production line /prəˈdʌkʃən
 laɪn/ 16, 18
productive /prəˈdʌktɪv/ 55
productivity /ˌprɒdʌkˈtɪvɪti/ 16
professional /prəˈfeʃənəl/ 41
professional guidelines
 /prəˌfeʃənəl ˈgaɪdlaɪnz/ 41
professional qualification
 /prəˈfeʃənəlˌkwɒlɪfɪˈkeɪʃən/ 53
professional skills /prəˈfeʃənəl
 skɪlz/ 54
profit (noun) /ˈprɒfɪt/ 7
profit and loss account (BrE)
 /ˌprɒfɪt ən ˈlɒs əkaʊnt/ 31
profit margin /ˈprɒfɪt ˌmɑːdʒɪn/ 27
profitable /ˈprɒfɪtəbl/ 28
profit-making /ˈprɒfɪtˌmeɪkɪŋ/ 28
project (noun) /ˈprɒdʒekt/ 42
project management /ˌprɒdʒekt
 ˈmænɪdʒmənt/ 42
project meeting /ˌprɒdʒekt
 ˈmiːtɪŋ/ 55
projector /prəˈdʒektə/ 60
promote /prəˈməʊt/ 21
promotion /prəˈməʊʃən/ 7, 21, 25
property (BrE) /ˈprɒpəti/ 13
proposal /prəˈpəʊzəl/ 65
proprietary /prəˈpraɪətri/ 15
prosumer /prəʊˈsjuːmə/ 18
prototype /ˈprəʊtətaɪp/ 14
protracted negotiations
 /prəˌtræktɪd nəˌgəʊʃiˈeɪʃənz/ 63
provide /prəˈvaɪd/ 16
provided that /prəˈvaɪdɪd ðət/ 65
provider /prəˈvaɪdə/ 16
providing that /prəˈvaɪdɪŋ ðət/ 65
provision /prəˈvɪʒən/ 16
psychometric test /saɪkəˌmetrɪk
 ˈtest/ 3
public holiday /ˌpʌblɪk
 ˈhɒlɪdeɪ/ 46
public limited company (PLC)
 /ˌpʌblɪk ˌlɪmɪtɪd ˈkʌmpəni/ 12
public telephone /ˌpʌblɪk
 ˈtelɪfəʊn/ 47
punctuality /ˌpʌŋktjuˈælɪti/ 46
purchaser /ˈpɜːtʃəsə/ 19

purchasing manager /ˈpɜːtʃəsɪŋ
 ˌmænɪdʒə/ 19
purpose /ˈpɜːpəs/ 57
put back /pʊt ˈbæk/ 50
put off /pʊt ˈɒf/ 50
put through /pʊt ˈθruː/ 48
put up money /ˌpʊt ʌp ˈmʌni/ 32

qualifications
 /ˌkwɒlɪfɪˈkeɪʃənz/ 3, 4
qualify /ˈkwɒlɪfaɪ/ 4
quality /ˈkwɒləti/ 42
quality of life /ˌkwɒləti əv ˈlaɪf/ 43
quality time /ˈkwɒləti taɪm/ 43
quarter /ˈkwɔːtə/ 31
questioner /ˈkwestʃənə/ 62

R&D (research and development)
 /ˌɑːrənˈdiː/ 15
racial discrimination /ˌreɪʃəl
 dɪskrɪmɪˈneɪʃən/ 8
racism /ˈreɪsɪzəm/ 8
racist /ˈreɪsɪst/ 8
racket /ˈrækɪt/ 40
racketeer /ˌrækəˈtɪə/ 40
raise capital /reɪz ˈkæpɪtəl/ 32, 36
rally /ˈræli/ 37
ramble (verb) /ˈræmbl/ 55
range of tasks /reɪndʒ əv tɑːsks/ 54
rapport /ræˈpɔː/ 60
rat race /ˈræt reɪs/ 43
raw material /ˌrɔː
 məˈtɪəriəl/ 17, 22
reach (an) agreement /ˌriːtʃ (ən)
 əˈgriːmənt/ 59
reach break-even point /ˌriːtʃ
 breɪkˈiːvən pɔɪnt/ 28
real estate (AmE) /ˈriːl ɪˌsteɪt/ 13
realistic plan /rɪəˌlɪstɪk ˈplæn/ 42
rebalancing /riːˈbæləntsɪŋ/ 43
recall (verb) /rɪˈkɔːl/ 14
receivables (AmE) /rɪˈsiːvəblz/ 29
receiver /rɪˈsiːvə/ 33
recession /rɪˈseʃən/ 39
recommended retail price
 /rekəˌmendɪd ˈriːteɪl praɪs/ 23
record high /ˈrekɔːd haɪ/ 37
recover /rɪˈkʌvə/ 33
recruit /rɪˈkruːt/ 3
recruiter /rɪˈkruːtə/ 3
recruitment /rɪˈkruːtmənt/ 3
recruitment agency
 /rɪˈkruːtmənt ˌeɪdʒəntsi/ 3
red ink /red ˈɪŋk/ 31

referee /ˌrefəˈriː/ 3
reference /ˈrefərənts/ 3
refocus /ˌriːˈfəʊkəs/ 34
Regards /rɪˈgɑːdz/ 52
regulate /ˈregjʊleɪt/ 40
related to /rɪˈleɪtɪd tʊ/ 61
relationship building /rɪˈleɪʃənʃɪp ˌbɪldɪŋ/ 64
relaxed look /rɪˌlækst ˈlʊk/ 60
release (verb) /rɪˈliːs/ 14, 15, 51
relocate /ˌriːləʊˈkeɪt/ 53
remain standing /rɪˌmeɪn ˈstændɪŋ/ 62
remote /rɪˈməʊt/ 44, 45
remote control /rɪˈməʊt kənˈtrəʊl/ 60
remuneration /rɪˌmjuːnərˈeɪʃən/ 5
remuneration package /rɪˌmjuːnərˈeɪʃən ˌpækɪdʒ/ 5
repetitive /rɪˈpetətɪv/ 2
repetitive strain injury (RSI) /rɪˌpetətɪv ˈstreɪn ˌɪndʒəri/ 8
replacement part /rɪˈpleɪsmənt ˌpɑːt/ 17
reply (noun) /rɪˈplaɪ/ 52
reply to all /rɪˌplaɪ tʊ ˈɔːl/ 52
report /rɪˈpɔːt/ 31
report results /rɪˌpɔːt rɪˈzʌlts/ 31
requirements /rɪˈkwaɪəmənts/ 18
rescue /ˈreskjuː/ 33
research and development (R&D) /rɪˌsɜːtʃ ən dɪˈveləpmənt/ 15
research centre (BrE) /rɪˌsɜːtʃ ˈsentə/ 15
researcher /rɪˈsɜːtʃə/ 14
reseller /ˈriːselə/ 24
reservation /ˌrezəˈveɪʃən/ 47
reservations line /rezəˈveɪʃənz ˌlaɪn/ 47
reserves /rɪˈzɜːvz/ 33
resign /rɪˈzaɪn/ 7
resolution /ˌrezəluːʃən/ 66
resolve /rɪˈzɒlv/ 56
respect /rɪˈspekt/ 62
responsibility /rɪˌspɒntsɪˈbɪlɪti/ 1
responsible for /rɪˈspɒntsɪbl fɔː/ 1
restructure /ˌriːˈstrʌktʃə/ 7, 34
restructuring /ˌriːˈstrʌktʃərɪŋ/ 7
results /rɪˈzʌlts/ 31
résumé (AmE) /ˈrezjuːmeɪ/ 3
retail /ˈriːteɪl/ 13
retail outlet /ˈriːteɪl ˌaʊtlet/ 24
retained earnings /rɪˌteɪnd ˈɜːnɪŋz/ 33

retire /rɪˈtaɪə/ 7
retirement /rɪˈtaɪəmənt/ 7, 35
revenue /ˈrevənjuː/ 27
rewarding /rɪˈwɔːdɪŋ/ 43
ridiculous /rɪˈdɪkjʊləs/ 58
right now /raɪt ˈnaʊ/ 49
ring (up) (BrE) /rɪŋ (ʌp)/ 47
rival (noun) /ˈraɪvəl/ 20
role of silence /ˌrəʊl əv ˈsaɪlənts/ 46
roles and responsibilities /ˌrəʊlz ən rɪˌspɒntsɪˈbɪlɪtɪz/ 64
rollout /ˈrəʊlaʊt/ 14
routine (adj) /ruːˈtiːn/ 2
royalties /ˈrɔɪəltɪz/ 15
RSI (repetitive strain injury) /ˌɑːresˈaɪ/ 8
rules of conversation /ˌruːlz əv kɒnvəˈseɪʃən/ 46
run /rʌn/ 1
run a meeting /ˌrʌn ə ˈmiːtɪŋ/ 55
run in parallel /rʌn ɪn ˈpærəlel/ 42
run out of time /rʌn aʊt əv ˈtaɪm/ 59

sack (BrE) /sæk/ 7
safe (adj) /seɪf/ 14
salary /ˈsæləri/ 5
(the) sales /ðə seɪlz/ 27
sales area /ˈseɪlz ˌeəriə/ 25
sales culture /ˈseɪlz ˌkʌltʃə/ 45
sales department /ˈseɪlz dɪˌpɑːtmənt/ 27
sales director /ˈseɪlz daɪˌrektə/ 27
sales figures /ˈseɪlz ˌfɪgəz/ 27
sales force /ˈseɪlz fɔːs/ 25
sales forecast /ˈseɪlz ˌfɔːkɑːst/ 27
sales growth /ˈseɪlz grəʊθ/ 27
sales manager /ˈseɪlz ˌmænɪdʒə/ 25
sales meeting /ˈseɪlz miːtɪŋ/ 27
sales outlet /ˈseɪlz ˌaʊtlet/ 24
sales team /ˈseɪlz tiːm/ 27
sales territory /ˈseɪlz ˌterətəri/ 25
sales volume /ˈseɪlz ˌvɒljuːm/ 27
salesman /ˈseɪlzmən/ 25
salesperson /ˈseɪlzpɜːsən/ 25
saleswoman /ˈseɪlzwʊmən/ 25
sample /ˈsɑːmpl/ 14
satisfying /ˈsætɪsfaɪɪŋ/ 2
saver /ˈseɪvə/ 35
savings account /ˈseɪvɪŋz əˌkaʊnt/ 35
scam /skæm/ 40
schedule (noun) /ˈʃedjuːl/ 42
scope /skəʊp/ 62
screen /skriːn/ 60

second-half results /ˌsekəndhɑːf rɪˈzʌlts/ 31
securities /sɪˈkjʊərɪtɪz/ 36
securities house /sɪˈkjʊərɪtɪz haʊs/ 36
security /sɪˈkjʊərɪti/ 32
selection process /sɪˈlekʃən ˌprəʊses/ 3
self-starter /self'stɑːtə/ 4
self-driven /self'drɪvən/ 4
self-employed /ˌselfɪmˈplɔɪd/ 11, 12
self-motivated /ˌself'məʊtɪveɪtɪd/ 4
sell your holding /ˌsel jɔː ˈhəʊldɪŋ/ 41
sell your stake /ˌsel jɔː ˈsteɪk/ 41
seller /ˈselə/ 19
selling price /ˈselɪŋ praɪs/ 27
sell-off /ˈselɒf/ 37
seminar /ˈsemɪnɑː/ 60
semi-skilled /ˌsemiˈskɪld/ 4
senior /ˈsiːniə/ 7
senior executive /ˌsiːniər ɪɡˈzekjʊtɪv/ 9
service /ˈsɜːvɪs/ 13, 16
service industry /ˈsɜːvɪs ˌɪndəstri/ 13
service sector /ˈsɜːvɪs ˌsektə/ 13
set up a meeting /set ˈʌp ə ˈmiːtɪŋ/ 55
settle a dispute /ˌsetl ə dɪsˈpjuːt/ 63
settle an invoice /ˌsetl ən ˈɪnvɔɪs/ 29
settlement /ˌsetlmənt/ 66
severance package /ˈsevərənts ˌpækɪdʒ/ 5
severance payment /ˈsevərənts ˌpeɪmənt/ 5
sex discrimination /ˌseks dɪskrɪmɪˈneɪʃən/ 8
sexual harassment /ˌsekʃəl ˈhærəsmənt/ 8
share /ʃeə/ 32, 36
share capital /ˈʃeə ˌkæpɪtəl/ 32
share options (BrE) /ˈʃeər ˌɒpʃənz/ 5
share price /ˈʃeə praɪs/ 37
shareholder /ˈʃeəˌhəʊldə/ 12, 32
shift /ʃɪft/ 2
ship (verb) /ʃɪp/ 29
shop (noun) (BrE) /ʃɒp/ 24
shopping centre /ˈʃɒpɪŋ ˌsentə/ 24
shopping mall /ˈʃɒpɪŋ ˌmɔːl/ 24
shortage /ˈʃɔːtɪdʒ/ 16
shortlist (verb) /ˈʃɔːtlɪst/ 3
show off /ʃəʊ ˈɒf/ 55

sick /sɪk/ 33
simultaneous /ˌsɪməl'teɪnɪəs/ 42
site /saɪt/ 6
situation /ˌsɪtju'eɪʃən/ 3
situations vacant /ˌsɪtju'eɪʃənz ˌveɪˌkənt/ 3
skill /skɪl/ 4, 53
skilled /skɪld/ 4
Skype /skaɪp/ 47
skyrocket (verb) /'skaɪˌrɒkɪt/ 39
slash (verb) /slæʃ/ 39
sleaze /sliːz/ 40
slide /slaɪd/ 60
slump (noun) /slʌmp/ 39
small investor /smɔːl ɪn'vestə/ 35
small or medium enterprise (SME) / smɔːl ɔː ˌmiːdiəm 'entəpraɪz/ 11
smartphone /smɑːtfəʊn/ 47
SME (small or medium enterprise) /ˌesem'iː/ 11
smiling /'smaɪlɪŋ/ 62
snowed under /snəʊd 'ʌndə/ 50
soar /sɔː/ 39
social issues /'səʊʃəl ˌɪʃuːz/ 41
social marketing /ˌsəʊʃəl 'mɑːkɪtɪŋ/ 21
social networking /ˌsəʊʃəl 'netwɜːkɪŋ/ 26
socially responsible /ˌsəʊʃəli rɪ'spɒnsɪbl/ 41
sole owner /ˌsəʊl 'əʊnə/ 12
sole proprietor /ˌsəʊl prə'praɪətə/ 12
sole trader (BrE) /ˌsəʊl 'treɪdə/ 12
sophisticated /sə'fɪstɪkeɪtɪd/ 23
spare part /ˌspeə 'pɑːt/ 17
special offer /ˌspeʃəl 'ɒfə/ 25
specifications /ˌspesɪfɪ'keɪʃənz/ 18
speculator /'spekjʊleɪtə/ 36
speed /ˌspiːd/ 60
spend /spend/ 28
sponsor (verb) /'spɒnsə/ 25
sponsorship /'spɒnsəʃɪp/ 25
the Square Mile /ðə skweə 'maɪl/ 36
stable (adj) /'steɪbl/ 39
staff /stɑːf/ 6
stage /steɪdʒ/ 42
stagflation /stæg'fleɪʃən/ 39
stagnation /stæg'neɪʃən/ 39
stake /steɪk/ 32, 41
stake in a company /'steɪk ɪn ə ˌkʌmpəni/ 34
stakeholder /'steɪkˌhəʊldə/ 41
stalemate /'steɪlmeɪt/ 66

standard (adj) /'stændəd/ 18
standardization /ˌstændədaɪ'zeɪʃən/ 18
standpoint /'stændpɔɪnt/ 57
start-ups /'stɑːtʌps/ 10
state pension /ˌsteɪt 'penʃən/ 35
state-of-the-art /ˌsteɪtəvðiː'ɑːt/ 15
state-owned /'steɪtˌəʊnd/ 11
steady (adj) /'stedi/ 39
steel /stiːl/ 13
step /step/ 42
stereotype /'steriətaɪp/ 45
stick to the point /ˌstɪk tə ðə 'pɔɪnt/ 55
stiff competition /'stɪf kɒmpəˌtɪʃən/ 20
stimulating /'stɪmjʊleɪtɪŋ/ 2, 43, 53
stock /stɒk/ 32, 36
stock market /'stɒk ˌmɑːkɪt/ 36
stock options (AmE) /'stɒk ɒpʃənz/ 5
stocks (BrE) /stɒks/ 17, 36
stoppage /'stɒpɪdʒ/ 6
store (noun) (AmE) /stɔː/ 24
store (verb) /stɔː/ 17
store brand (AmE) /'stɔː ˌbrænd/ 22
street vendor /'striːt vendə/ 19
stress (noun) /stres/ 43
stressful /'stresfəl/ 43
stress-induced /'stresɪndjuːst/ 43
stretched /stretʃt/ 43
strike (noun) /straɪk/ 6
structure /'strʌktʃə/ 60
subcontracting /'sʌbkənˌtræktɪŋ/ 17
subject /'sʌbdʒekt/ 52
subordinate /sə'bɔːdɪnət/ 44
subsidiary /səb'sɪdiəri/ 34
sum up /sʌm 'ʌp/ 59
supermarket /'suːpəˌmɑːkɪt/ 24
supplier /sə'plaɪə/ 17
support staff /sə'pɔːt stɑːf/ 6
supposing that /sə'pəʊzɪŋ ðət/ 65
surge /sɜːdʒ/ 39
surname /'sɜːneɪm/ 51
surplus /'sɜːpləs/ 16
survey /'sɜːveɪ/ 14
sweatshop labour /ˌswetʃɒp 'leɪbə/ 41
sweetener /'swiːtnə/ 40
swipe card /swaɪp kɑːd/ 2
systematic /ˌsɪstə'mætɪk/ 4

tactfully /'tæktfəli/ 56
tailor-made /ˌteɪlə'meɪd/ 18

take downmarket /teɪk daʊn'mɑːkɪt/ 23
take longer than planned /teɪk ˌlɒŋgə ðən 'plænd/ 42
take part in /teɪk 'pɑːt ɪn/ 14
takeover /'teɪkəʊvə ˌbɪd/ 34
takeover bid /'teɪkəʊvə ˌbɪd/ 34
takeover negotiations /ˌteɪkəʊvə nəˌgəʊʃi'eɪʃənz/ 63
talented /'tæləntɪd/ 4
target (noun) /'tɑːgɪt/ 27
target (verb) /'tɑːgɪt/ 24
task /tɑːsk/ 42
team meeting /ˌtiːm 'miːtɪŋ/ 55
team of equals /ˌtiːm əv 'iːkwəlz/ 45
team player /'tiːm pleɪə/ 4
technical support /'teknɪkl sə'pɔːt/ 6
technology /tek'nɒlədʒi/ 15
telecommunications /ˌtelɪkəˌmjuːnɪ'keɪʃənz/ 13
telecommuting /ˌtelɪkə'mjuːtɪŋ/ 2
telemarketing /'telɪˌmɑːkɪtɪŋ/ 24
telephone /'telɪfəʊn/ 47
telephone survey /'telɪfəʊn ˌsɜːveɪ/ 47
teleworking /'telɪˌwɜːkɪŋ/ 2
temporary contract /ˌtempərəri 'kɒntrækt/ 7
temporary job /ˌtempərəri 'dʒɒb/ 1
tense negotiations /ˌtens nəˌgəʊʃi'eɪʃənz/ 63
terminate /'tɜːmɪneɪt/ 7
test (verb) /test/ 14
text (noun) /tekst/ 47
text message /'tekst ˌmesɪdʒ/ 47
textile /'tekstaɪl/ 13
3G /ˌθriː'dʒiː/ 47
time /taɪm/ 42, 46
time management /ˌtaɪm 'mænɪdʒmənt/ 42
timeframe /'taɪmfreɪm/ 42
timescale /'taɪmskeɪl/ 42
timetable /'taɪmˌteɪbl/ 42
tip (noun) /tɪp/ 5
tiring /'taɪərɪŋ/ 2
toll-free number /ˌtəʊl'friː 'nʌmbə/ 47
tone /təʊn/ 48
tone of voice /ˌtəʊn əv 'vɔɪs/ 60
top-down /ˌtɒp'daʊn/ 44
top-end /ˌtɒp'end/ 23
total costs /ˌtəʊtəl kɒsts/ 27
tough /tʌf/ 2

Business Vocabulary in Use Intermediate 173

tough competition /ˈtʌf ˌkɒmpəˌtɪʃən/ 20
tough negotiator /ˈtʌf nəˌɡəʊʃiˈeɪtə/ 63
tourism /ˈtʊərɪzəm/ 13
trade balance /ˈtreɪd ˌbæləns/ 38
trade credit /treɪd ˈkredɪt/ 29
trade deficit /ˈtreɪd ˌdefɪsɪt/ 38
trade dispute /treɪd dɪsˈpjuːt/ 63
trade down /treɪd ˈdaʊn/ 23
trade gap /ˈtreɪd ɡæp/ 38
trade negotiations /treɪd nəˌɡəʊʃiˈeɪʃənz/ 63
trade surplus /ˈtreɪd sɜːpləs/ 38
trade union (BrE) /treɪd ˈjuːniən/ 6
trade up /treɪd ˈʌp/ 23
trademark /ˈtreɪdmɑːk/ 15
trade-off /ˈtreɪdɒf/ 65
trader /ˈtreɪdə/ 36
trading /ˈtreɪdɪŋ/ 37
train (verb) /treɪn/ 4
trainee /ˌtreɪˈniː/ 54
traineeship /ˌtreɪˈniːʃɪp/ 54
training /ˈtreɪnɪŋ/ 4, 54
transaction /trænˈzækʃən/ 35
transparency /trænˈspærəntsi/ 61
treadmill /ˈtredmɪl/ 43
trial /ˈtraɪəl/ 14
troubled /ˈtrʌbld/ 33
trough /trɒf/ 39
true and fair view /truː ən ˌfeə ˈvjuː/ 31
trust /trʌst/ 46
try out /traɪ ˈaʊt/ 14
turn down /tɜːn ˈdaʊn/ 3
turn round /tɜːn ˈraʊnd/ 33
turn to /ˈtɜːn tʊ/ 61
turnover (BrE) /ˈtɜːnˌəʊvə/ 27, 37
tycoon /taɪˈkuːn/ 10

under budget /ˌʌndə ˈbʌdʒɪt/ 28
under licence (BrE) /ˌʌndə ˈlaɪsənts/ 15
under stress /ˌʌndə ˈstres/ 43
undercut /ˌʌndəˈkʌt/ 23
underlying shares /ˌʌndəˌlaɪɪŋ ˈʃeəz/ 36
underspend /ˌʌndəˈspend/ 28
uneconomic /ˌʌnˌiːkəˈnɒmɪk/ 38
uneconomical /ˌʌnˌiːkəˈnɒmɪkəl/ 38
(the) unemployed /ði ˌʌnɪmˈplɔɪd/ 38
unemployment /ˌʌnɪmˈplɔɪmənt/ 38
unethical /ˌʌnˈeθɪkəl/ 41

uninteresting /ˌʌnˈɪntərestɪŋ/ 2
unit sales /ˌjuːnɪt seɪlz/ 27
unit trust (BrE) /juːnɪt ˈtrʌst/ 35
unpaid /ʌnˈpeɪd/ 54
unprofessional /ˌʌnprəˈfeʃənəl/ 41
unprofessional conduct /ˌʌnprəˈfeʃənəl ˈkɒndʌkt/ 41
unskilled /ʌnˈskɪld/ 4
unstimulating /ʌnˈstɪmjʊleɪtɪŋ/ 2
unstressful /ʌnˈstresfəl/ 43
upfront /ʌpˈfrʌnt/ 29
upmarket (BrE) /ʌpˈmɑːkɪt/ 23
useful discussion /ˌjuːsfəl dɪsˈkʌʃən/ 55
user /ˈjuːzə/ 19

vacation (AmE) /veɪˈkeɪʃən/ 46
values /ˈvæljuːz/ 45
variable costs /ˌveəriːəbl kɒsts/ 27
variety /vəˈraɪəti/ 60
vending machine /ˈvendɪŋ məˌʃiːn/ 19
vendor /ˈvendə/ 19
venue /ˈvenjuː/ 56
vice president (VP) (AmE) /ˌvaɪs ˈprezɪdənt/ 9
videoconferencing /ˈvɪdiəʊˌkɒnfərəntsɪŋ/ 47
video-sharing /ˌvɪdiːəʊˈʃeərɪŋ/ 26
vision /ˈvɪʒən/ 44
visionary /ˈvɪʒənri/ 44
visual aid /ˌvɪʒuəl ˈeɪd/ 60
vocational qualification /vəʊˈkeɪʃənəl ˌkwɒlɪfɪˈkeɪʃən/ 54
voicemail /ˈvɔɪsmeɪl/ 47
VoIP /vɔɪp/ 47
voluntary sector /ˈvɒləntri ˌsektə/ 12
volunteer /ˌvɒlənˈtɪə/ 12
VP (vice president) (AmE) /ˌviːˈpiː/ 9

wage bargaining /weɪdʒ ˈbɑːɡɪnɪŋ/ 63
wage negotiations /ˌweɪdʒ nəˌɡəʊʃiˈeɪʃənz/ 63
wages /ˈweɪdʒɪz/ 5
walk-out /ˈwɔːkaʊt/ 6
Wall Street /ˈwɔːl striːt/ 36
wander off the point /ˌwɒndər ɒf ðə ˈpɔɪnt/ 55
warehouse /ˈweəhaʊs/ 17
waste of time /ˌweɪst əv ˈtaɪm/ 55
Web 2.0 /ˈweb ˌtuː pɔɪnt ˌəʊ/ 26
webcam /ˈwebkæm/ 47

What do you do? /ˌwɒt də jə ˈduː/ 1
whiteboard /ˈwaɪtbɔːd/ 60
white knight /waɪt ˈnaɪt/ 34
widen /ˈwaɪdən/ 38
Wikinomics /wɪkɪˈnɒmɪks/ 18
wind up /waɪnd ˈʌp/ 33
windfall /ˈwɪndfɔːl/ 35
window dressing /ˈwɪndəʊ ˌdresɪŋ/ 31
win-win /wɪnˈwɪn/ 65
win-win solution /wɪnˌwɪn səˈluːʃən/ 65
wipe off /waɪp ˈɒf/ 37
withdraw from a market /wɪðˈdrɔː frəm ə ˌmɑːkɪt/ 20
work /wɜːk/ 1
work environment /wɜːk ɪnˈvaɪrənmənt/ 54
work experience /wɜːk ɪkˈspɪəriənts/ 4
work placement /wɜːk ˈpleɪsmənt/ 54
worker /ˈwɜːkə/ 6
workforce /ˈwɜːkfɔːs/ 6
working at full capacity /ˈwɜːkɪŋ ət fʊl kəˈpæsɪti/ 16
working breakfast /ˌwɜːkɪŋ ˈbrekfəst/ 46
working conditions /ˈwɜːkɪŋ kənˈdɪʃənz/ 5
working from home /ˌwɜːkɪŋ frəm ˈhəʊm/ 2
working hours /ˈwɜːkɪŋ ˌaʊəz/ 2, 46
work-in-progress (BrE) /ˌwɜːkɪnˈprəʊɡres/ 17
work–life balance /wɜːkˈlaɪf ˈbæləns/ 43
workshop /ˈwɜːkʃɒp/ 16, 60
write down /raɪt ˈdaʊn/ 30
write off (verb) /raɪt ˈɒf/ 29, 30
write-off (noun) /ˈraɪt ɒf/ 30
wrongdoer /ˈrɒŋˌduːə/ 40
wrongdoing /ˈrɒŋˌduːɪŋ/ 40

Yours /jɔːz/ 52
Yours faithfully (BrE) /ˌjɔːz ˈfeɪθfəli/ 52
Yours sincerely (BrE) /ˌjɔːz sɪnˈsɪəli/ 52, 53

Acknowledgements

The author would like to thank Liz Driscoll, and Chris Capper, Chris Willis and Neil Holloway at Cambridge University Press for guiding the book smoothly through the editorial process.

The authors and publishers acknowledge the following sources of copyright material and are grateful for the permissions granted. While every effort has been made, it has not always been possible to identify the sources of all the material used, or to trace all copyright holders. If any omissions are brought to our notice, we will be happy to include the appropriate acknowledgements on reprinting and in the next update to the digital edition, as applicable.

Key: B = Below, C = Centre, L = Left, R = Right, T = Top.

Text

The Financial Times for the text on pp. 19, 71 and 76 adapted from 'Kevin Davis Quits as MF Global Chief' by Hal Weitzman, *The Financial Times* 30.10.2008. Copyright © The Financial Times. Reproduced with permission; The Guardian for the text on p. 19 adapted from 'Underachieved? Have a performance-related bonus' by Richard Watchman, *The Guardian* 23.04.2006 Copyright © The Guardian. Reproduced with permission; The Guardian for the text on p. 19 adapted from 'When old dogmas die, there is room for all kinds of radical new thinking' by Jonathan Freedland, *The Guardian* 15.10.2008. Copyright © The Guardian; The Independent for the text on p. 55 adapted from 'Starbucks chokes on its latte' by Louise Dransfield, *The Independent* 01.08.2017. Copyright © The Independent; Cellular News for the text on p. 65 adapted from 'Nokia says replacement phone sales key in emerging markets' by Adam Ewing and Dow Jones. Copyright © 01.04.2008 Cellular News. Reproduced with kind permission of Cellular News via the Copyright Clearance Centre; Lonrho Limited for the text on the p. 76 from 'History', http://www.lonrho.com/About_Lonrho/History/Default.aspx?id=744. Copyright © 2016 Lonrho Ltd. Reproduced with kind permission; Daily Mail for the text on p. 129 from 'Make sure you get the message across' by Lynn Bateson, *Daily Mail* 27.01.2000. Copyright © Daily Mail. Reproduced with permission.

Photographs

All the photographs are sourced from GettyImages.

p. 10: Mario Tama/Getty Images News; p. 11: Ezra Bailey/Taxi; p. 12: PhotoTalk/E+; p. 14 (T): AndreyPopov/iStock/Getty Images Plus; p. 14 (B): bowdenimages/iStock/Getty Images Plus; p. 17: Ron Krisel/The Image Bank; p. 18: Alistair Berg/DigitalVision; p. 23: Tetra Images/Brand X Pictures; p. 28: Hero Images; p. 29 (Gular): Anadolu Agency; p. 29 (Cath Kidston): Fred Duval/FilmMagic; p. 29 (Jack Ma): Lintao Zhang/Getty Images News; p. 29 (Elon Musk): Bill Pugliano/Getty Images News; p. 29 (Zhang Xin): Bloomberg; p. 29 (Mark Zuckerberg): Miquel Benitez/WireImage; p. 32: jacoblund/iStock/Getty Images Plus; p. 34 (L): Dmitri Kessel/The LIFE Picture Collection; p. 34 (C): Bloomberg; p. 34 (R): Dabldy/iStock Editorial/Getty Images Plus; p. 36 (T): Sturti/E+; p. 36 (B): Compassionate Eye Foundation/Hero Images/Taxi; p. 40: Marin Tomas/Moment; p. 41: Bloomberg; p. 42 (T): Bruno Vincent/Getty Images News; p. 42 (B): Jetta Productions/The Image Bank; p. 44 (T): LEON NEAL/AFP; p. 44 (B): Marga Buschbell Steeger/Photographer's Choice; p. 46: Jason Hawkes/The Image Bank; p. 50: Photography by Steve Kelley aka mudpig/Moment; p. 51: Yuri_Arcurs/E+; p. 52 (T): Urfinguss/iStock/Getty Images Plus; p. 52 (C): Firmafotografen/iStock/Getty Images Plus; p. 52 (B): Victor Georgiev/iStock Editorial/Getty Images Plus; p. 57: AdrianHancu/iStock Editorial/Getty Images Plus; p. 58 (Classified): Devonyu/iStock/Getty Images Plus; p. 58 (displays): Henrik Sorensen/Stone; p. 58 (hoardings): Art Directors & TRIP/Alamy Stock Photo; p. 58 (commercial): Morrowind/Shutterstock; p. 58 (neon signs): Marco wong/Moment; p. 62: Morsa Images/DigitalVision; p. 66 (L): Lane Oatey/Blue Jean Images/Collection Mix: Subjects; p. 66 (R): Hill Street Studios/Blend Images; p. 67: ImagesBazaar/Images Bazaar; p. 70: Jetta Productions/David Atkinson; p. 78: YinYang/E+; p. 80: Spencer Platt/Getty Images News; p. 81: Christoph Wilhelm/Photographer's Choice; p. 83: Bloomberg; p. 90 (T): Bloomberg; p. 90 (B): Bernhard_Staehli/iStock/Getty Images Plus; p. 92 (T): MeePoohyaphoto/iStock/Getty Images Plus; p. 92 (B): roman023/iStock Editorial/Getty Images Plus; p. 94 (T): PeopleImages/E+; p. 94 (B): amriphoto/E+; p. 96: John van Hasselt - Corbis/Sygma; p. 103: AndreyPopov/iStock/Getty Images Plus; p. 104 (L): Jon Feingersh/Blend Images; p. 104 (R): GlobalStock/E+; p. 106: PeopleImages/DigitalVision; p. 108: Compassionate Eye Foundation/Hero Images/Taxi; p. 116 (T): Image Source/DigitalVision; p. 116 (B): Caiaimage/Tommerton/Caiaimage; p. 117: Hero Images; p. 119: Portra Images/Taxi; p. 120: Klaus Vedfelt/Taxi; p. 130: PeopleImages/DigitalVision; p. 131: KatarzynaBialasiewicz/iStock/Getty Images Plus; p. 132: PeopleImages/DigitalVision; p. 134: gilaxia/E+; p. 136: Echo/Cultura; p. 141: Kelly Funk/All Canada Photos.

Illustrations

eMC Design Ltd, John Goodwin (Eye Candy Illustration), Gavin Reece (New Division), Kathy Baxendale, Gecko Ltd, Laura Martinez, Roger Penwill and Mark Watkinson.

Also available

You can buy this book with or without an ebook. You can also buy the ebook separately in the Cambridge Bookshelf app on an iPad or Android tablet. The ebook has the same vocabulary explanations and practice exercises as the printed book.

978-1-316-62997-0

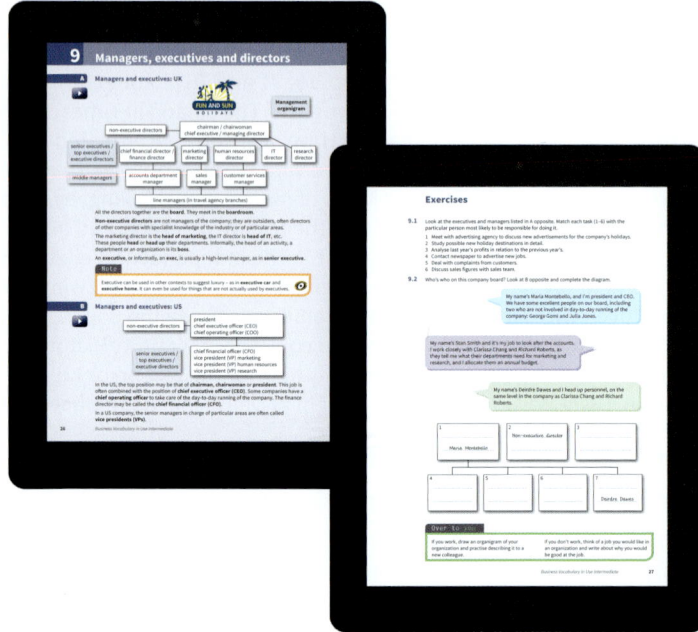

More *in Use* books are available for this level, including the ones below. You can buy *English Vocabulary in Use* with or without an ebook. *English Pronunciation in Use* includes free downloadable audio.

978-1-316-62831-7

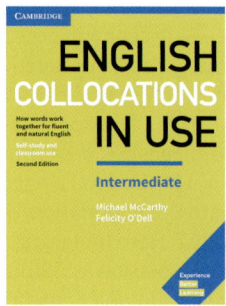

978-1-316-62975-8

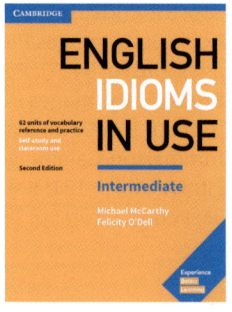

978-1-316-62988-8

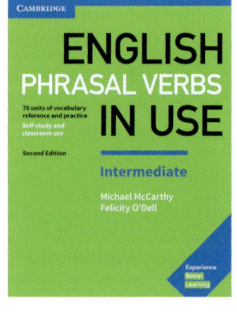

978-1-316-62815-7

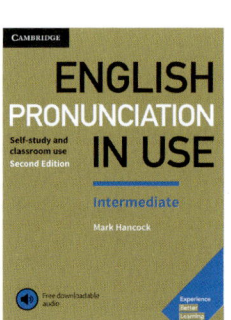

978-1-108-40369-6